Video training courses are available on the subjects of these
in the James Martin ADVANCED TECHNOLOGY LIBRARY fr
Deltak Inc., East/West Technological Center, 1751 West Dieh
Naperville, Ill. 60566 (Tel: 312-369-3000).

TEMS MANIFESTO

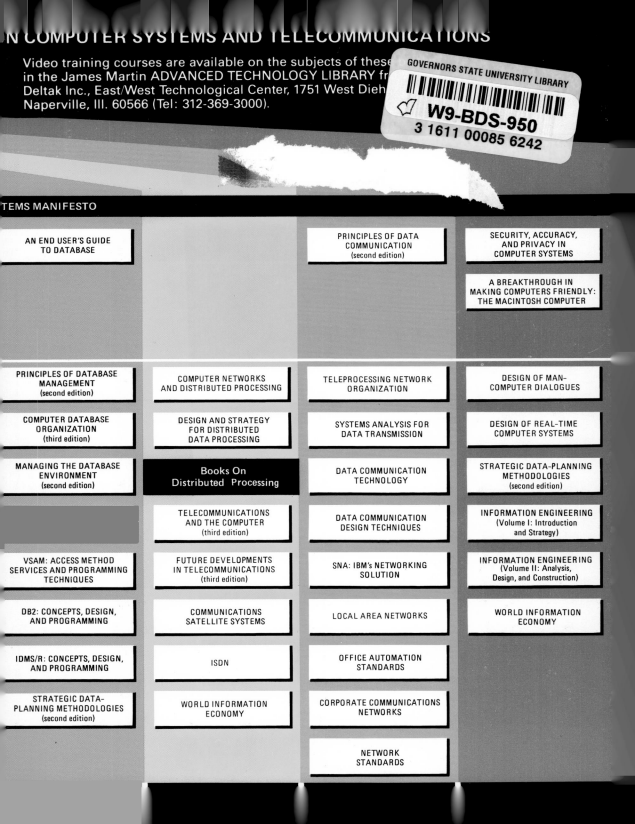

AN END USER'S GUIDE
TO DATABASE

PRINCIPLES OF DATA
COMMUNICATION
(second edition)

SECURITY, ACCURACY,
AND PRIVACY IN
COMPUTER SYSTEMS

A BREAKTHROUGH IN
MAKING COMPUTERS FRIENDLY:
THE MACINTOSH COMPUTER

PRINCIPLES OF DATABASE
MANAGEMENT
(second edition)

COMPUTER NETWORKS
AND DISTRIBUTED PROCESSING

TELEPROCESSING NETWORK
ORGANIZATION

DESIGN OF MAN-
COMPUTER DIALOGUES

COMPUTER DATABASE
ORGANIZATION
(third edition)

DESIGN AND STRATEGY
FOR DISTRIBUTED
DATA PROCESSING

SYSTEMS ANALYSIS FOR
DATA TRANSMISSION

DESIGN OF REAL-TIME
COMPUTER SYSTEMS

MANAGING THE DATABASE
ENVIRONMENT
(second edition)

Books On
Distributed Processing

DATA COMMUNICATION
TECHNOLOGY

STRATEGIC DATA-PLANNING
METHODOLOGIES
(second edition)

TELECOMMUNICATIONS
AND THE COMPUTER
(third edition)

DATA COMMUNICATION
DESIGN TECHNIQUES

INFORMATION ENGINEERING
(Volume I: Introduction
and Strategy)

VSAM: ACCESS METHOD
SERVICES AND PROGRAMMING
TECHNIQUES

FUTURE DEVELOPMENTS
IN TELECOMMUNICATIONS
(third edition)

SNA: IBM's NETWORKING
SOLUTION

INFORMATION ENGINEERING
(Volume II: Analysis,
Design, and Construction)

DB2: CONCEPTS, DESIGN,
AND PROGRAMMING

COMMUNICATIONS
SATELLITE SYSTEMS

LOCAL AREA NETWORKS

WORLD INFORMATION
ECONOMY

IDMS/R: CONCEPTS, DESIGN,
AND PROGRAMMING

ISDN

OFFICE AUTOMATION
STANDARDS

STRATEGIC DATA-
PLANNING METHODOLOGIES
(second edition)

WORLD INFORMATION
ECONOMY

CORPORATE COMMUNICATIONS
NETWORKS

NETWORK
STANDARDS

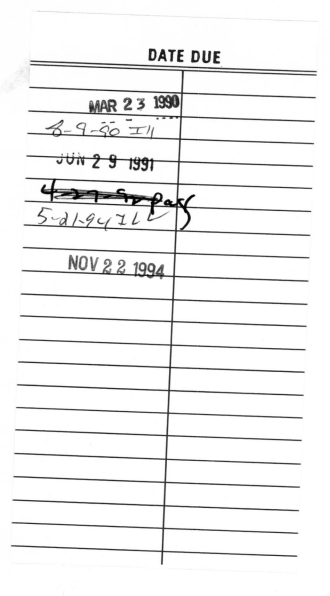

DATE DUE

MAR 23 1990

6-9-90 Ill

JUN 29 1991

5-21-94 IL

NOV 22 1994

PRINCIPLES
OF DATA
COMMUNICATION

A  BOOK

THE JAMES MARTIN BOOKS

- Application Development Without Programmers
- Communications Satellite Systems
- Computer Data-Base Organization, Second Edition
- Computer Networks and Distributed Processing: Software, Techniques, and Architecture
- Design and Strategy of Distributed Data Processing
- Design of Man-Computer Dialogues
- Design of Real-Time Computer Systems
- An End User's Guide to Data Base
- Fourth-Generation Languages, Volume I: Principles
- Future Developments in Telecommunications, Second Edition
- Information Engineering
- An Information Systems Manifesto
- Introduction to Teleprocessing
- Managing the Data-Base Environment
- Principles of Data-Base Management
- Programming Real-Time Computer Systems
- Recommended Diagramming Standards for Analysts and Programmers
- Security, Accuracy, and Privacy in Computer Systems
- Strategic Data-Planning Methodologies
- Systems Analysis for Data Transmission
- System Design from Provably Correct Constructs
- Technology's Crucible
- Telecommunications and the Computer, Second Edition
- Telematic Society: A Challenge for Tomorrow
- Teleprocessing Network Organization
- Viewdata and the Information Society

with Carma McClure

- Action Diagrams: Clearly Structured Program Design
- Diagramming Techniques for Analysts and Programmers
- Software Maintenance: The Problem and Its Solutions
- Structured Techniques: The Basis for CASE, Revised Edition

with The ARBEN Group, Inc.

- A Breakthrough in Making Computers Friendly: The Macintosh Computer
- Data Communication Technology
- Fourth-Generation Languages, Volume II: Representative Fourth-Generation Languages
- Fourth-Generation Languages, Volume III: 4GLs from IBM
- Principles of Data Communication
- SNA: IBM's Networking Solution
- VSAM: Access Method Services and Programming Techniques

with Adrian Norman

- The Computerized Society

PRINCIPLES OF DATA COMMUNICATION

JAMES MARTIN
with
Joe Leben
The ARBEN Group, Inc.

PRENTICE HALL, Englewood Cliffs, New Jersey 07632

Library of Congress Cataloging-in-Publication Data

MARTIN, JAMES (date)
  Principles of data communication.

  "James Martin books."
  Includes index.
    1. Data transmission systems. I. Leben, Joe.
II. Arben Group. III. Title. IV. Title: James
Martin books.
  TK5105.M3559 1988   004.6   87-7289
  ISBN 0-13-709891-X

Editorial/production supervision: *Kathryn Gollin Marshak*
Jacket design: *Bruce Kenselaar*
Manufacturing buyer: *Richard Washburn*

Previously published under the title:
Introduction to Teleprocessing

Printed in the United States of America

10 9 8 7 6 5 4 3 2 1

ISBN 0-13-709891-X   025

PRENTICE-HALL INTERNATIONAL (UK) LIMITED, *London*
PRENTICE-HALL OF AUSTRALIA PTY. LIMITED, *Sydney*
PRENTICE-HALL CANADA INC., *Toronto*
PRENTICE-HALL HISPANOAMERICANA, S.A., *Mexico*
PRENTICE-HALL OF INDIA PRIVATE LIMITED, *New Delhi*
PRENTICE-HALL OF JAPAN, INC., *Tokyo*
SIMON & SCHUSTER ASIA PTE. LTD., *Singapore*
EDITORA PRENTICE-HALL DO BRASIL, LTDA., *Rio de Janeiro*

TO
CORINTHIA

ABOUT THIS BOOK

Principles of Data Communication

Principles of Data Communication was first published in 1972 under the title *Introduction to Teleprocessing.* The second edition has been completely rewritten. The technical content for this book has been derived from the more detailed books *Data Communication Technology* and *Data Communication Design Techniques,* described below, and has been edited to constitute an introduction to data communication. This book can be read by programmers, analysts, managers, and telecommunications technical staff members who require an introduction to data communication facilities. Technical terms are used, but all are clearly defined. This book has no prerequisites other than a general understanding of data processing fundamentals, and no programming background is required. *Principles of Data Communication* could be used as the text for an introductory course on data communication.

ABOUT RELATED BOOKS

Data Communication Technology

Data Communication Technology is for data processing and telecommunications administration technical staff members who require an in-depth understanding of the complex technology surrounding data communication networks. This book uses examples and case studies to show how data communication technology supports modern data processing applications. It will enable the reader to select appropriate communication lines, equipment, and software in constructing data communication systems. A general background in data processing fundamentals is assumed, but no programming background or knowledge of data communication techniques is required. *Data Communication Technology* could be used as the text in an in-depth course on the use of data transmission in information processing systems.

Data Communication Design Techniques

Data Communication Design Techniques was first published in 1972 under the title *Systems Analysis for Data Transmission.* The second edition has been completely rewritten. This book is for data processing and telecommunications administration technical staff members. It has a how-to-do-it orientation and shows the technical staff member how to perform the systems analysis and design tasks that are required in designing data communication systems and telecommunications networks. The book includes the source code for a series of programs, written in BASIC for an IBM or IBM-compatible personal computer, that can be used in performing many of the tasks necessary in designing minimum-cost networks. This book assumes a basic knowledge of data communication, which can be gained by reading either *Principles of Data Communication* or *Data Communication Technology*. *Data Communication Design Techniques* could be used as the text for an in-depth course on the design of systems that use data transmission and the design of telecommunications networks.

CONTENTS

PART **II** **EQUIPMENT**

PART **III**   PROGRAMMING

EPILOGUE

PREFACE

A vast network of telecommunications links spans the industrialized countries of the world, carrying telephone, telegraph, television, news photographs, and radio programs. This network is constantly being expanded, and new inventions are increasing its capacity at a breathtaking rate. As yet computer systems have made only minor use of this immense network. For several decades, data has been transmitted over communication lines. There were many problems in the beginning, but slowly solutions have been found. We have learned to use the links more efficiently, and the costs have dropped dramatically. It is now practical for one computer to dial up another computer—just as we dial one another on the phone—and transmit information. Even with the speed restrictions of a conventional telephone line, the computer can often code its information so that it sends hundreds or thousands of times as much in a given time as human speakers.

Perhaps more important, *we* are now able to dial the computers and communicate with them. In offices, shops, factories, and individual homes, there are personal computers and inexpensive terminals designed to enable people to communicate with distant computers. We are now able to ask them questions, to consult enormous banks of stored information, to perform calculations, and to enter data that the computers store, process, and act on. In more advanced applications, we are seeing a new type of thinking in which the creative ability of the human user interacts with the enormous logic power of the machine and provides access to its vast store of data. This interaction can produce results that neither people nor computers could achieve alone.

This book should provide the easiest possible way to learn about data communication from the beginning. All of the subject matter has been taken from the authors' other books but has been rewritten here to constitute an introduction to the subject. Although some technical terms are used, all are clearly defined when they are first used, and a glossary at the back of the book can be used for reference. The book can be read by nontechnical persons, and it is hoped that the book can be enjoyable reading rather than a chore.

James Martin
Joe Leben

PROLOGUE

1 COMPUTERS OF THE WORLD, UNITE!

One of the most exciting technological developments of the latter portion of this century is the use of telecommunications facilities to tie together the world's computers. Both the telecommunications industry and the computer industry are developing at a fast and furious rate. Calculated speculation about what either of them is likely to lead to brings awe-inspiring conclusions. Either the computer industry or the telecommunications industry, alone, is capable of bringing about massive changes to our society, our working habits, and our governments. But when the two techniques are used together, they add power to each other. Telecommunications links are bringing the capabilities of computers and the information in huge databanks to the millions of locations where they can be used, and computers are in turn being used to control the immense switching centers and help divide the enormous capacities of new transmission facilities into usable channels.

FUNDAMENTAL TERMINOLOGY

When discussing computer systems that use data communication facilities, the terms *telecommunications, data communication,* and *teleprocessing* are often misused. Consequently, we will begin this book by defining these important terms.

- **Telecommunications.** *Telecommunications* refers to the electronic transmission of any kind of electronic information, including telephone calls, television signals, data, electronic mail, facsimile, and telemetry from spacecraft.

- **Data Communication.** The term *data communication* refers to the electronic transmission of *data. Data transmission* is a synonym. Both terms are usually used in reference to data that is manipulated by computers. However, in the true sense of the term, data communication also encompasses telegraphy, telemetry, and similar forms of electronic data transmission.

- **Teleprocessing.** *Teleprocessing* is a newer term. Originally coined by IBM, it refers to the accessing of computing power and computerized data files from a distance, generally using terminals and telecommunications facilities.

Note from these definitions that *teleprocessing* is a more inclusive term than *data communication*. Generally, when we examine the *data communication* aspects of a system, we are referring to only those parts of the system that are involved in the transmission of data from one point to another. However, when we discuss a *teleprocessing* system, we are referring to the total system, including computers, terminals, telecommunications lines, and all associated hardware and software used to implement a complete data processing application.

COMPUTERS AND COMMUNICATION

In a sense, all computer systems use data transmission techniques. A modern computing system consists of a number of devices wired together with cables. Generally these cables are out of sight under the computer room floor. These cables are actually data transmission lines that operate at very high speeds.

As we will discuss later, if we had long-distance communication lines with characteristics similar to computer room cables, we could connect devices at remote locations directly to the computer, and data communication would not be a topic of special interest. But, of course, such channels do not exist—at least not in so simple a form as a computer room cable. So a system that connects a computer with devices at remote locations has characteristics different from those of a system that connects local devices only.

DATA COMMUNICATION SYSTEMS

Systems that use data transmission facilities are built for a variety of purposes and perform different functions. Today, the most common data transmission system takes the form of people at terminals communicating with a distant computer. The computer usually responds quickly, with a dialog taking place between each terminal user and the remote computer. Many of today's systems connect terminal users to multiple computers in a distributed processing environment. Figure 1.1 shows how six criteria can be used to separate data transmission systems into categories. These categories are described in Box 1.1.

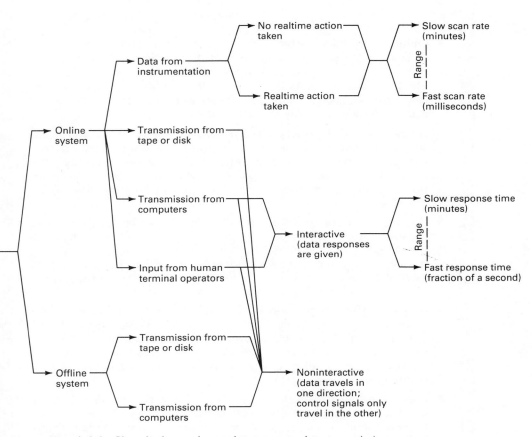

Figure 1.1 Six criteria can be used to separate data transmission systems into categories.

FUNCTIONAL LAYERS AND PROTOCOLS

In the early days of data communication, individual computer manufacturers produced communication products that worked only on their equipment. In this environment, data communication connections between the equipment of different manufacturers was difficult. Today, networks have evolved and have increased in capability and complexity. Many diverse types of equipment are interconnected.

In modern data communication systems, the functions relating to data transmission for each station connected to a communication line are performed by software or firmware installed in the communicating stations. The functions performed by that software or firmware are divided into independent *layers,*

BOX 1.1 Categorizing data transmission systems

- **Online and Offline Systems.** The communication links in a system can be either *online* or *offline* to a computer. In an *offline* system, the data is collected by a device that simply stores the data on an intermediate storage device and is processed at a later time. In an *online* system, the data enters the computer directly from its point of origination and/or output data is transmitted directly to where it is used.

- **Interactive and Noninteractive Systems.** An offline system is of necessity also *noninteractive,* but an online system can also be noninteractive. For example, the computer might receive a batch transmission and might not need to respond to it. But most systems that support transmission from operators at terminals are *interactive,* often with a high flow of data in both directions.

- **Quantity of Data Transmitted.** The quantity of data required to be transmitted varies enormously. At one extreme, whole files are transmitted. At the other, one bit will suffice to indicate a yes or no condition. In many systems a *dialog* takes place between a terminal user and a computer, the sizes and contents of the messages exchanged depending on the design of the user interface.

- **Response Time Requirements.** The time available for transmission is generally referred to as the *response time*. A response time of 1 or 2 seconds is typical in today's interactive systems, although subsecond response times are desirable for certain types of interactions. Systems that are not interactive might have a *delivery time* specified instead of a response time.

- **User Independence.** Most systems with terminals are *time-shared,* meaning that more than one user is using them at the same time. In some systems, the processing requested by one terminal user is quite unrelated to the processing requested by other users. In other systems, the users may not be independent. There are four types of online systems, differing by the degree of user independence:
  — Systems that carry out a carefully specified and limited function, such as an airline reservation system
  — Systems for a specific limited function in which the users have personal, independent files
  — Systems in which users employ terminals to perform a variety of tasks that are limited to a narrow range of functions
  — General-purpose systems in which the users employ various types of terminals for a wide range of purposes

- **Communication Line Sharing.** Communication lines are often shared. The degree of independence of users on a shared communication line varies. On some shared lines, all users must employ the same terminal type with the same line control procedure. On others, the terminals can be different but must use the same character code. With some systems, they can be entirely independent, each using different codes. Finally, they could be entirely independent users sharing public data transmission facilities.

much like the skins of an onion. Each layer isolates the layers above it from the complexities below.

At each layer, a set of *rules* must be agreed to and followed by both parties in order for communication to be successful. The rules that govern communication are called *protocols*. Each set of protocols can be thought of as a rule book that governs communication at a given layer.

NETWORK ARCHITECTURES

The need is now apparent for a high degree of standardization in the protocols that govern the operation of a communication system. This is the role of a *network architecture*. A network architecture is an overall plan that governs the design of the hardware and software components that make up a data communication system. Several such network architectures are in existence today, and we will introduce two important ones in this chapter. Before we discuss these two specific architectures, we will examine the functions that are performed in a data communication system and see how those functions are performed by independent software layers.

TRANSPARENT AND VIRTUAL

In discussing complex systems that use layered software, it is important to have a clear understanding of the meaning of the terms *transparent* and *virtual*. A *transparent* facility is one that actually exists but appears not to exist. A *virtual* facility is one that appears to exist but in fact does not. The concept of transparent and virtual facilities make it easier to understand the principles involved in data communication.

TRANSPARENT FACILITIES

Much of the complexity involved in data communication is *transparent* to the communicating parties because many aspects of the complex chain of events that implements the interaction between two communicating stations are handled automatically. The idea of transparent facilities is important because transparent facilities isolate higher-level layers from the complexities of the lower-level layers. Transparent facilities are used in all modern computer systems to isolate higher-level functions, and ultimately the end user, from the complexities of the lower-level functions. A modern, sophisticated data communication system might use a number of independent software layers that are all quite complex. All but the topmost layer are transparent to the user. The total system can be made to *appear* quite simple. The user might see only a simple set of commands for requesting easy-to-use network services.

VIRTUAL FACILITIES

A virtual facility is a seemingly simple facility that may actually be implemented by something quite complex. For example, when you place a long-distance telephone call and the party at the other end picks up the receiver, it seems as though a single set of wires exists between you and the other party. We can call this make-believe set of wires a *virtual* connection; it does not actually consist of a single set of wires but only appears to. The connection is implemented by a transparent, but quite complex, system of local telephone lines, amplifiers, signal converters, switching centers, and long-distance transmission facilities.

Virtual facilities provide a simple way of viewing a complex system. A given network might actually look like that shown in Fig. 1.2. However, a network user needs a simpler way to view the part of the network being used. A given user who needs to use a terminal to access one of the computers might perceive the network as if it appeared as shown in Fig. 1.3. The user views the network as if a simple point-to-point connection (a *virtual channel*) exists between the terminal and the computer. The user can ignore the complexities of the hardware and software facilities that implement the virtual channel—they are transparent to the user.

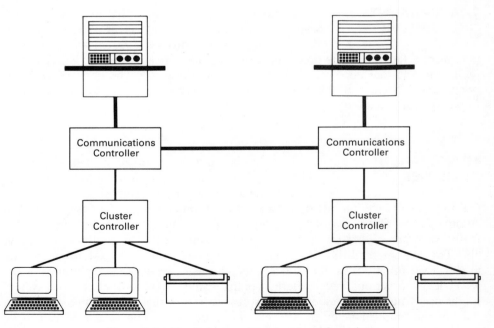

Figure 1.2   Physical computer network configuration.

Figure 1.3   The user perceives only a simple virtual channel connecting the terminal and the computer.

COMMUNICATION SYSTEM SOFTWARE LAYERS

A data communication system can be viewed on a number of levels. At each level, a layer of software works together with hardware to provide a useful set of functions, and each software layer is independent of all the others. Independence of the layers gives a modern data communication system great flexibility. All data communication systems have at least two layers in common: the *physical* layer and the *data link* layer.

THE PHYSICAL LAYER

The lowest layer of any data communication system implements a physical connection between two devices that allows electrical signals to be exchanged between them. Figure 1.4 shows a simple point-to-point link that connects a terminal to a small computer. The hardware consists of a cable, appropriate connectors, and the two communicating devices, each of which is capable of both generating and detecting voltages on the connecting cables. The mechanisms operating at the physical layer, shown in Fig. 1.5, are simple and consist of firmware permanently installed in both the computer and the terminal. This firmware controls the generation and detection of voltages on the cable that represent zero bits and one bits.

The physical layer does not assign any significance to the bits. For example, this layer is not concerned with how many bits make up each unit of data,

Figure 1.4 A simple point-to-point data link connecting a terminal and a small computer.

nor is it concerned with the meaning of the data being transmitted. In the physical layer, the sender simply transmits a string of bits, and the receiver detects them.

THE DATA LINK LAYER   We use the term *data link* to refer to a communication line with associated equipment that allows computer data to be sent over the link. The second layer of software or firmware in any data communication system is generally called the *data link* layer (see Fig. 1.6). Software in the data link layer implements a logical connection between the two communicating devices that can be used to transmit meaningful data between them. The data link layer is also normally implemented by firmware permanently installed in the communicating machines. This firmware is concerned with how bits are grouped into collections called *frames*. There are any number of ways that bits can be grouped to form meaningful data, so standards are as important for the data link layer as they are for the physical layer. A number of standards, called *data link protocols*, have been published that describe how bits should be grouped for various purposes.

As an example of what happens at the data link layer, suppose a terminal is connected to a computer via a simple point-to-point connection. The process that occurs is illustrated in Fig. 1.7. The terminal user presses the A key on the keyboard, and the keyboard sends the bits that make up the letter A to the firmware operating in the data link layer. The data link firmware interprets these bits and causes the firmware operating in the physical layer to send the appropriate electrical signals out on the physical connection. Firmware operating in the physical layer in the computer detects the signals and passes them up to the

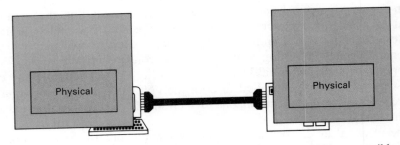

Figure 1.5 The physical layer in a data communication system is responsible for generating and detecting voltages on the connecting cable.

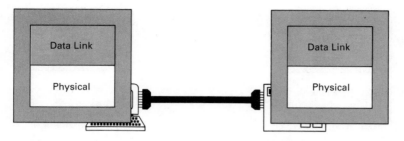

Figure 1.6   The data link layer in a data communication system is concerned with how bits are grouped into collections called frames.

firmware operating in its data link layer. The data link layer firmware in the computer then interprets the signals as the bit configuration for A.

HIGHER-LEVEL LAYERS

Figure 1.8 shows that there are functions above the levels of the data link layer that must operate in both the sender and the receiver. In the simplest case, these functions may be performed by the human terminal operator. For example, some functions must be performed by the sender in deciding that an appropriate action is to press the A key on the keyboard. And on the receiving end, some higher-level function, either in higher-level data communication software or in an application program, must attach some significance to receiving the letter A.

LAYER INDEPENDENCE

Earlier in this chapter we introduced the principle of *layer independence*. As an example of layer indepen-

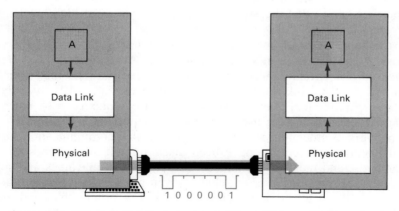

Figure 1.7   The data link layer in the sending machine sends data via the physical link to the data link layer in the receiving machine.

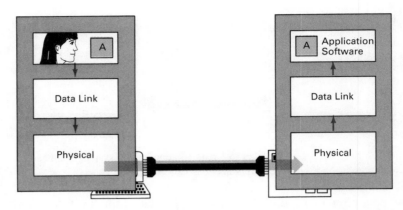

Figure 1.8 In a typical data communication system, there are functions operating above the data link layer in both the sending and receiving machines.

dence, the physical layer can be changed by installing a new cable with different connectors or by changing the signals that are used for transmitting bits. The same techniques could still be used at the data link layer over the new physical connection. At the data link layer, many data link protocols exist. The data link protocol can be changed without affecting the software layers that operate above the data link layer.

The principle of layering allows the functions that are performed by lower layers in a data communication system to be transparent to the upper layers. At the level of the user at the terminal and the application program in the computer, the functions performed by the data link layer and by the physical layer are transparent. The system can be viewed as if a virtual channel existed between the user at the keyboard and the high-level software in the computer (see Fig. 1.9). The user knows that pressing the A key will cause the high-level software to receive the letter A.

In the same manner, the functions performed by the physical layer are transparent to the firmware in the data link layer. At this level, the system can be viewed as if a virtual connection existed between the data link layer in the terminal and the data link layer in the computer (see Fig. 1.10). It is the principle of transparency that allows systems of great complexity to be built, while at the same time isolating the user from those complexities.

A network architecture defines the way in which communication functions are divided into the layers we have been discussing. It also defines the protocols, standards, and message formats to which different machines and software modules must conform in order to achieve given goals. When new products are created that conform to the architecture, they will be compatible, and they can be interlinked to share data, resources, and programs that already exist.

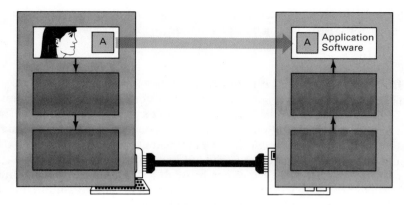

Figure 1.9   A data communication system can be viewed as if a virtual channel existed between the uppermost layers in the sender and the receiver.

The goals and standards of a network architecture are important to both the users of data communication systems and the companies that provide data communication equipment and services. The architecture must provide users with a variety of choices in the configuration of data communication systems, and it must allow them to change a configuration with relative ease as their systems evolve. Architectures permit the mass production of hardware and software building blocks that can be used in a variety of systems. They also provide standards and definitions that allow development laboratories to create new machines and software that will be compatible with existing machines. These new

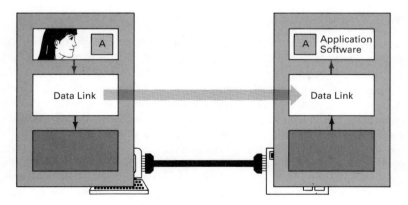

Figure 1.10   At the data link level, the system can be viewed as if a virtual channel existed between the data link layer in the sender and the data link layer in the receiver.

products can then be integrated into existing data communication systems without the need for costly interfaces and program modifications.

THE NATURE OF ARCHITECTURE

The term *architecture* is often used to describe database management systems, operating systems, and other highly complex software/hardware mechanisms. Architecture is a particularly important concept in describing data communication and computer network systems because in these systems so many potentially incompatible hardware devices and software packages must fit together to form an easily used and easily modified whole. A good architecture ought to relate primarily to the needs of the end users rather than to enthusiasms for particular techniques. A well-architected house, for example, is one that reflects the desired life style of its owners rather than one that is designed to exploit a building technique that is currently in vogue.

DEVELOPERS OF ARCHITECTURES

Because of the importance of network architectures, several types of organizations have gotten involved in standards and architecture development. Of these organizations, two are especially important: *standards organizations* and *computer manufacturers*. Architectures designed by these groups have many characteristics in common. They all define the rules of a network and define how the components of a network can interact. But there are also major differences between these two types of architecture developers.

Standards Organizations

Many organizations in the United States and Europe are actively involved in developing standards for data communication and computer networking. The most important of these is the *Comité consultatif international télégraphique et téléphonique* (CCITT) (generally translated as International Telegraph and Telephone Consultative Committee). The CCITT publishes a series of important *recommendations* that constitute international standards for data communication. Several CCITT recommendations are described in this book.

The CCITT publishes its recommendations at four-year intervals and changes the color of the covers of its documents when each new set of recommendations is published. The color of the covers was yellow for the set of documents that covered recommendations developed during the period 1976–1980. The set of CCITT recommendations for that time period was referred to as the *Yellow Book;* the *Yellow Book* was in common use until 1985. The color of the cover of the current set of CCITT recommendations is red; thus the

CCITT recommendations are currently called the *Red Book*. The *Red Book* contains the most up-to-date set of CCITT recommendations and will be useful through about 1989, when a new series of recommendations will replace it.

A convenient source of information about CCITT standards is *McGraw-Hill's Compilation of Data Communication Standards,* edited by Harold C. Folts (New York: McGraw-Hill, 1982). This book contains reprints of the most commonly used standards from a variety of standards organizations. Be warned, however, that this publication is over 2000 pages in length and is 3 inches thick, even though printed on thin paper. The CCITT *Red Book,* however, is published in many volumes and is *much* larger than that. Standards documents should not as a rule be read late at night, unless used as a cure for insomnia.

Computer Manufacturers

Computer manufacturers began providing advanced data communication capabilities long before the development of today's standardized network architectures. For this reason, computer manufacturers were forced to develop their own architectures to give an overall cohesiveness to their product lines. The most commonly used manufacturer's network architecture is IBM's *Systems Network Architecture* (SNA). The first products that conformed to the SNA architecture were released in 1975. Computer manufacturers' architectures are specifically designed for data communication systems that are built from components supplied by that manufacturer. Since an individual organization frequently owns and implements its own network, often from components obtained from a single vendor, a manufacturer's architecture may allow systems to be built that meet the user's specific needs.

However, a manufacturer's architecture can make it difficult to interconnect machines offered by competing vendors. The protocols used by communicating machines are highly complex and are often completely different from one manufacturer to another. It may be relatively easy to hook a simple terminal from one manufacturer to a computer from another. It is quite difficult, however, to connect a computing system that conforms to Digital Equipment Corporation's DECNET architecture to an SNA network. (Many computer manufacturers do, however, provide facilities called *gateways* that allow such connections to be made.)

Now that we have described network architectures in general, we will examine the software layers defined by two important network architectures: the OSI Reference Model and IBM's SNA.

THE OSI REFERENCE MODEL

The OSI Reference Model, often simply called the OSI model, was developed by a committee of the *International Standards Organization* (ISO) and was subsequently adopted by the CCITT. Descriptions of the OSI model are now published by both the ISO and the CCITT. The OSI model defines an overall architecture for the complex software that modern computer networks require. This architecture describes how communicating machines can communicate with one another in a standardized and highly flexible way by defining the layers of software that should be implemented in each communicating machine.

There is no requirement on the part of any hardware or software vendor to adhere to the principles set forth by the OSI model. However, the worldwide trend in the computer industry today is toward acceptance and conformity to this architecture. The OSI model was adopted first by organizations outside the United States, but now U.S. computer manufacturers are increasingly working toward acceptance of the OSI model.

The OSI model defines the seven independent software layers that are shown in Fig. 1.11. Each layer performs a different set of functions and is independent of all other layers. The OSI model does not define the software itself, nor does it define detailed standards for that software; it simply defines the broad categories of functions that each layer should perform. The OSI model can incorporate different sets of standards at each layer that are appropriate for given situations. In a very simple data communication system, for example, one that uses a simple point-to-point link, the software at many of the higher-level layers might be very simple or even nonexistent. In very complex systems, all

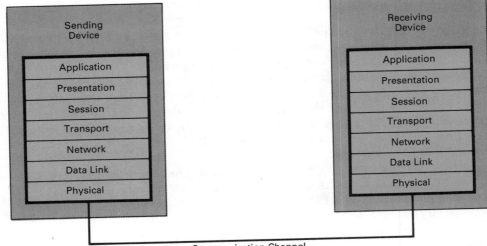

Figure 1.11   The OSI Reference Model defines seven independent layers of software, each of which performs a separate set of functions and is independent of the other layers.

seven layers can be implemented, some of which may contain highly complex software. Many alternative standards already exist for the various layers, and more are under development. Box 1.2 contains brief descriptions of the functions performed by each of the seven layers in the OSI model. The OSI model is discussed further in Chapter 12.

BOX 1.2　OSI model software layers

- **Layer 7—Application.** This is the layer that user processes plug into. The application layer in a computer might consist of query software that a terminal operator uses. The application layer in a terminal might implement the control mechanisms that allow a person to enter requests and display answers.

- **Layer 6—Presentation.** This is the layer that might, in a computer, compress data or encipher it for security. Presentation-layer software in a terminal might reexpand the data and add screen-formatting information.

- **Layer 5—Session.** Software in this layer performs services that make possible an interaction between users. For example, the terminal user might start a session by specifying the name of the database that will be accessed.

- **Layer 4—Transport.** This layer pretends that there is a direct connection between two users. Software running in this layer is responsible for transmitting a message between one network user and another. For example, a message entered by the terminal operator might be divided by transport-layer software into smaller units called *packets* for transmission through the network.

- **Layer 3—Network.** Software running in this layer is responsible for transmitting a message, or an individual packet, from its source to its destination. Layer 3 might take a single packet of a message and transmit it through the network from the location of the terminal to the location of the other user. The most commonly used standard for layer 3 and the layers below it is published by the CCITT and is called *Recommendation X.25*.

- **Layer 2—Data Link.** Software or hardware control mechanisms in this layer handle the physical transmission of frames over a single data link. A commonly used standard for the data link layer is called *High-level Data Link Control* (HDLC).

- **Layer 1—Physical.** Control mechanisms in the physical layer handle the electrical interface between a terminal and a piece of data communication equipment. A commonly used standard for the physical layer is the EIA RS-232-C interface (see Chapter 5).

SYSTEMS NETWORK ARCHITECTURE (SNA)

IBM's SNA is an important network architecture because it is currently more widely used than any other. However, it is possible that this may change as support for the OSI model grows. SNA is similar to the OSI model in that it is an architecture for data communication systems that defines a framework into which various protocols fit. Many of the functions performed by SNA software have counterparts in the OSI layers. However, SNA software functions are divided up between the various layers somewhat differently. Figure 1.12 shows the major layers of software that are used in systems that conform to SNA. Box 1.3 contains brief descriptions of the functions performed by each of the five major SNA layers. Notice that SNA defines five major layers, but there are two additional layers that are defined outside the SNA architecture.

Do not be misled because we have described seven software layers for both the OSI model and SNA. Although the two architectures are similar through the data link layer, they are quite incompatible at higher-level layers and distribute functions among the higher layers in different ways. It is likely that SNA and the OSI model will become more compatible over the years. For example, one of IBM's SNA protocols, called *Advanced Program-to-Program Communication* (APPC), has been selected by the CCITT as one of the accepted international standards for the higher-level layers of the OSI architecture. However, for now, the OSI model and SNA represent two fundamentally different network architectures. SNA is discussed further in Chapter 13.

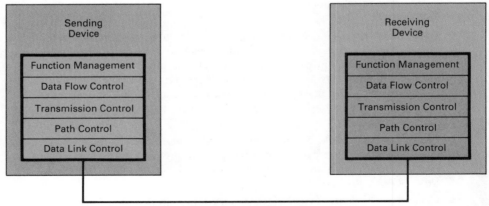

Figure 1.12 IBM's SNA defines five software layers whose functions are distributed somewhat differently from those of the OSI Reference Model.

BOX 1.3   SNA software layers

- **Layer 5—Function Management.** This layer coordinates the interface between network users and the network, presents information to the user, controls and coordinates the activities of the network, and provides high-level services to the layers below it.

- **Layer 4—Data Flow Control.** This layer is concerned with the overall integrity of the flow of data during a session between two users. This can involve determining the mode of sending and receiving, managing groups of related messages, and determining the type of responses to use.

- **Layer 3—Transmission Control.** This layer keeps track of the status of sessions between users, controls the pacing of data flow, and sees that units of data are sent and received in the proper sequence.

- **Layer 2—Path Control.** This layer is concerned with routing data from one node to the next in the path that a message takes through the network. In a complex network, this path often passes through several nodes over many separate data links.

- **Layer 1—Data Link Control.** This layer of SNA is comparable to the data link layer of the OSI model and is responsible for the transmission of data between two devices over a single physical link. A standard for SNA's data link control layer is the *Synchronous Data Link Control* (SDLC) protocol. SDLC is a functional subset of HDLC, the data link protocol defined by the International Standards Organization (ISO).

- **Physical Control.** This layer operates below SNA's lowest layer and is comparable to the physical layer of the OSI model. The techniques used for physical transmission, though important, are defined outside the SNA architecture.

- **Application.** This layer operates above the function management layer of SNA and represents the users that interface with the SNA network. As with the physical control layer, the application layer is outside SNA's architectural definition.

The data communication systems of today are powerful and complex, and they employ many components. Chapter 2 examines one of the most important components in any data communication system, the communication channel itself.

PART **I** INFORMATION PATHWAYS

2 COMMUNICATION CHANNELS

Imagine someone with a long fire hose going into a building. Now suppose that this is not a firefighter but an espionage agent who is trying to transmit data to an accomplice inside the building. Our espionage agent can send the data by means of a piston. As the piston at one end of the hose is pushed and pulled, the pulses are transmitted to a receiving piston at the other end.

Now, if the hose were absolutely rigid and the water in it absolutely incompressible, the movement of the receiving piston would follow the movement of the sending piston exactly. And if the water had no viscosity and moved completely without friction, the piston would be able to transmit pulses at a very high speed. However, a hose is not rigid; it is slightly elastic, and the water contains air bubbles and is slightly compressible. So the receiving piston does not follow the movement of the transmitting piston exactly. Furthermore, viscosity and friction prohibit the piston from moving and transmitting at a limitless speed. A communication line has properties that are loosely analogous to our fire hose.

THE IDEAL COMMUNICATION CHANNEL

What we would really like in constructing a data communication facility is a channel similar to an incompressible fire hose. Such a channel would have similar characteristics to the extremely high speed buses that connect the various pieces of equipment in the computer room. A device at one end of the connection generates a stream of bits that is transmitted at millions of bits per second to the other end, where the bits are interpreted correctly.

The purpose of a data communication channel is the same. We want to take a bit stream from a data processing machine at one location and transmit that bit stream without error to another data processing machine at a distant location.

CHANNEL CHARACTERISTICS

Technical and economic factors generally make it necessary to transmit the bit streams much more slowly than data can be transmitted over the connections in the computer room. Electrical properties called *capacitance, resistance,* and *inductance* cause transmitted data to be distorted, just as data flowing along a fire hose would be distorted. It might be possible to transmit data quite successfully at 5 bits per second over a 1000-foot fire hose, but if the hose were 3 miles long, the same technique would not work. Only a very slow bit rate would be detectable.

In addition, there is *noise* on the line. Suppose that the fire hose is vibrating because of the motion of a nearby pump. At high transmission speeds, the strength of the received pulses becomes comparable in magnitude with this vibration noise, and errors in the interpretation of the data will occur.

DIGITAL COMMUNICATION CHANNELS

Now, given these factors, how would a channel for transmitting computer data over long distances be built? Since we can transmit high bit rates only for relatively short distances before the noise and distortion interfere with the signal, we might provide *bit repeaters* (also called *regenerative repeaters*) at frequent intervals along the line. A bit repeater is a device that detects the bits that are being sent and then retransmits them with their original strength and sharpness. The bit repeater catches the bit stream before it is submerged in the noise and then separates it from the noise by creating it afresh. A very high bit rate can be transmitted over unlimited distances provided that the bit repeaters are sufficiently close together (see Fig. 2.1).

There is one advantage to sending signals in digital form—it is simple and inexpensive. Digital signals can be sent over ordinary wires of a few miles in length at relatively high speeds without harmful distortion. The speed can be increased enormously by using coaxial cables (such as the cable used for cable television) rather than ordinary wire or by installing a bit repeater every few thousand feet.

CHANNEL CAPACITY

We can describe the *capacity* of a communication channel as the maximum rate at which we can send information over it without error. For data communication purposes, this is most often measured in *bits per second* (bps), and this is the unit of measure we will use in this book.

The term *baud* is sometimes used in data communication literature in quoting the speed of a transmission line. A certain transmission line is said to have a speed of so many *baud*. The term *baud* refers to the signaling speed of a line. Signaling speed, or baud, refers to *the number of times in each second the line condition changes*. If the line condition represents the presence or absence of 1

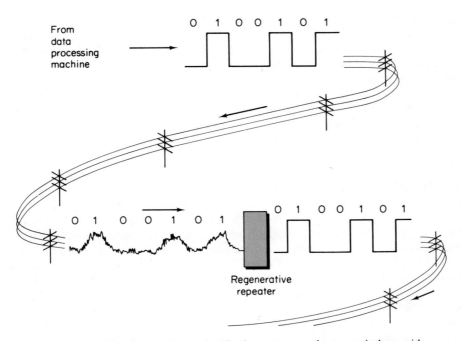

Figure 2.1 Bit repeaters detect the bits that are sent and retransmit them with their original strength and sharpness.

bit, the line's signaling speed in *baud* is the same as the line's capacity in *bits per second*. If, however, the line can be in one of *four* possible states, then one line condition can be used to represent 2 data bits, and 1 baud equals 2 bits per second. In actual practice, data is often transmitted over communication lines in this manner. If the signals are coded into eight possible states, then one line condition represents 3 bits, and 1 baud equals 3 bits per second.

Some literature uses the term *baud* to mean *bits per second*. Though this is true with two-state signaling, it is definitely *not* true in general. Since the term *baud* can be confusing, we will avoid using it in this book.

ANALOG COMMUNICATION CHANNELS Unfortunately, most of the lines that are used to transmit data are not digital. The most commonly used data communication channel is the ordinary telephone circuit, which has as its major function the transmission of human voice, not computer data.

Light, sound, radio waves, and analog signals passing along telephone wires are all described in terms of *frequencies*. In all these means of transmission, the *amplitude* of the signal at a given point oscillates rapidly, just as the displacement of a plucked violin string oscillates. The rate of oscillation is referred to as the *frequency* of the signal and is described in terms of *cycles per second,* or *hertz.* The unit *hertz* is often abbreviated *Hz.* One thousand cycles per second is called one *kilohertz* (kHz), and one million cycles per second is called one *megahertz* (MHz).

With light we see different frequencies as different *colors.* Violet light has a higher frequency than green; green has a higher frequency than red. With sound, higher frequencies are heard as higher *pitch.* A flute makes sounds of higher frequency than a trombone.

BANDWIDTH

Analog lines are designed to carry specific ranges of frequencies. The capacity of an analog line is measured by the range of frequencies that the line is designed to carry. This is called its *bandwidth.* Most of the energy of human speech is concentrated between the frequencies 300 and 3100 hertz, and telephone channels are designed to transmit approximately this range (see Fig. 2.2). The telephone companies made this decision based on economics. It permits the maximum number of telephone conversations to be sent simultaneously over a transmission medium while still making the human voice intelligible and the speaker recognizable.

The difference between 3100 hertz and 300 hertz is 2800 hertz, or approximately 3 kilohertz, the bandwidth of a normal telephone line. (The bandwidth of a telephone channel is actually about 4 kilohertz, but part of that bandwidth

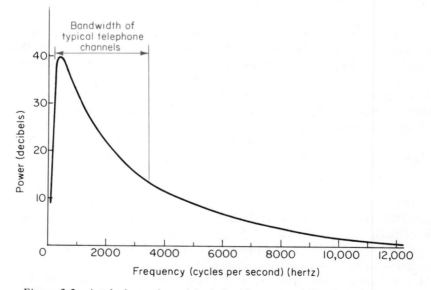

Figure 2.2   A telephone channel is designed to transmit human speech frequencies in the range of 300 to 3100 hertz.

is used to provide adequate separation between the channels when multiple channels share the same transmission facility.) The bandwidth of an analog channel is always the difference between the upper and lower limits of the frequencies it is designed to carry. If a line is designed to carry the frequencies between 80,300 and 83,100 hertz, its bandwidth is still approximately 3 kilohertz.

The number of bits per second that an analog line can carry is related closely to the line's bandwidth. In general, the higher the bandwidth of the channel, the higher the bit rate that can be carried.

CARRIER FREQUENCIES

The bandwidth of an analog channel refers to the *range* of frequencies that are transmitted. As we have seen, a telephone channel capable of sending signals from 300 to 3100 Hz has a bandwidth of approximately 3 kHz. The bandwidth of a channel does not have anything to do with the actual frequencies that are used for transmission. For example, FM radio is capable of reproducing sound in the range of about 30 to 18,000 Hz. However, the waves of FM radio do not actually travel at these frequencies; the transmission occurs at frequencies of about 100 million Hz. A similar consideration is true with the high-frequency media that are used in transmitting telephone signals.

A transmission medium might work efficiently only at high frequencies of perhaps 70 to 150 MHz. Somehow this high frequency must be made to *carry* the lower frequencies. This is done through a process of *modulation*. The low frequencies are used to modulate, or make changes to, the high-frequency signal, which is known as the *carrier frequency*. In this way, the modulation process produces a signal that can be transmitted efficiently and from which, after transmission, the original lower frequencies can be recovered.

Let us suppose that a bandwidth of 4000 Hz is to be used for voice transmission (3100 Hz plus some extra to separate channels from one another) and that the carrier frequency is 30 kHz. The conversion process might change the original frequencies from 0–4000 Hz to 30,000–34,000 Hz. The bandwidth is still 4000 Hz and will still carry the same quantity of information if it is voice or data.

SENDING DATA THROUGH TELEPHONE CHANNELS

When data is sent over ordinary telephone channels, the digital data must be converted into analog signals that must fit into the available bandwidth of the telephone channel. Because telephone channels are so widespread, it is desirable to have a method that will enable the highest data rate to be squeezed into the available bandwidth, but without incurring an excessive error rate.

This is normally achieved through another modulation process, similar to the process used by the telephone company in converting the speech spectrum into the frequency range used in the transmission medium. This time, however, the modulation process converts the bit stream produced by a data machine into audible tones that can be transmitted over a standard telephone channel.

MODEMS

In order to use an analog line to transmit the discrete voltage levels that a data processing machine creates, the bits must first be converted into a continuous range of frequencies. The process of converting a digital bit stream into an analog signal is a form of *modulation*. The process of performing the opposite conversion at the other end is called *demodulation*. The device that performs this conversion is called a *modem,* short for *modulator/demodulator*. To connect two digital machines using an analog line, there must be a modem between the data machine and the line at each end (see Fig. 2.3).

Some telephone companies, AT&T for one, have referred to the modem as a *data set*. This is an unfortunate choice of terminology, since in many operating systems, the term *data set* is used to refer to data files. Fortunately, the term *data set* in referring to a modem is now seldom used.

A modem to be used on a speech channel converts the bit stream produced by a data processing machine into a modulated-sine-wave carrier that fits within the allowable frequencies that can be sent over a standard voice channel. The maximum speed of modems designed to operate on speech channels is about 19,200 bps. However, most modems operate at speeds much lower than this. The most commonly used modem speeds are 300, 1200, and 2400 bps.

DIGITAL CHANNELS

It is possible to change the electronics on a line so that it becomes a high-speed digital channel rather than an analog circuit. It is common to transmit more

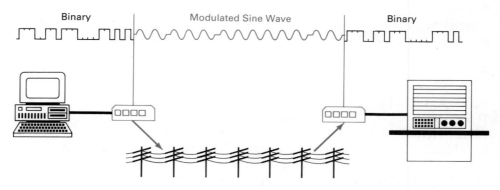

Figure 2.3 To connect two digital machines using an analog transmission facility, there must be a modem at each end of the line.

than 1.5 million bits over such a line. As we have seen, we can transmit a digital bit stream over an analog circuit using modems to perform the necessary signal conversion. It is also possible to transmit voice signals on a digital line. To do this a device called a *codec* (for *coder/decoder*) is used at each end of the line to convert the voice signal into a digital bit stream.

Most of the world's telecommunications facilities are analog, mainly for historical reasons. It is now economically advantageous to switch from analog to digital transmission in the telephone network, for two main reasons. First, the circuitry used to handle digital signals is much cheaper than the complex amplifiers and filters used for analog signals. As the cost of microelectronics drops, digital techniques become more attractive. Second, the use of data transmission is increasing rapidly. It is obviously more efficient to carry computer data in its original digital form.

SHARING CHANNEL CAPACITY

In many systems that use data transmission facilities, the cost of the communication channels themselves represents a large percentage of the total cost of the system. The channels must be shared as much as possible to ensure that their capacity is fully utilized. The sharing of transmission lines can be carried out in a variety of ways. Basically, two problems are involved. The first is the technical problem of combining different transmissions on the same line. This is relatively easily solved. When several separate transmissions are sent over the same line *at the same time,* this is referred to as *multiplexing*. The second problem is that of bringing together a sufficient number of users to fill the group of channels that has been derived from the line.

The need for communication line multiplexing is a basic factor in achieving economic usage of remote computers. A *very* high degree of multiplexing is necessary to take advantage of the digital transmission media that today's technology makes possible. Microwave links and coaxial cables that carry a billion bits per second are today routinely used in the public telephone network. Consequently, data transmission networks are passing through a number of stages. These stages are summarized in Box 2.1. We will now turn our attention to the technology that is used in sharing communication facilities.

MULTIPLEXING

The physical cables and radio links that are used in the public telephone network for transmitting signals have a high bandwidth—many times higher than the 4-kHz bandwidth needed for telephone speech. To use them economically, many speech channels are transmitted together as a single signal occupying all (or most) of the available bandwidth. For efficiency, the speech channels are packed together as tightly as possible, like sardines in a can. Each speech channel occupies no more than 4 kHz of the available bandwidth. The term *multiplexing* refers to any process

BOX 2.1   Evolution of computer networks

- **Private Single-Use Networks.** First, we have seen private networks in which terminals are linked to one system designed for one set of functions—for example, today's airline and banking systems, each using its own computer center.

- **Private Networks Interlinking Systems.** Next, we see private networks in which more than one system is interlinked within an organization. For example, a private network might interlink separate time-sharing facilities or database systems.

- **Private Shared Networks.** Then come private networks in which systems in different organizations share network facilities. In this category are interbank systems and interairline systems that share network facilities. This type of network might interconnect time-sharing systems or the computer centers in different organizations.

- **Limited Public Networks.** Next come the public data transmission networks that offer services in large metropolitan areas using digital technology.

- **Nationwide Public Networks.** It is then a logical step to nationwide public networks in which access is provided virtually everywhere in a country. It may be some time before public data networks become as ubiquitous as the telephone network, but eventually terminals and personal computers in most homes and offices will be interlinked.

- **International Public Networks.** The next step is toward international public data networks. The problems with international incompatibility are being solved with interface computers. Political problems are also being overcome. The work being done toward the creation of international telecommunications standards is a step in the right direction toward the creation of international public networks.

- **Integrated Services Digital Network (ISDN).** A future goal of networking is to have universal access to an integrated network that allows a user anywhere to plug in any type of device—telephone, data terminal, computer, facsimile machine, or video equipment—and to communicate with a similar device anywhere in the world. A channel with the appropriate bit rate will be assigned automatically by the network. ISDN development is actively under way in a number of countries, including the United States, and pilot ISDNs are in operation; within the foreseeable future, this goal of a universal ISDN may be realized. ISDN technology is discussed in Chapter 20.

that permits more than one separate signal to be transmitted simultaneously over a single physical channel. There are three multiplexing methods:

- **Space-Division Multiplexing.** With *space-division multiplexing,* multiple physical circuits are carried in the same cable. For example, a telephone cable may contain 100 or more wire pairs, each of which carries a separate signal.

- **Frequency-Division Multiplexing.** *Frequency-division multiplexing* is used with analog channels. Each speech channel is typically raised in frequency to a 4-kHz slot assigned to it (see Fig. 2.4). All of these slots can then be carried simultaneously over a single circuit. In Fig. 2.4, three carriers are shown, with frequencies of 30, 34, and 38 kHz. Each is modulated by the speech band at frequencies 300 to 3100 Hz to form a block of frequencies slightly higher than the carrier frequency. These three signals are transmitted together in a block of frequencies ranging from 30,000 to 42,000 Hz. In actual practice, many more than three different signals would be carried together over a channel of much higher bandwidth than in this example.

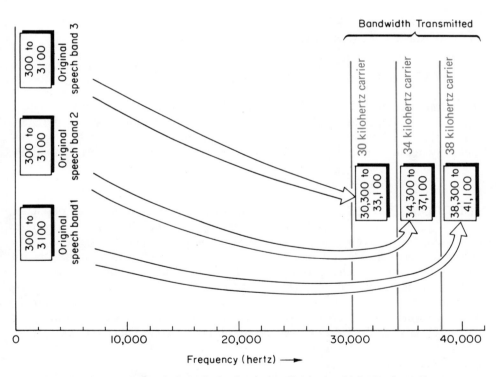

Figure 2.4   With analog channels, frequency-division multiplexing is used to carry multiple signals on the same transmission facility.

- **Time-Division Multiplexing.** *Time-division multiplexing* is used with digital channels. A bit stream is subdivided to carry lesser bit streams with their bits interleaved. For example, every tenth bit in a high-speed bit stream might be a bit from one subchannel. The bit after that is from the second channel and so on, until ten subchannels are derived.

SWITCHING

Another way to share communication channels among many users, but for a different purpose, is to interconnect them by means of *switching*. The user has a line to a telephone exchange, and there the user's line can be connected to that of another subscriber. The switching can take place in the network facilities, for example, in a telephone exchange, or it can take place on the subscriber's premises, enabling many users to share a small number of access lines. The type of switching used on the public telephone network in interconnecting subscribers is not the only kind of switching that can be used. In general, there are four types of switching:

- Conventional circuit switching
- Fast-connect circuit switching
- Message switching
- Packet switching

These four switching techniques are introduced in Box 2.2. Packet switching is a particularly important technology for data communication and is the most commonly used switching technique for implementing public data networks. Packet switching and public data networks are discussed in detail in Chapter 14.

MULTIPOINT LINES

Another way that communication lines can be shared is by using a multipoint line. Figure 2.5 illustrates the difference between using multiple *point-to-point* connections and a single *multipoint* connection to interconnect devices. When a point-to-point connection is used, data can be exchanged only between devices that are directly connected, unless data is relayed from one device to another. The situation is different when multipoint connections are used. (A multipoint line is sometimes called a *multidrop line*.) When data is transmitted from terminal A using a multipoint line, terminals B, C, and D all receive the transmission. Therefore, more complex procedures are needed to ensure that terminal C, for example, ignores all transmissions that are not intended for it.

The use of multipoint lines can often make it possible to reduce line costs

BOX 2.2   Switching techniques

- **Conventional Circuit Switching.** With this technique, all the lines are connected to exchanges, or switching offices. The exchanges are used to connect, on demand, any subscriber to any other subscriber. Although this type of switching is most often associated with the public telephone network, individual subscribers can also use conventional telephone switching techniques. Individual users can lease telephone channels and install switches to construct private switched networks of their own.

- **Fast-Connect Circuit Switching.** This technique is logically similar to conventional circuit switching. All the lines are connected to switching centers, and circuits are established on demand between any two subscribers. However, with telephone switching it may take as long as 30 seconds to establish a connection. With fast-connect switching, a typical connection is established in a fraction of a second. The extremely fast switching time makes this switching technique particularly well suited to data transmission.

- **Message Switching.** With *message switching,* users can be interconnected on demand without using circuit switches. Messages that enter a message switching system each have a *destination address* attached to them. They are then *forwarded* to their final destinations. Electronic mail systems have been built that use message switching techniques to route letters and memos between users.

- **Packet Switching.** *Packet switching* is a particular form of message switching that is often used to interconnect users on a general-purpose public data network. Messages are divided into *packets,* which are routed independently through the network for transmission to their final destinations. At their destinations, the packets are reassembled into their original form. Although packets may be routed through many intermediate nodes in reaching their destinations, it looks to the user as if a direct connection exists between the sender and the receiver.

substantially. As shown in Fig. 2.6, it would be more expensive to interconnect terminals A, B, C, and D with point-to-point connections, especially if the distances involved are long.

DYNAMIC CHANNEL ALLOCATION

Dynamic channel allocation is another method for increasing the utilization of an expensive channel. This technique is often used when a telephone line is long

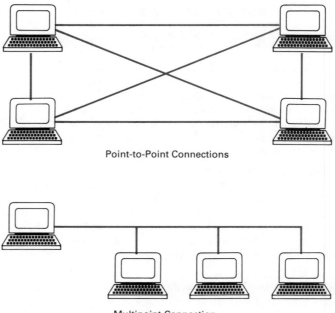

Point-to-Point Connections

Multipoint Connection

Figure 2.5 Multiple point-to-point connections or a single multipoint connection can be used to interconnect devices.

and expensive, such as a transatlantic cable. With dynamic channel allocation, the link is subdivided into many channels in both directions. When you talk, a circuit detects that you are talking and allocates a channel to you. When you stop talking, even for a second or two, the channel is made available to other users. When the party you are talking to replies, a channel is dynamically allocated in the opposite direction. The channel allocations are done at electronic speed within a tiny fraction of a second.

Most telephone speakers spend about 55 percent of their time pausing or listening. Dynamic channel allocation done very rapidly can more than double the capacity of a channel. The front of some words will be removed, as the channel allocation cannot be done instantaneously. Usually, only a few milliseconds is removed, but occasionally many milliseconds are lost because, by chance, most persons are speaking in one direction and there is no free channel space until one of them pauses briefly. If no more than about 50 milliseconds is chopped off the front of every word spoken, most speech is still quite intelligible and recognizable.

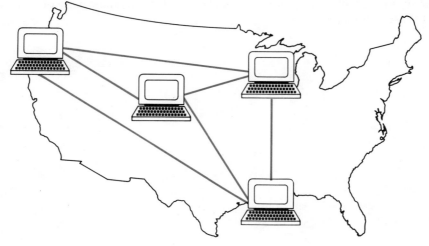

Point-to-Point

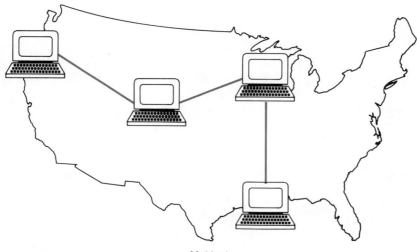

Multipoint

Figure 2.6 A multipoint connection is often less expensive than point-to-point connections.

In this chapter, we have examined the general characteristics of the communication channels that we use. In Chapter 3, we discuss the various types of transmission facilities that are used in the public telephone network to implement these channels.

3 TRANSMISSION FACILITIES

In this chapter, we examine the nature of the communication facilities that are used for carrying telephone voice and computer data. To establish a framework into which we can fit the various types of communication facilities that we will discuss, we will classify communication links according to the following criteria:

- Analog or digital
- Channel capacity
- Switched versus leased lines
- Transmission mode
- Physical transmission medium

ANALOG OR DIGITAL

As discussed in Chapter 2, telecommunications channels can be designed to carry analog signals, or they can carry digital data directly. This is a fundamental difference that has much to do with the way the communication link is engineered. Most of today's telecommunications links are analog, but this is rapidly changing; digital links will become much more common in the future. Computer data can be carried on either analog or digital channels, but as we have seen, data is carried more economically on a channel that has been designed with digital data in mind.

CHANNEL CAPACITY

The transmission speeds that are available today range from just a few bits to millions of bits per second. For convenience, we generally separate transmission lines into three categories. In the first category are *sub-voice-grade* lines, ones that transmit at rates from about 45 to 600 bps. These are lines that do not have sufficient capacity to carry telephone calls. Some telegraph circuits consist of sub-voice-grade lines.

In the second category are *voice-grade* lines, which are generally normal telephone channels. They are typically used to carry telephone voice signals, but they can also be used to carry computer data at speeds of from 300 to a maximum of 19,200 bps.

In the third category are *wideband* lines. These lines have higher capacities than normal telephone channels. Speeds of 48,000, 56,000, and 64,000, and 1.5 million bps are common on wideband channels. Some of the long-distance communication channels in use today support bit rates much higher than these, sometimes into the billions of bits per second. But most of these high-capacity links are used only by telephone companies to multiplex large numbers of voice channels or to transmit television signals.

SWITCHED VERSUS LEASED LINES

When you make a telephone call, you make use of a *public, switched line*. When you dial, a communication line is made available to you through the facilities of switching offices between you and your destination. As soon as you hang up, the switches disconnect your circuit so that it can be used by someone else. When a *leased line* is used, a permanent circuit is established between one user and another, and a fixed monthly charge is assessed for the connection. The line may still go through the switching offices, but the switches are permanently set so that the circuit is always connected.

TRANSMISSION MODE

There are three modes of transmission: *simplex, half-duplex,* and *full-duplex*. A *simplex* line is capable of transmitting in only one direction. A *half-duplex* line can transmit in both directions, but only in one direction at a time. A *full-duplex* line can transmit in both directions at once. Most communication lines that are used today for data transmission are either half-duplex or full-duplex. Simplex lines are not very useful because even in the simplest data communication application, where data is transmitted in only one direction, control signals must ordinarily flow the opposite way.

PHYSICAL TRANSMISSION MEDIUM

Early telecommunications systems used wires called *open pairs,* which consisted of pairs of relatively thick wires that were capable of carrying signals a long distance without amplification. Today, most open-wire pairs have been replaced with cables containing a number of *twisted-*

wire pairs. The wire pairs are twisted to minimize *crosstalk* (interference between circuits) when many twisted-wire pairs are packed together in a single cable. These cables use thinner wire and require amplifiers that are spaced closer together. Twisted-wire pairs have a limited bandwidth because as the frequencies transmitted increase, the current tends to flow on the outer skin of the wire, and the effective resistance of the wire increases.

Twisted pairs that are used to connect individual subscribers to the local switching office are called *local loops* or *subscriber lines.* Local loops are not ordinarily shared; they are used to transmit one call only between a subscriber and the switching office. Twisted pairs are sometimes also used to connect switching offices with one another. Circuits used for this purpose are called *trunks* or *toll circuits.* Twisted pairs used as trunks often carry either 12 or 24 simultaneous telephone calls.

To carry higher frequencies, and hence deliver a higher bandwidth than twisted pairs, coaxial cables can be used. A coaxial cable consists of a wire surrounded by a hollow copper cylinder. The wire is insulated from the cylinder by air or plastic. Several coaxial cables are often bound together along with a number of twisted-wire pairs in a single cable. A special form of coaxial cable is used in the submarine cables used for overseas communication.

In many cases, radio is used as the transmission medium. Regular high-frequency radio communication is used for mobile telephone service and ship-to-shore operations. Microwave radio channels span the nation and carry much of our long-distance telephone traffic. The disadvantage of microwave radio is that transmission must be on a line-of-sight basis with the microwave towers relatively close together. Tropospheric scatter circuits use the reflective nature of the earth's troposphere to make radio communication possible over long distances.

Very high frequency radio waves can be used in rectangular and helical waveguides. Their advantage is that the higher frequencies used allow for extremely high bandwidths. But almost as soon as waveguides were becoming popular, optical fibers made them seem obsolete. As we will discuss later in this chapter, optical fibers are made of glass and carry signals on a modulated light beam.

WIDEBAND ANALOG CHANNELS AND TRUNKS

The wideband analog telecommunications facilities that allow data communication systems to carry high bit rates of 50,000 bps and more are derived mainly from the high-capacity trunks that carry telephone signals over long distances. The main telecommunications highways of the world carry many signals simultaneously, and these signals are gathered into standardized groupings. The composition of a grouping is precisely defined in terms of the number of channels, the frequencies used, and the multiplexing techniques employed to form the grouping.

To a major extent, international standardization has been achieved, but some of the North American standards are different from the CCITT standards adopted by much of the rest of the world. This is because many of the North American high-capacity facilities were designed and installed before the international standards came into existence.

- **North American Analog Channel Groups.** Figure 3.1 shows the main blocks of analog channels that form the standards for North America. At the bottom of the diagram is the telegraph channel. Either twelve 150-Hz telegraph channels or twenty-four 50-bps telex channels can be derived from one voice channel. Twelve voice channels can be multiplexed together to form a *channel group,* sometimes called simply a *group.* This was the highest level of multiplexing in the 1930s; since then larger and larger blocks have come into use.
- **CCITT Standard Analog Channel Groups.** The CCITT groupings are shown in Fig. 3.2. Note that the CCITT international standards are the same as the North American ones for the group and supergroup but are different for higher-capacity groups. Consequently, a mastergroup or higher cannot travel directly from North American to European telephone networks. They must first be demultiplexed down to the supergroup level and then remultiplexed using CCITT groupings.

WIDEBAND CHANNELS

Most providers of telecommunications services lease their channel groups and supergroups to provide wideband services. Three grades of wideband services are commonly used in North America. The series 8000 channel is equivalent to one channel group, the type 5700 channel to a supergroup, and the type 5800 to four supergroups.

When an organization leases a wideband channel, such as these, it also typically leases appropriate channel terminals. A variety of terminating equipment is available. The channels can be used as wideband channels, or they can be subdivided by the user into private channels of lower bandwidth to be used for telephone calls or for lower-speed data transmission. The various channel groupings that are available can use terminating equipment that enable channels to be used for a number of purposes. Some of these are listed in Box 3.1.

So far, we have been discussing the wideband *analog* transmission facilities that are used in the public telephone network. However, high-speed digital transmission now dominates the long-haul facilities of most telecommunications providers.

DIGITAL TRANSMISSION FACILITIES

In its first half century, telecommunications was dominated by analog transmission and frequency-division multiplexing. Multibillions of dollars are still tied up in such equipment. However, if the telecom-

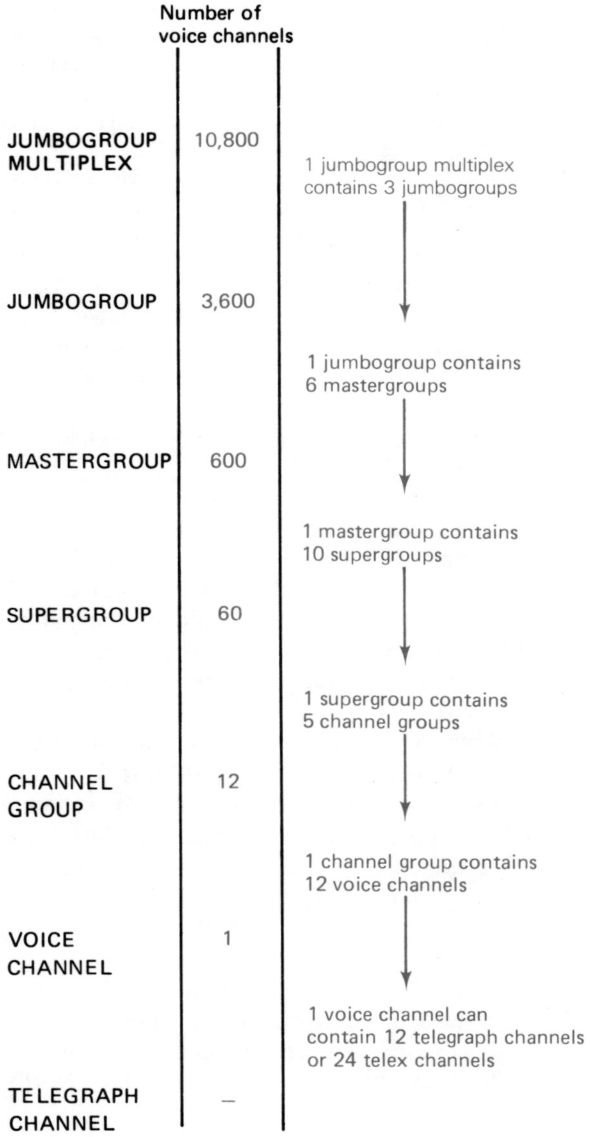

Number of voice channels

JUMBOGROUP MULTIPLEX	10,800
JUMBOGROUP	3,600
MASTERGROUP	600
SUPERGROUP	60
CHANNEL GROUP	12
VOICE CHANNEL	1
TELEGRAPH CHANNEL	—

1 jumbogroup multiplex contains 3 jumbogroups

1 jumbogroup contains 6 mastergroups

1 mastergroup contains 10 supergroups

1 supergroup contains 5 channel groups

1 channel group contains 12 voice channels

1 voice channel can contain 12 telegraph channels or 24 telex channels

Figure 3.1 Hierarchy of North American frequency-division multiplexing groups.

Number of Voice Channels	CCITT Standard	AT&T Standard
12	Group	Channel group (sometimes called "Group")
60	Supergroup	Supergroup
300	Mastergroup	
600		Mastergroup
900	Supermaster group (sometimes called "Mastergroup" or "Hypergroup")	
1800		Mastergroup multiplex
3600		Jumbogroup
10,800		Jumbogroup multiplex

Figure 3.2   CCITT standards for frequency-division multiplexing groups.

munications industry were to start again today building the world's transmission links, frequency-division multiplexing would have limited use, and all trunks would transmit *digital* bit streams instead of analog signals. Most links, with the possible exception of some local loops, would be incapable of transmitting analog signals without conversion to digital form. After converting an analog signal using a codec, the telephone voice becomes a bit stream that looks like computer data.

A telephone call, when digitized, needs a bit rate of 64,000 bps for transmission (56,000 bps for the voice signal and 8000 bps for control functions on most North American digital transmission facilities). This rate is much higher than 9600 or 19,200 bps, typical maximum rates at which data travels over analog telephone lines. The balance of cost between telephone voice transmission and data transmission is thus swinging substantially in favor of data.

AT&T DIGITAL CARRIERS   AT&T has defined standards for four levels of digital transmission channels. These are referred to as the T1, T2, T3, and T4 carriers. The same standards are used by many of the other telecommunications vendors in North America.

THE T1 CARRIER   The most widely used digital transmission system at present is the *T1* carrier. This carrier uses wire pairs with digital repeaters spaced 6000 feet apart to carry 1,544,000 bps. Twenty-

BOX 3.1　Common uses of channel groupings

Channel Group Uses

1. Twelve telephone channels between two points
2. Forty-eight 150-bps channels between two points
3. 144 teletype channels between two points
4. Equivalent combinations of the above
5. Data transmission at 40,800 bps plus one telephone channel for coordination purposes
6. Two-level facsimile signals in the frequency range of approximately 29 to 44 kHz plus one telephone channel for coordination purposes
7. Two-level facsimile signals requiring up to 50,000 bps plus one telephone channel
8. A channel of bandwidth up to 20 kHz of high quality having only minor deviations in gain and delay characteristics

Supergroup Uses

1. Data transmission at approximately 105,000 bps plus a control channel and a telephone channel for coordination purposes
2. Two-level facsimile requiring up to 250,000 bps plus four channels of teletype grade for control and coordination
3. A channel of bandwidth up to 100 kHz having only minor deviations in gain and delay characteristics

four speech channels can be encoded on this bit stream. The T1 carrier has been highly successful, and millions of voice-channel-miles of it are in operation. Most readers of this book have talked over a digital T1 carrier without knowing it.

When AT&T first introduced T1 facilities, they were installed mainly in the public telephone network to implement connections between switching offices; these high-speed facilities were not initially available to individual subscribers. The T1 carrier has been so successful, however, that individual users of telecommunications can now lease T1 facilities from a variety of vendors. These leased T1 communication facilities, though relatively expensive, are now used routinely to implement communication links where high data rates are required.

HIGHER-CAPACITY DIGITAL TRANSMISSION

The T1 carrier was only the beginning. A hierarchy of interlinked digital channels is used in the public telephone network. The next step up is the T2 carrier, which operates at 6.3 million bps and carries the signals from four T1 carriers. Millions of T2 voice-channel-miles are operational. The T2 carrier typically uses wire-pair circuits that are specifically engineered for digital transmission.

The T3 and T4 carriers are too fast for wire-pair circuits. They must use more sophisticated transmission media. The T3 carrier has approximately seven times the capacity of the T2 carrier; it can carry 672 telephone channels. This carrier standard is little used in actual practice and serves mainly as a bridge between the T2 and T4 carriers.

The T4 carrier has a capacity roughly 42 times that of the AT&T T2 carrier and can carry 4032 digital voice channels. It is coming into common use for long-haul circuits and can be carried by a variety of transmission media, including coaxial cable, microwave relay, waveguide, satellite, and optical fiber.

CCITT DIGITAL RECOMMENDATIONS

The CCITT has made two recommendations for digital transmission, one for transmission at the T1 carrier speed of 1,544,000 bps and one for transmission at 2,048,000 bps. As is often the case, the CCITT recommendation for 1,544,000-bps transmission is slightly different from the North American standard set by AT&T.

A great many complex technologies are used to implement the world's telecommunications facilities. Two of the newest technologies for telecommunications are having a major impact on the reduction in cost of long-haul transmission. These are the technologies of communication satellites and optical fibers.

COMMUNICATIONS SATELLITES

A *communications satellite* provides essentially a very high capacity cable in the sky. The unique thing about a satellite link is that the cost of a channel can be independent of distance. On April 6, 1965, the world's first commercial satellite, *Early Bird,* rocketed into the evening sky at Cape Kennedy. The success of the transmission experiments that followed this has been spectacular. Before long, earth stations were being built around the world, and new and more powerful satellites were on the drawing boards.

TRANSPONDERS

A communications satellite is really no more than a microwave relay in the sky. It receives microwave signals from equipment on the earth in a given frequency band and retransmits them at a different frequency. It must use a different frequency for retransmission; otherwise the powerful transmitted signal would interfere with the weak incoming signal. The equipment on the ground, consisting of a receiver, a transmitter, and an antenna, is referred to as an *earth station*.

The device in the satellite that receives a signal, amplifies it, changes its frequency, and retransmits it is called a *transponder*. Most satellites have more than one transponder. The bandwidth handled by a transponder has differed from one satellite design to another, but many contemporary satellites have transponders with a bandwidth of 36 MHz. How this bandwidth is used depends on the nature of the earth station equipment. For example, a typical transponder can carry any of the following:

- One color television channel
- 1200 voice channels
- One channel of 50 million bps
- 16 T1 channels of 1,544,000 bps
- 400 channels of 64,000 bps
- 600 channels of 40,000 bps

WORLD COVERAGE

Communications satellites are stationed in a *geosynchronous orbit* about 23,000 miles over the equator. They revolve around the earth in exactly the time it takes for the earth to rotate and hence appear to hang stationary in the sky. Because they are so high, they can transmit to much of the earth. Three satellites can cover all of the inhabited regions of the world, with the exception of a few dwellings close to the poles.

The cost of satellite channels is dropping remarkably fast. A main thrust of the technology is to find ways to make the receiving equipment on earth cheap and mass-producible. Costs have already dropped sufficiently so that many corporate and government organizations have their own earth stations.

PROPERTIES OF SATELLITE LINKS

Satellite channels have unique properties. Some of these properties have an effect on how those channels can be employed for data communication. Box 3.2 lists some of the properties of satellite channels. Two of the characteristics listed in Box 3.2 deserve further discussion. These are the costs of satellite channels and the 270-millisecond propagation delay inherent in satellite links.

Satellite Channel Costs

One of the favorable characteristics of a communications satellite channel is its potentially very low cost. Figure 3.3 shows how dramatically the investment

BOX 3.2   Characteristics of satellite channels

- Transmission cost is independent of distance. A link from Washington to Baltimore costs the same to engineer as a link from Washington to Vancouver.
- There is a 270-millisecond *propagation delay* of the signal due to the great distance the signal must travel.
- Very high bandwidths or bit rates are available to users if they can have an earth station at their premises or a microwave link to an earth station, thereby avoiding the local loops.
- A signal sent to a satellite is transmitted to all receivers within range of the satellite.
- Because of the broadcast property, dynamic assignment of channels is necessary between geographically dispersed users.
- Also because of the broadcast property, security procedures must be taken seriously.
- Most satellite transmissions are sent in digital form. Digital techniques can therefore be used to manipulate and interleave the signals in a variety of ways.
- A transmitting station can receive its own transmission and hence monitor whether the satellite has transmitted it correctly. This fact can be used in certain forms of transmission control.

cost per satellite channel (for the satellite and its launch) has been dropping. The extraordinary cost reduction shown in Fig. 3.3 will probably continue, but not at such a spectacular rate. The cost of an earth station has dropped even more spectacularly than that of a satellite, as shown in Fig. 3.4. Early earth stations cost more than $10 million, and some early experimental earth stations cost several times that. Costs have now dropped to a small fraction of that, especially for small receive-only stations.

Propagation Delay

A disadvantage of satellite transmission is that a delay occurs because the signal has to travel far out into space and back. The signal propagation time is about 270 milliseconds, varying slightly with the earth station locations. If you make a telephone call that uses a satellite link in both directions, you wait for the reply of the person you are talking to for an extra 540 milliseconds. This delay

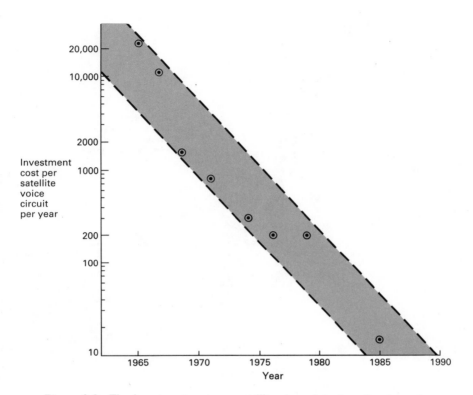

Figure 3.3 The investment cost per satellite channel is dropping dramatically.

of more than half a second can be annoying in telephone conversations, but most people who regularly use satellite circuits for voice communication get used to it. The delay has more serious consequences for the users of data communications. In interactive data transmission via satellite, a terminal user will experience a constant increase in response time of 540 milliseconds. A system designer has to take this into account in determining the overall system response time.

In many interactive systems it is desirable that the mean response time for certain interactions be no greater than 2 seconds. This is achieved satisfactorily on many interactive systems using satellites today. However, appropriate line control procedures have to be used on satellite channels. Some equipment for data transmission over telephone lines performs very poorly if used on a satellite channel because it uses a control procedure that is inappropriate if the channel has a long delay. But satellite channels can perform very well for data communication if appropriate equipment and control procedures are used.

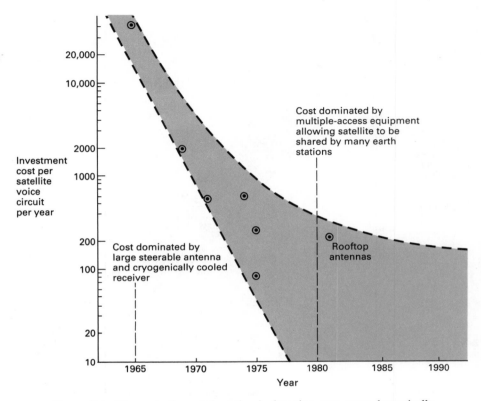

Figure 3.4 The cost of an earth station is dropping even more dramatically than satellite costs.

FIBER OPTICS

An optical fiber is a long strand of glass that carries a signal in the form of a modulated light beam. The optical fiber has two advantages over traditional forms of terrestrial telecommunications circuits. First, the fiber can be manufactured at lower cost than traditional copper wire or other types of cable. Second, since the frequency of a light beam is much higher than other forms of electromagnetic radiation, an optical fiber can support a much higher bandwidth. The frequency of light is 10 million times greater than the frequencies used on coaxial cables. Furthermore, a coaxial cable has 10,000 times the cross-sectional area of the glass fibers used for optical transmission, so many more fibers than coaxial tubes can be packed in one cable. Figure 3.5 shows how an optical fiber cable is constructed.

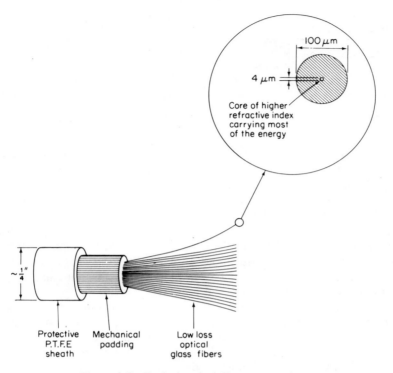

Figure 3.5 Typical optical fiber construction.

ABSORPTION, REFLECTION, AND DISPERSION

In the early stages of optical fiber development, fibers worked successfully for telecommunications only over short distances. The main reason for this was the *absorption* that occurred in the glass. In the 1970s and 1980s, however, phenomenal progress occurred in glass fiber manufacture. It is now clear that optical fibers represent one of the most important technologies of telecommunications. Optical fiber transmission links are now in common use throughout the world.

Why does the light stay inside the fiber? It travels down a cylinder of glass that is surrounded by a substance, usually also glass, of low refractive index. When the beam strikes the edge of the cylinder, it is totally reflected and remains inside, as shown in Fig. 3.6. This total internal reflection occurs in a similar manner at the surface of a pond. If you put your head under the water and look at the surface some distance away, it will appear to be a totally reflect-

Light rays are reflected down a glass fiber with total internal
reflection at the surface:

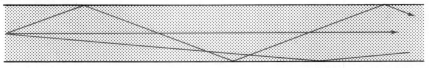

Figure 3.6   Internal reflection keeps the light beam inside the optical fiber.

ing mirror. Not a ray of light is refracted out of the pond at all because of its low striking angle; all light is reflected back into the water.

The light beam travels down a fiber and is confined within it by total internal reflection. However, it is absorbed somewhat by the fiber; consequently, bit repeaters must be used at appropriate intervals.

The potentially usable bandwidth of glass fibers is very high. If the potential bandwidth could be fully utilized, one fiber could transmit on the order of 10^{14} bps. The glass fibers in use today transmit bit rates that are far below this theoretical maximum. One factor that limits the transmission capacity is *dispersion* of the signal as it travels down the fiber.

Rays of light traveling down a fiber can be transmitted by different paths. A ray traveling straight down the axis of the fiber will reach its destination before a ray that bounces down the fiber with many reflections. A very short pulse transmitted down a fiber will therefore be spread out in time, as shown in Fig. 3.7. The farther it is transmitted, the more it will be spread out.

In a typical fiber of 100 microns (0.1 millimeter) diameter, the axial ray

However some light rays travel by shorter paths than others,
This causes the signal to become increasingly dispersed:

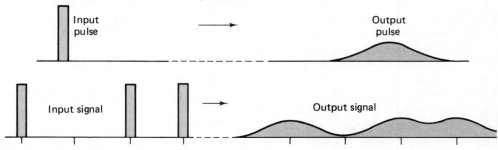

This dispersion puts an upper limit on the signaling rate of a
glass fiber. Fibers can be constructed with very low dispersion.
Such fibers can carry a very high rate.

Figure 3.7   Dispersion of the light beam limits the maximum bit rate of an optical fiber.

is transmitted 1 kilometer in several nanoseconds less time than the ray that takes the longest path. Pulses less than a few nanoseconds apart will interfere with one another and become indistinguishable. If the repeaters on the fiber are to be 10 kilometers apart, this pulse spreading limits the transmission rate to well below 100 million bps per fiber.

LASERS

It is necessary to have a source of light that has a long enough life to act as a transmitter and that can be modulated to operate at a high information rate. Most of today's fibers are designed to work with laser beams.

Laser stands for *"light amplification by stimulated emission of radiation."* A laser produces a narrow beam of light that is *coherent*. In a coherent light beam, all the waves travel in unison, like the waves traveling away from a stone dropped in a pond. The beam is also sharply *monochromatic;* that is, it occupies a single color or frequency or consists of multiple monochromatic emissions.

A problem with optical fibers is how to get a powerful signal inside such a tiny fiber. The beam for a typical fiber must be shone down the very central

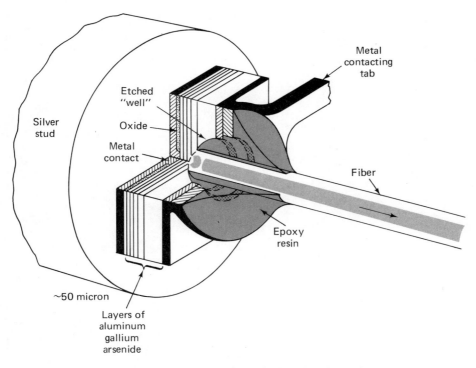

Figure 3.8   Construction of a typical semiconductor laser.

portion of the glass fiber, in a beam as narrow as 5 microns (0.005 millimeters) in diameter. Lenses and mirrors could be used, but much of the light from an incoherent source would be lost. A laser can provide a very tiny but intensely bright source that emits light in a narrow parallel beam and can be attached directly to the fiber.

The type of laser most commonly used for this purpose is the *semiconductor laser*. It is tiny and inexpensive to manufacture, using similar methods to those used for producing today's microelectronic chips. As in the production of LSI circuitry, quantities of such chips are produced simultaneously by depositing the various chemical layers on a wafer of the substrate material and then dicing the wafer into many chips. The construction of a typical semiconductor laser is shown in Fig. 3.8.

Chapter 4 introduces the telecommunications industry and examines the companies that provide the telecommunications services that we have been discussing.

4   THE TELECOMMUNICATIONS INDUSTRY

In this chapter, we examine the vendors, telecommunications administrations, regulatory authorities, and other organizations that make up the telecommunications industry. We begin with the largest class of organizations, the *common carriers* that make up the telephone companies of the United States.

UNITED STATES COMMON CARRIERS

The companies in North America that furnish communication services to the public are referred to as *common carriers*. The telecommunications common carriers offer facilities for the electronic transmission of information of all types, including voice, data, facsimile, television, and telemetry. Many find it surprising that there are thousands of telecommunications common carriers in the United States. Many other countries have only one such organization, which is run by the government. Most of the common carriers in the United States are very small; only about 250 of them have more than 5000 subscribers.

BELL OPERATING COMPANIES

The *American Telephone and Telegraph Company* (AT&T) had for years operated one of the largest telecommunications networks in the world. The network was called the *Bell System* after Alexander Graham Bell, the inventor of the telephone. In 1982, a federal court forced AT&T to divest itself of the *Bell Operating Companies* (BOCs) that provided local loop telephone service to individual subscribers. The divestiture officially began on November 21, 1983, and the former Bell System is now organized as AT&T and seven *Regional Holding Companies* (RHCs). The RHCs together operate the 23 Bell Operating Companies. The organization of AT&T and the RHCs is shown in Box 4.1.

BOX 4.1   The Bell System breakup

- **AT&T.** The *American Telephone and Telegraph Company* no longer controls the Bell Operating Companies (BOCs) that install and maintain the telephone local loops that provide telephone service to individuals, corporations, and government organizations. AT&T continues to operate its own research and development organization and Western Electric, AT&T's manufacturing organization. The BOCs are now organized in the form of the seven Regional Holding Companies (RHCs) described below.

- **Ameritech.** *American Information Technologies* (Ameritech) owns the five Midwestern BOCs that provide telephone service to Illinois, Indiana, Michigan, Ohio, and Wisconsin.

- **Pacific Telesis.** *Pacific Telesis* owns the BOC that provides telephone service to California and Nevada.

- **Bell South.** *Bell South* owns the BOCs that provide telephone service to Alabama, Florida, Georgia, Kentucky, Louisiana, Mississippi, North Carolina, South Carolina, and Tennessee.

- **Bell Atlantic.** *Bell Atlantic* owns the BOCs that provide telephone service to Connecticut, Delaware, Maryland, New Jersey, Pennsylvania, West Virginia, and Virginia.

- **NYNEX.** *NYNEX* owns the BOCs that provide telephone service to Maine, Massachusetts, New Hampshire, New York, Rhode Island, and Vermont.

- **Southwestern Bell Corporation.** *Southwestern Bell Corporation* owns the BOCs that provide telephone service to Arkansas, Kansas, Missouri, Oklahoma, and Texas.

- **US West.** *US West* owns the BOCs that provide telephone service to Arizona, Colorado, Idaho, Iowa, Minnesota, Montana, Nebraska, New Mexico, North Dakota, Oregon, South Dakota, Utah, Washington, and Wyoming.

The RHCs must now provide equal access for their customers to any of the various long-distance telephone common carriers (described later in this chapter) that now offer long-distance services in competition with AT&T.

THE AMERICAN TELEPHONE AND TELEGRAPH COMPANY

Up until the divestiture, AT&T employed over a million people; its assets were over three times greater than those of General Motors, America's largest industrial corporation. The Bell System once referred to the vast network of telephone and data circuits with many switching offices and to the television and other links that were operated across the United States by AT&T and its subsidiaries and associated companies. AT&T is now prohibited by law from using the name Bell or the familiar bell logo in advertising any of its products or services; the Bell name and logo are for the exclusive use of the seven regional holding companies that own the Bell Operating Companies.

Although AT&T does not now own any portion of the 23 Bell Operating Companies, it still operates its *Long Lines Department*, which provides much of the U.S. interstate long-distance service. AT&T still also owns Western Electric, the main manufacturing company for AT&T. It manufactures and installs most of the equipment that it uses in providing long-distance telephone service.

In addition to providing telecommunications products and services, the divested AT&T currently also manufactures and markets a wide range of computing equipment, including many personal computer and minicomputer models. AT&T also provides a series of ACCUNET digital communication services, including the ACCUNET public data network.

GENERAL TELEPHONE AND ELECTRONICS CORPORATION

The network of the *General Telephone and Electronics Corporation* (GTE) is known as the *General System*. This organization operates approximately 8 percent of American telephones. General System equipment is compatible with the equipment of the Bell Operating Companies in most areas and allows direct interconnection. GTE's two manufacturing subsidiaries are the Automatic Electric Company and the Lenkhurt Electric Company. GTE now operates the Telenet public data network and the US Sprint long-distance telephone service.

THE INDEPENDENTS

All other telephone companies are usually referred to as *independent* telephone companies. These serve more than half of the U.S. geographical area and operate about 17 percent of the telephones. The number of independents has been decreasing ever since 1920, when there were 9211 of them, but their combined revenue has been growing more rapidly than that of AT&T and the Bell Operating Companies. The independents today are bigger than AT&T was in 1940. Virtually all the independents interconnect with the rest of the public telephone system and transmit signals compatible with it.

WESTERN UNION

The *Western Union Telegraph Company* operates a national telegraph message service to all parts of the United States. Western Union also leases private communication links, and it operates two public dial-up telegraph networks, a *telex* network compatible with the worldwide telex network, and the *TWX* (Teletypewriter Exchange) network, which it bought from AT&T. The Western Union leased-line facilities now include voice, data, and facsimile services with a wide range of speeds.

Western Union has done much experimenting with online computer systems and offers a wide range of computer services. It also acquired the PS Newswire Association. To do this it had to form a holding company, Western Union Corporation, which is separate from the common carrier, the Western Union Telegraph Company. Western Union International Inc. is also a separate company that handles international cablegrams and data traffic.

GOVERNMENT AGENCIES

With so many common carriers, many of which monopolize the services they offer, it is necessary to have some regulating authority. There is at least one such authority for each American state, as well as a national authority for controlling interstate lines and foreign facilities originating in the United States. The latter is the *Federal Communications Commission* (FCC).

Federal Communications Commission

The FCC is an independent federal agency that regulates radio, television, telephone, telegraph, and other transmissions by wire or radio. The powers of the FCC are defined in the Communications Act of 1934. Figure 4.1 shows the organization of the FCC. The FCC has jurisdiction over *interstate* and *foreign* telecommunications but not telecommunications within a state. The latter are regulated by *state public utility commissions*.

State Public Utility Commissions

What the FCC does for interstate links and foreign links originating in the United States, the state public utility commissions do for links within a state. Different states have different tariffs for the same grade of service, and there can be a wide difference in the price of facilities from one state to another. Interstate tariffs, however, are uniform across America.

Office of Telecommunications Policy

The *Office of Telecommunications Policy* (OTP) formulates plans, policies, and programs designed to maximize the value of telecommunications to the public interest, the U.S. economy, and national security. The OTP has no executive authority. It can issue recommendations, not directives. The OTP has stimulated the launching of domestic communications satellites, the growth of the specialized common carriers, the rise of the value-added common carriers, and the regulations encouraging the growth of cable television operators.

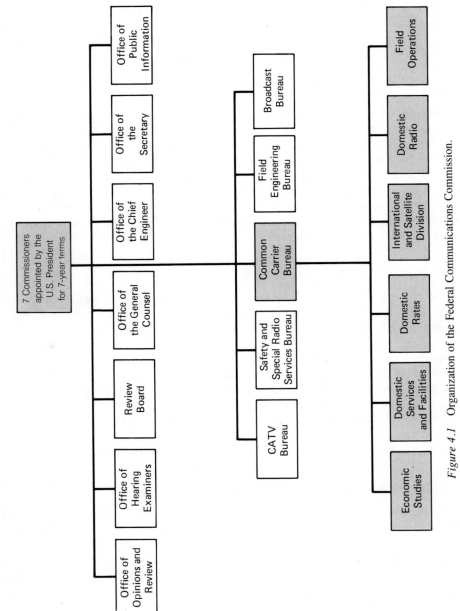

Figure 4.1 Organization of the Federal Communications Commission.

TELECOMMUNICATIONS ORGANIZATIONS IN OTHER COUNTRIES

In a few countries, telecommunications is organized in a similar manner to that of the United States. In others, it is quite different. We will next look at the organizations that control telecommunications in some representative countries, beginning with Canada.

Canada

The structure of the telecommunications industry in Canada is somewhat similar to the United States, except that some of Canada's common carriers are government-owned. Sixty-nine percent of Canada's telephones are operated by Bell Canada, which is entirely separate from AT&T or the Bell Operating Companies in the United States. Twelve percent of the telephones are operated by GTE. Four percent are operated by small independent common carriers and almost 16 percent by provincial or municipal governments. Telsat Canada, a mixed private and government-owned corporation, established the free world's first domestic communications satellite system in 1972.

British Post Office Corporation

In many countries the job of delivering mail and providing telecommunications is undertaken by the same organization. Among these is the *British Post Office Corporation* (BPOC), which has departments for handling mail and for handling telecommunications. In 1969, the BPOC changed its status from a government department to a nationalized commercial company.

For data transmission, the BPOC offers a variety of links under the heading of *datel services*. It also operates a telex system similar to that of the United States. The BPOC provides facilities for sending data over the dial-up public telephone network, and it offers private leased lines of varying speeds. The lines are not always compatible with the American ones, and sometimes equipment that works well in the United States cannot be installed in Britain.

Other Countries

Most of the countries of the world have a government-controlled monopoly that provides their telecommunications, in a similar manner to Britain's BPOC, and offers facilities for data transmission that are broadly similar. In Germany there is the *Deutsche Bundespost* and in France the *Postes, télégraphes et téléphones*. In most countries, financing comes from government, not public, sources. For the *Swedish Telecommunications Administration*, for example, the state, through the Riksdag (Parliament), decides the amount of investments and makes the necessary grants.

INTERNATIONAL TELECOMMUNICATIONS UNION

Although incompatibilities certainly exist, the degree of *compatibility* that exists in the world's telecommunications facilities is remarkable. This is largely due to the efforts of the *International Telecommunications Union* (ITU). This organization, headquartered in Switzerland, has over 100 member countries throughout the world. Its consultative committees carry out detailed studies of world telecommunications and make recommendations for standardization. The recommendations are put into practice widely throughout the world.

The CCITT (see Chapter 1) is an organization within the ITU, which is in turn divided into a number of study groups that make recommendations on various aspects of telephony and telegraphy. The CCITT study group that is most concerned with data communication is the special committee on data transmission. It has produced reports of great thoroughness, giving recommendations for standards for data transmission that are widely accepted throughout the world. We will make frequent mention of important CCITT recommendations throughout this book.

NEW BREEDS OF COMMON CARRIERS

In the 1970s, the telecommunications industry of the United States changed from being a somewhat placid growth industry to an industry in upheaval. In the 1980s, the breakup of the Bell System caused further far-reaching changes in the industry.

Changes in the regulatory climate encouraged three new breeds of common carriers to come into existence: the *long-distance telephone common carriers,* the *satellite carriers,* and the *value-added carriers.* The new "specialized" common carriers seized on the rigidity of the United States telephone system, claiming that separate microwave and other transmission links were needed for specialized purposes, including business telephone and data transmission. Most specialized carriers are concentrating on voice transmission and data transmission up to 9600 bps because this is where most of the business revenue is.

Long-Distance Telephone Carriers

A long-distance telephone common carrier does not provide the broad range of telecommunications services that the conventional common carriers offer. Instead they provide specialized transmission facilities that are designed to compete with the long-distance telephone services originally offered only by AT&T. Two of the largest of these long-distance carriers are described in Box 4.2.

Satellite Carriers

A particularly interesting form of specialized common carrier is the satellite carrier. Several new corporations obtained permission to become satellite car-

BOX 4.2 Two long-distance common carriers

Microwave Communications Incorporated

The pioneer and pacesetter of the specialized common carriers is *Microwave Communications Incorporated* (MCI). In 1969, after six years of legal battling, the FCC gave MCI permission to build a microwave system between St. Louis and Chicago. This historic decision triggered a flood of new microwave station applications. MCI was soon a large group of corporations building a nationwide microwave network and selling a wide variety of bandwidths to any customer who could use them. MCI's prices, like those of the other specialized carriers, were just sufficiently lower than those of the established carriers to attract customers. Today MCI's network is nationwide and provides long-distance services to and from any telephone in the country, just as AT&T's network does. MCI now also operates the satellite carrier Satellite Business Systems (SBS). IBM currently owns about 20 percent of MCI.

US Sprint

Another extremely successful long-distance telephone carrier began operations in 1970 as the *Southern Pacific Communications Company* (SPC). SPC began its operations by offering telecommunications services whose circuits used the Southern Pacific railroad's right-of-way between California and the Southwest. In 1978, SPC began offering a low-cost long-distance telephone service called *Sprint* to the general public. In 1983, SPC was acquired by General Telephone and Electronics, and today the Sprint long-distance telephone service is known as US Sprint. The majority of US Sprint's long-distance calls are transmitted over fiber optic circuits, and the company's advertising has stressed the high quality of signals that the US Sprint network provides in addition to the lower cost.

riers, but the first domestic satellites were launched by already existing corporations, such as Western Union, RCA, and COMSAT. The Canadian ANIK satellite—the first domestic satellite—and later Canada's CTS satellite were planned and launched by the Canadian government. The satellite carriers will enable organizations to have their own earth stations on their premises.

Value-added Common Carriers

The value-added carriers are different from other common carriers in that they are not ordinarily in the business of building new communication links. Instead, they lease channels from other common carriers and then provide additional services to customers that use these leased channels. The networks operated by the value-added common carriers are normally referred to as *public data networks*. When you use the services of a public data network, you do not pay for a communication channel. Instead, you pay the carrier to transmit a given number of bits from here to there.

Box 4.3 lists the most widely used public data networks in North America, including one operated by AT&T and one by IBM. All the networks, with the exception of the IBM Information Network, implement packet switching techniques that conform to CCITT *Recommendation X.25*. Not surprisingly, the IBM Information Network uses the SNA architecture instead of *X.25* (see Chapter 13). The widespread availability of the services of public data networks promises to revolutionize data transmission. These networks are already spreading throughout the world, and a wide variety of services will be available from many carriers.

The public data networks take advantage of economies of scale. When many users share the same wideband communication channels, they can communicate more cheaply. The wider the bandwidth they share, the faster the response time of the network. Also, the communication path can be made more reliable, because the network can be designed to bypass failures. Users who could not otherwise communicate because they have incompatible machines can be interconnected. For example, the Telenet network routinely interconnects all varieties of incompatible computers and terminals.

TARIFFS

In the United States, the services offered by a telecommunications common carrier are described in *tariffs*. Tariffs are documents that a common carrier files with a regulating authority. By law, a tariff must be registered and approved by either the FCC or a state public utilities commission before a new telecommunications service can be made available to the public. In most other countries, the telecommunications facilities are set up by government bodies and thus are directly under their control.

In the United States, the subject of communication rates has become very complex. The amount and structure of charges differ from one state to another. In most other countries, the rates for more conventional channels remain relatively straightforward; however, often the carriers are government organizations who are not obliged to publish tariffs for all their facilities. The price for less common channels, such as wideband links, may have to be obtained by special

BOX 4.3   North American public data networks

- **Telenet.** The *Telenet Public Data Network,* the oldest value-added network in operation in the United States, began operation in 1975. GTE acquired Telenet in 1979. In addition to offering general packet-switched communication services in conformance with Recommendation *X.25*, Telenet also offers an electronic mail service called Telemail. Information about Telenet can be obtained from Telenet Communications Corporation, 8229 Boone Boulevard, Vienna, VA 22180; telephone: (703) 442-1000.

- **Tymnet.** The *Tymnet* network is operated by a wholly owned subsidiary of McDonnel Douglas Automation. Originally called Tymshare, the network was developed to support the time-sharing services marketed by Tymshare, Inc., and has evolved to a general-purpose *X.25* public data network. Like Telenet, Tymnet also offers an electronic mail service it calls OnTyme-II. Information about Tymnet can be obtained from Tymnet, Inc., 2710 Orchard Parkway, San Jose, CA 95134; telephone: (408) 946-4900.

- **ADP Autonet.** The *ADP Autonet* network is operated by a subsidiary of Automatic Data Processing, Inc. (ADP). The ADP Autonet network evolved from a private network that ADP developed to service its own clients and now conforms to *X.25*. ADP Autonet operates an electronic mail service that it calls Auto Mail. Information about ADP Autonet can be obtained from ADP Autonet, 175 Jackson Plaza, Ann Arbor, MI 48106; telephone: (313) 769-6800.

- **AT&T ACCUNET Packet Service.** The *AT&T ACCUNET Packet Service* is the newest of the major packet-switched public data networks described here. The service can be accessed using any *X.25* device via dedicated lines that operate at 2400, 4800, or 56,000 bps. Information about the ACCUNET Packet Service can be obtained from AT&T Communications, 295 North Maple Avenue, Basking Ridge, NJ 07920.

- **IBM's Information Network.** Unlike the other four networks, IBM's public data network does not use packet switching. Instead it conforms to the SNA architecture and handles the routing of data using a nationwide system of interconnected IBM host processors and communication controllers. Information about the IBM Information Network can be obtained from IBM Corporation, P.O. Box 30104, Tampa, FL 33630-9984.

request to the carrier. In general, it is desirable, when designing a system, that the organization in question be called in to quote a price for the facilities needed.

GUIDE TO COMMUNICATION SERVICES

A particularly useful source of current information on telecommunications services in the United States is a book called the *Guide to Communication Services* published by the Center for Communications Management, Inc., P.O. Box 324, Ramsey, NJ 07446. This reference guide contains a description of all currently available telecommunications tariffs along with their costs. The CCMI guide is published in looseleaf form on an annual subscription basis and is kept up-to-date with monthly replacement pages.

MEASURED-USE TARIFFS

When you dial a friend and talk on the telephone, you speak over a line connected by means of the public exchanges. As we have seen, this line, referred to as a *public* or *switched* line, can also be used for the transmission of data by using appropriate modems. This type of telecommunications service is typically called a *measured-use service*. With a measured-use service, the telephone company keeps track of the time a circuit is connected and thus "measures" the use of the circuit. The public telephone network provides a very high degree of flexibility for data transmission, as a computer can be dialed from practically any telephone in the world. There are other measured-use services that common carriers provide. Box 4.4 lists some of the more popular measured-use services in the United States.

Hot-Line Service

An interesting type of measured-use service, called a hot-line service, is offered by some carriers. A hot line gives the impression that a dedicated channel exists between two points. When a subscriber picks up the phone at one end, a particular phone at the other end rings automatically. In fact, a switched connection is automatically established between the two points as soon as the receiver is picked up. The user is billed for a monthly service fee plus a measured-use charge based on the amount of time the circuit is actually used. In some cases, a hot-line service can be used for data transmission when instant communication is required between two data machines but the cost of a private line is not justified.

Wide Area Telephone Service (WATS)

Another measured-use tariff in the United States, *Wide Area Telephone Service* (WATS), provides dial-up facilities for a fixed monthly fee. When a company

BOX 4.4   Measured-use services

- **Toll telephone.** The public telephone service.
- **WATS (Wide Area Telephone Service).** An AT&T reduced-rate, bulk-billing, long-distance telephone service in which the United States is divided into billing zones. There are tariffs for either measured-time or full-period charges.
- **Hot Line.** A service providing fixed point-to-point telephone grade connections on a measured-time basis.
- **Broadband Exchange Service.** A Western Union service in which the user can dial the bandwidth required.
- **Telex.** The international 50-bps service used over much of the world.
- **TWX (Teletypewriter Exchange Service).** A Western Union 150-bps teletypewriter service with dial-up connections like telex.
- **Infomaster—formerly Telex Computer Services (TCS).** A message switching service for Western Union telex subscribers, offering telex-to-TWX conversion.
- **Public data networks.** These networks generally use packet switching techniques to transmit messages between two subscribers.

is given an *OUTWATS* access line, people in that company may make as many calls as desired to a specified zone. With an *INWATS* line, anyone in a specified zone is permitted to call into that line without being charged for the call. WATS permits data transmission using the same types of modems that are used with normal telephone lines. It is not possible to make person-to-person, conference, third-party, credit, or collect calls under the WATS tariff.

Measured-Use Wideband Services

The main drawback to using a normal switched circuit for data transmission purposes is that most of the services available use standard telephone circuits of 4-kHz bandwidth. The highest practical bit rate normally used on this type of channel is 4800 bps. A rate of 9600 bps or 19,200 bps is sometimes achievable, but at the cost of a higher error rate. However, there are switched services available that allow much higher bit rates. For example, AT&T offers a switched service that provides 48-kHz channels into customer locations and is available in most of the larger cities over the local loops operated by the local telephone companies. Such a wideband channel can be used for economical data transmission at bit rates up to about 50,000 bps.

Measured-use wideband services will become more and more important to data transmission as switched services supporting high bit rates become more widespread. But today, most high-speed data transmission between two points is accomplished via leased lines.

LEASED LINES   Instead of using a measured-use service, a *private* or *leased* line is often connected permanently or semi-permanently between two data machines. The private line might be connected via the local switching office, but it is not ordinarily connected to the switching gear and signaling devices of that office. An interoffice leased connection does use the same physical links as the switched circuits. It would not, however, have to carry the signaling that is needed on a switched line. This frees up the signaling frequencies for use by the subscriber, thus making slightly more bandwidth available than is available over a public, switched connection.

Line Conditioning

Since a leased channel is permanently connected, the subscriber can pay extra for special *line conditioning* that improves the quality of the channel. With proper conditioning and appropriate modem equipment, bit rates of 9600 and 19,200 bps are achievable. AT&T has two types of conditioning, referred to as C and D conditioning. C conditioning attempts to equalize attenuation and delay at different frequencies; D conditioning controls the signal-to-noise ratio and the harmonic distortion of the line. Various levels of C and D conditioning are available, and both may be used together if required. Both types of conditioning are designed to permit higher data speeds to be used on the line with acceptably low error rates.

Wideband Lines

If a higher bandwidth than that of a telephone channel is desired, *channel groups* can be leased. A group of 12 channels provides a total bandwidth of about 48 kHz. A group of 24 channels provides a total bandwidth of about 96 kHz. A supergroup of 60 voice channels, for a total bandwidth of 240 kHz, is also generally available. With private analog channels, it is up to the user to decide how to use the available bandwidth, and generally, voice and data can be combined. Various types of modems are available to support various bit rates up to as high as 230,400 bps when a supergroup is used.

The North American common carriers offer several tariffs for leased wideband lines. Some of these can be subdivided by the carrier into bundles of lower bandwidth. They can also be subdivided into channels for voice transmission, teletypewriter, control, signaling, facsimile, or data. With some tariffs, the user pays a lower price for the bundles than for the individual channels.

Satellite Channels

Another type of leased-line channel that is now available from several common carriers, including AT&T, is a leased satellite channel. Satellite channels are generally more economical than terrestrial channels of equivalent capacity. Bandwidths as great as 1.2 MHz are available, and this type of channel can provide bit rates into the millions of bits per second for users that require them. A satellite channel has the capability of dropping in cost much more rapidly than high-capacity channels of most other types.

DIGITAL CHANNELS

Most leased channels, including those supplied by many satellite carriers, are analog and require modems for data transmission. But many carriers are also supplying channels that are designed specifically for digital transmission. AT&T offers a number of options for digital data transmission in its ACCUNET group of digital services. Some of the available AT&T ACCUNET services are described in Box 4.5. Modems are not required, and users are connected to the network via digital adapters. AT&T calls these adapters *Digital Service Units* (DSUs). The digital adapters can usually be acquired from the common carrier that offers the digital service or from a variety of telecommunications equipment vendors.

As we have discussed, AT&T is in the process of swinging from analog to digital transmission for many telephone trunks. The ACCUNET collection of services is a by-product of this process of voice digitization. The T1 and T2 carriers discussed in Chapter 3 are used to create the ACCUNET network.

Unfortunately, these digital channels are available only in certain locations. Depending on where the subscriber is located, it may not be possible to obtain a local channel to such a network. The alternative is to use a telephone connection to the nearest access point of the digital network. When this is done, however, many of the advantages are lost. If a telephone connection is needed at each end, a total of four modems is required, where two would suffice had an ordinary telephone line been used to implement the entire connection.

It can be expected that the digital networks will grow and become more widespread so that increasing numbers of users will be able to connect to them directly.

SWITCHED PRIVATE SYSTEMS

Many firms have private lines that are switched with private exchanges. In this way they build their own switched systems, which are often called *corporate tie-line networks*. The lines that are used can be either privately owned or leased from common carriers. The reason for designing a switched private system is

BOX 4.5   AT&T ACCUNET Services

- **Dataphone Digital Service.** The *Dataphone Digital Service* (DDS) provides leased digital lines at bit rates of 2400, 4800, 9600, or 56,000 bps.

- **ACCUNET Switched 56 Service.** The *ACCUNET Switched 56 Service* provides digital data transmission at the bit rate of 56,000 bps via a switched network. The network is accessed via a dedicated digital line to a local ACCUNET switching office. A subscriber can access any other subscriber to the Switched 56 Service in a similar manner to placing a long-distance call.

- **ACCUNET Packet Service.** The *ACCUNET Packet Service* provides a packet-switched public data network that can be accessed via dedicated lines that operate at 2400, 4800, or 56,000 bps.

- **ACCUNET T1.5 Service.** The *ACCUNET T1.5 Service* offers leased digital lines that operate at the speed of the T1 carrier—1,544,000 bps. The service can be used for data transmission as well as for conventional telephone channels, color video, audio, facsimile, and graphics signals for video teleconferencing applications.

- **ACCUNET Reserved 1.5 Service.** The *ACCUNET Reserved 1.5 Service* offers the same T1 channel as the ACCUNET T1.5 service but allows the subscriber to schedule the use of the channel in half-hour increments whenever the channel is required, rather than leasing a dedicated line on a monthly basis.

either to lower the total telephone bill or to have a switched system of higher bandwidth than the telephone system provides.

Telephone companies facilitate the building of private switched networks within organizations by providing *common control switching arrangements* (CCSAs). Such an arrangement uses switching equipment at telephone exchanges to switch calls in a private leased network. All stations connected to the private network may call one another without having to use the public toll facilities.

Part II of this book discusses the equipment used to construct computer systems that use data transmission. Chapter 5 begins Part II by examining terminal equipment.

PART **II** EQUIPMENT

5 TERMINAL EQUIPMENT

In a system that supports a dialog between a human operator and a computer, terminal features form an essential element of the dialog. The terminal is very important to the user. It is typically the only component of the system that the user sees. Users often form their impressions of the system entirely from the terminal. A poorly planned terminal configuration can have a serious effect on the efficient operation of the system. It can slow the system down, introduce errors, lessen its usefulness, and significantly add to the system's overall cost. At worst, it can reduce users to a state in which they want to put a fist through the screen.

For efficient operation, the terminal must be as unconfusing as possible and must give a suitably fast response time. For most uses, it is desirable that it be possible to operate the terminal with one hand for some functions. If it has a display screen (which is probable), the screen should be large enough to support the user interface, and there should be an easy way of responding to the screen content.

Any number of types of terminal devices are available, ranging from simple teletypewriter devices to display screen terminals that support alphanumeric displays and, on the more expensive devices, graphics displays as well. In today's environment, a very common terminal device is a personal computer. An important characteristic of a personal computer used as a terminal is that the personal computer can be programmed in a variety of ways to support the interaction between the central computing system and the user. The storage and processing power of the personal computer are important assets in the implementation of an efficient user interface.

Many types of special-purpose terminal devices are also available, including devices that read the bar code printed on all items for sale in supermarkets and banking terminals designed to be used by the consumer.

CLUSTER CONTROLLERS

A device used in all but the simplest data communication systems is the *cluster controller*. It often consists of a small computer whose sole job is to control the operation of a group, or *cluster,* of terminals. Instead of attaching each terminal directly to the central computer using a separate communication link, cluster controllers are used at each remote location (see Fig. 5.1). This allows a single link to connect a group of terminals to the central computer. The cluster controller can also free the central computer from performing many functions that are better done at the remote location itself. For example, the cluster controller may have disk storage capabilities and may run application programs that perform functions such as screen formatting and data collection. The use of cluster controllers is a step in the direction of distributed processing, where computing power is used at each point in the system where it can serve some need.

COMMUNICATIONS CONTROLLERS

In some very simple systems, the communication lines from terminals and cluster controllers can be attached directly to a host computer. However, it is much more common to use a device at the location of the host computer called a *communications controller* (also called a *front-end processor* or a *line control computer*). A communications controller is often a stored-program device that performs many communication-related functions, thus freeing up the host computer for application-related work. A typical data communication system using a communications controller and cluster controllers is shown in Fig. 5.2.

TYPES OF TERMINALS

Terminals can be devices into which data is entered by human operators or devices that collect data automatically from instruments. Terminals designed for

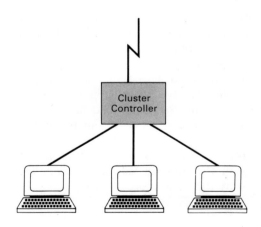

Figure 5.1 A cluster controller controls the operation of a group of terminals.

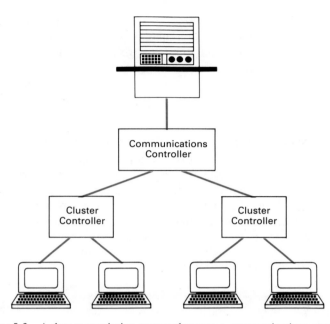

Figure 5.2   A data transmission system that uses a communications controller and cluster controllers.

human use often permit a fast two-way dialog with the computer or may be a remote equivalent of the computer room input/output devices. For example, keyboards, magnetic tape drives, or diskette readers can be used to provide input over communication lines. Printers and display screens of various types can be used to provide output.

TELEGRAPH EQUIPMENT

In the early days of data transmission, the most common terminal combined a typewriter-like keyboard and a slow-speed printer. The telecommunications industry has produced a range of such machines for telegraphy. In North America, these are generally called *teletype* machines; the term *teleprinter* is common elsewhere. Many terminals that emulate earlier teletype terminals are still in use.

Telegraph signals are formed simply by switching an electrical current on and off or by reversing its direction of flow. The means for producing these current changes are some form of make-and-break contact. The instruments for sending signals, such as teleprinters or paper-tape readers, make or break the circuit at appropriate times. The on and off pulses form a code that is appropriately interpreted by the receiving device.

DISPLAY TERMINALS

Today, the vast majority of terminals combine a keyboard and a display screen to form what is commonly referred to as a *display terminal*. Many display terminals today take the form of personal computers that are doing double duty by functioning also as display terminals in mainframe-based online systems. The use of personal computers as terminals is discussed more fully in Chapter 11.

ASYNCHRONOUS DISPLAY TERMINALS

The most common, and generally least expensive, form of display terminal communicates with a host computer using a line control technique called asynchronous transmission (discussed in Chapter 9). With asynchronous transmission, characters are transmitted one at a time between the host computer and the terminal. When the terminal operator presses a key, the corresponding character is transmitted immediately to the host computer. When the host computer transmits a character, it is immediately sent to the terminal and is displayed on the terminal's screen.

ANSI DISPLAY TERMINAL STANDARDS

Literally thousands of different types of asynchronous terminals are available in the marketplace, each type generally supporting its own set of control codes. In an attempt to eliminate the confusion caused by the thousands of incompatible terminal control code schemes, the American National Standards Institute (ANSI) has defined a standard set of terminal control codes that could be used to control the standard functions performed by most display terminals. Many of today's asynchronous display terminals support the ANSI standard codes, sometimes as an option in addition to the terminal manufacturer's own set of terminal controls. Box 5.1 shows a few of the ANSI standard codes for controlling the functions of a simple display terminal.

PROTOCOL CONVERTERS

Many asynchronous terminals are attached directly to host computers or host computer communication controllers, as shown in Fig. 5.3. The asynchronous communication techniques that are used in such a system are inefficient, and it is desirable to communicate with the host computer using a more efficient synchronous technique. With synchronous transmission, characters are stored up in a buffer until an entire group is assembled, possibly corresponding to a complete line or an entire screen of information. The group is then sent as a unit in a single *transmission frame*. Synchronous transmission techniques are discussed in detail in Chapter 9.

Protocol converters are available to perform the necessary conversion be-

BOX 5.1   ANSI standard terminal control codes

In the following control code descriptions, ESC stands for the ASCII escape character, and the symbol # stands for an integer value.

Code	Function
ESC[#,#H	Moves the display cursor to the position indicated by the two numeric values. The first value indicates the row and the second the column.
ESC[#A	Moves the display cursor up the number of rows specified by the numeric value.
ESC[#B	Moves the display cursor down by the number of rows specified by the numeric value.
ESC[#C	Moves the display cursor forward by the number of columns specified by the numeric value.
ESC[#D	Moves the display cursor back by the number of columns specified by the numeric value.
ESC[2J	Erases the screen and moves the display cursor to the home position (row 1, column 1).
ESC[K	Erases from the position of the display cursor to the end of the line.

tween asynchronous and synchronous transmission. These converters ordinarily function as cluster controllers or concentrators for groups of asynchronous terminals (see Fig. 5.4). They allow simple asynchronous terminals to be attached to the protocol converter, thus allowing the protocol converter to handle the buffering of data and the sending and receiving of data in larger blocks between the protocol converter and the host computer.

THE 3270-TYPE TERMINAL

One of the most widely used types of terminal for IBM mainframe applications is the 3270-type display terminal marketed by IBM. Many other terminal manufacturers also offer terminals that are compatible with 3270-type equipment. Due to the extremely large numbers of 3270s and 3270-compatible computers that are now installed, the 3270 has become somewhat of a standard terminal design. Data is ordinarily sent from the host computer to the 3270 terminal a screen at a time using synchronous transmission. When the operator enters data at the keyboard, the data is stored in a buffer at the terminal location until an attention key (such as ENTER) on the terminal is pressed.

In most applications, multiple 3270 terminals are attached to a control unit

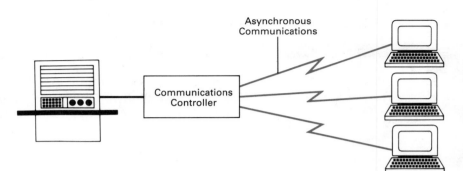

Figure 5.3 Terminals can be connected to the host computer using individual point-to-point connections.

that functions as a cluster controller. The control unit can be connected directly to a host computer's I/O channel, or modems and a communication line can be used to connect a control unit at a remote location to the host computer's communications controller. Terminal models are also available with integral control units when a single terminal is required at a given location. These options are shown in Fig. 5.5.

In Chapter 11, we will discuss add-on circuit boards that allow personal computers to emulate 3270 terminals. One such board is a communications adapter that allows a personal computer to plug into a 3270 control unit. Another type of communications adapter contains an integral synchronous modem that allows the personal computer directly to emulate a 3270 cluster controller and to communicate directly with the host computer's communications controller over a communication line.

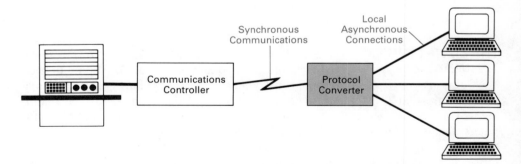

Figure 5.4 A protocol converter can serve as a concentrator that handles several asynchronous terminals with a single data link that uses synchronous transmission.

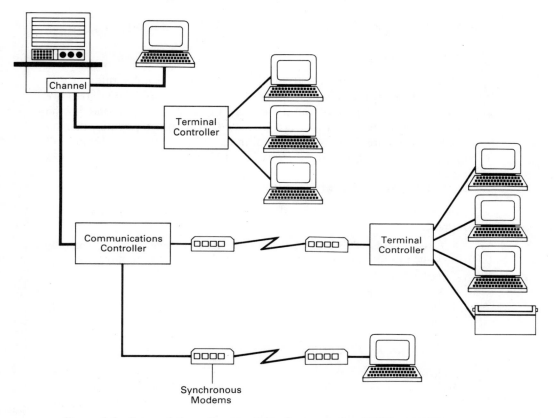

Figure 5.5 Some of the options available for connecting 3270-type terminals.

The 3270 terminal hardware supports a screen buffer that can store an entire screen of data within the terminal. The cursor control and data character keys allow the terminal operator to enter data into the screen buffer, and modify it as required, without causing it to be transmitted to the host computer. When finished entering data and possibly editing it for correctness, the operator presses one of the attention keys. This sends to the host computer, in a single transmission frame, selected fields from the screen buffer. Box 5.2 provides additional information about 3270-type terminals.

SPECIALIZED TERMINALS

Most computer peripherals can be taken out of the computer room and attached to a communication line. With the addition of a control console, they can

BOX 5.2   3270-type terminals

3270 Terminal Screen

When referring to the 3270 terminal screen, we usually refer to display positions in terms of *rows* and *columns*. Several screen sizes are supported by the 3270 family of terminals, and both monochrome and color display options are provided. The most popular display screen sizes are 24 rows by 80 columns, 32 rows by 80 columns, 43 rows by 80 columns, and 27 rows by 132 columns.

3270 Terminal Screen Fields

Information is displayed on the 3270 screen in various *fields* of two types:

- **Literal fields.** This type of field has a predefined value and is generally written to the screen as part of a display that provides information to the terminal operator.

- **Variable fields.** This type of field (sometimes called a *data field*) is defined without a specific value and is often used to contain data entered by the terminal operator.

3270 Field Attributes

Each field on the terminal screen begins with an attribute byte, which occupies a screen position but is not displayed. It describes the field's physical characteristics, such as the type of data the field can contain, the brightness of the field, and whether the field should blink.

The 3270 Keyboard

The keyboards of 3270-type terminals vary in layout from one model to another. The keys on any 3270 keyboard can be divided into the following three categories:

- **Data Character Keys.** These include the keys for letters, numbers, and special characters. They are similar to the corresponding keys on a typewriter keyboard and are used to enter data into fields on the 3270 screen.

- **Cursor Movement Keys.** These include the up, down, left, and right arrow keys and various tab keys. They move the display cursor from place to place and determine where data is entered on the screen.

- **Attention Keys.** These include ENTER, CLEAR, program attention (PA), and program function (PF) keys. They cause data to be transmitted from the screen buffer to the host computer.

make up an offline data preparation terminal, or with a cluster of manual-input devices, they can form a data collection system. Tape cartridge or small diskette devices can be added. Logic circuitry and memory can be added in varying quantities to form various types of *intelligent terminals*. Microprogramming can be used, or a stored-program minicomputer or microprocessor. The variations on these possibilities are proliferated by the fact that the components can be supplied from hundreds of manufacturers. The units are often modular so that, as with a hi-fi system, a variety of devices may be added. The user's choice can be complex.

The information, whether from automatic devices or from manually operated keyboards, can be transmitted immediately to the computer or can be stored in some medium for transmission later. In other words, the preparation of data can be *online* or *offline*. Readings of instruments, for example, can be transcribed onto a magnetic medium and the data later transmitted to the computer. Similarly, data collected from manually operated devices can be stored on a diskette. In this case, the diskette device is the terminal. The output can also make use of an interim medium, such as magnetic tape, or it can directly control the environment in question. Very often it is necessary to make a printed copy of the computer output for later analysis. In this case, part of the terminal equipment may be a printer of some kind.

Many types of specialized terminals are today used for various applications. In many cases, these specialized terminals are operated by the general public. A few of these specialized terminal types are listed in Box 5.3.

BOX 5.3 Specialized terminal types

- Bank teller terminals
- Supermarket bar code readers and checkout stations
- Fast-food computerized cash register terminals
- Consumer check verification terminals
- Consumer airline ticketing terminals
- Stock quote terminals that read radio data broadcasts
- Factory floor data collection terminals
- Rapid-transit automatic ticketing terminals
- Credit card verification terminals
- Police radio terminals for car license verification
- Radio terminals supporting field engineering personnel

PHYSICAL-LAYER STANDARDS

A number of standards are important in governing the way in which a terminal device is attached to a computer or a piece of data communication equipment. As we discussed in Chapter 1, standards are important in each of the many layers that make up a data communication system. We will conclude this chapter by discussing the standards that apply to the physical layer, the layer that controls the electrical connection between a terminal and some other piece of equipment.

The simplest type of connection takes the form of a cable that connects a terminal to some other device. Figure 5.6 shows a direct cable connection between a small computer and a printer. We will use this simple form of connection to summarize the functions performed by the physical layer in a data communication system. The following are the major functions of the physical layer:

- To provide an electrical connection between two or more devices
- To transmit electrical signals over the electrical connection
- To detect electrical path failures

THE RS-232-C STANDARD

The *Electronic Industries Association* (EIA) publishes standards that are analogous to those developed by the CCITT. A common EIA standard for the physical layer is called *RS-232-C*. The RS-232-C standard has CCITT counterparts called *Recommendation V.24* and *Recommendation V.28* that together are equivalent to the RS-232-C standard.

The RS-232-C standard defines 25 circuits that can be used to connect two communicating stations and describes the electrical characteristics of the signals carried over those circuits. The 25 circuits are defined in the standards by circuit number. The RS-232-C interface allows for data transmission at speeds up to about 20,000 bps at a distance of typically 50 feet or less. Each of the circuits is assigned a specific function.

Figure 5.7 shows some of the commonly used functions of the interface and the pins to which those functions are assigned. Although the connector itself is not specified in the standard, a 25-pin connector, such as that shown in Fig. 5.8, has become a generally accepted standard for implementing an RS-232-C connection. Note that RS-232-C is a *physical layer standard* and does not define functions that are performed in the higher-level layers in a data communication

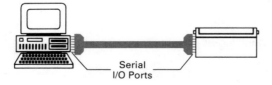

Serial
I/O Ports

Figure 5.6 The simplest form of physical connection takes the form of a cable that connects two data devices directly.

Pin	Description	Ground	Data	Control	Timing
1	Protective ground	●			
7	Signal ground	●			
2	Transmitted data		●		
3	Received data		●		
4	Request to send			●	
5	Clear to send			●	
6	Data set ready			●	
20	Data terminal ready			●	
22	Ring indicator			●	
8	Received line signal detector			●	
21	Signal quality detector			●	
23	Data signal rate selector			●	
24	Transmitter signal element timing (DTE)				●
15	Transmitter signal element timing (DCE)				●
17	Receiver signal element timing				●

Figure 5.7   RS-232-C interface pin functions.

system. For example, the RS-232-C standard does not specify how bits are generated or detected, nor does it specify how bits are to be grouped into characters or frames. These concerns are handled by software or firmware in the *data link layer,* the layer above the physical layer. Data link–layer standards are discussed in Chapter 9.

When two devices communicate using the RS-232-C standard, they each contain circuitry that can generate and detect the voltages specified by the RS-232-C standard. They also typically use a cable that connects two 25-pin connectors in a standard way. There are many different implementations of the

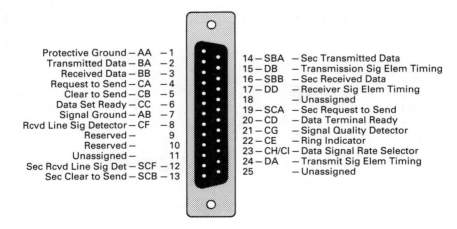

Protective Ground — AA — 1
Transmitted Data — BA — 2
Received Data — BB — 3
Request to Send — CA — 4
Clear to Send — CB — 5
Data Set Ready — CC — 6
Signal Ground — AB — 7
Rcvd Line Sig Detector — CF — 8
Reserved — 9
Reserved — 10
Unassigned — 11
Sec Rcvd Line Sig Det — SCF — 12
Sec Clear to Send — SCB — 13

14 — SBA — Sec Transmitted Data
15 — DB — Transmission Sig Elem Timing
16 — SBB — Sec Received Data
17 — DD — Receiver Sig Elem Timing
18 — Unassigned
19 — SCA — Sec Request to Send
20 — CD — Data Terminal Ready
21 — CG — Signal Quality Detector
22 — CE — Ring Indicator
23 — CH/CI — Data Signal Rate Selector
24 — DA — Transmit Sig Elem Timing
25 — Unassigned

Figure 5.8   Typical 25-pin RS-232-C cable connector.

RS-232-C standard. For example, not all 25 circuits need be used by the two communicating devices. As few as three of the circuits, and thus a three-wire cable, can be used for communication between two devices and still be in conformance with the standard. However, some devices use more than the minimum three. One of the difficulties in using the RS-232-C recommendation is that the two communicating devices must agree in advance as to which circuits will be used. Since devices that use the RS-232-C standard are designed and manufactured by a great many competing companies, the proper wiring of an RS-232-C cable and its two connectors has been referred to by some as a "black art."

COMMUNICATING OVER LONGER DISTANCES

Communicating over an RS-232-C cable is limited to a distance of less than 50 feet. At first glance, it would appear that the RS-232-C standard is much too restrictive to be of use in data communication applications, where distances are sometimes measured in hundreds or thousands of miles. However, when we introduce the true purpose of the RS-232-C standard, the applicability of the standard will become more clear. The RS-232-C standard is designed for connecting a device in a class called *data terminal equipment* (DTE) to a device in a complementary class called *data circuit terminating equipment* (DCE). The communication ports in terminals and computers are common examples of DTEs; modems are common examples of devices that implement DCEs.

Figure 5.9 illustrates a typical long-distance implementation of a physical connection between two communicating stations. In this case, the computer on the left has circuitry installed in it that performs the functions of a DTE. It is connected via a cable that uses two 25-pin RS-232-C connectors to a complementary device that has circuitry installed in it that performs the functions of a DCE. On the right, the printer also has a DTE that is connected by another RS-

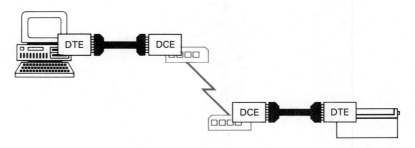

Figure 5.9 Using modems and a telephone line to interconnect two data devices wired as DTEs.

232-C cable to a DCE. The DCEs are connected to each other by a telephone line of arbitrary length. In this example, the DTE on the left consists of a communication port installed in the computer, the two DCEs are implemented in a pair of compatible modems, and the DTE on the right consists of a communication port installed in the printer.

Notice that there are three physical connections in this configuration. The DTE on the left is connected to its DCE by an RS-232-C cable, the two DCEs are connected by a telephone line, and the DTE on the right is connected to its DCE by another RS-232-C cable.

ANALOG AND DIGITAL SIGNALS

As we saw in Chapter 2, when communicating over long distances, it is often necessary to convert the digital signals used by the DTEs to analog signals that can be transmitted over an ordinary telephone circuit. An RS-232-C connection is intended to carry *digital* data. A positive voltage on the appropriate RS-232-C circuit ordinarily indicates a zero bit, and a negative voltage indicates a one bit. To send digital signals over analog telephone lines, modems are used to convert the voltages generated by the DTE into analog signals. The analog signals are continuous audio tones that are similar to the tones generated by a push-button telephone.

VIRTUAL CHANNEL

When two communicating devices (DTEs) are connected using two modems and a telephone line, it appears to the two DTEs as if a simple hard-wired cable connects them. In effect, the two modems and the telephone line are transparent to the two DTEs; the modems implement a virtual channel between the two devices that appears just as if a simple cable connects them. When the DTE on the left in Fig. 5.9 generates a bit stream, its DCE converts the bit stream to a continuous analog signal and transmits it to the DCE on the right. The DCE on the right reconstructs the original bit stream and applies the appropriate voltages to the cable connected to its DTE. The DTE on the right has no way of knowing that the voltages were not generated directly by the DTE on the left. In effect, the physical connection appears just as though a very long RS-232-C cable were used to connect the two DTEs. The use of two modems and a telephone line is *transparent* to the two DTEs. They implement a simple, point-to-point *virtual channel,* as shown in Fig. 5.10. We can change the modems, perhaps using exotic technology to increase transmission speed, and this change would not be apparent to the two communicating devices. We could even substitute a digital communication line of arbitrary length for the two modems and the telephone line, and the two DTEs would still communicate in the same manner.

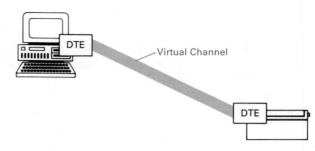

Figure 5.10   The two modems and the telephone line are transparent to the
DTEs and implement a virtual channel between the two data devices.

DIRECT RS-232-C CONNECTIONS

Direct RS-232-C connections are often used to connect communicating devices. For example, Fig. 5.6
showed how we might connect a small computer to a
printer via a direct RS-232-C cable connection. As we mentioned earlier, the
RS-232-C standard is meant for connecting a DTE to a DCE. However, if the
serial ports in both devices happen to be wired as DTEs (as shown in Fig. 5.11),
or perhaps both as DCEs, they can still be connected simply by using a cable
that has the appropriate circuits crossed. An RS-232-C cable that has its circuits
crossed in the appropriate way is sometimes known as a *null modem* because it
simulates the presence of a pair of modems connected by an analog circuit.

Notice that the direct cable connection in Fig. 5.11 is conceptually identical to the virtual channel in Fig. 5.10. The computer and printer need have no
knowledge of how the physical connection is implemented. The two devices
function in an identical manner whether they are in the same room connected
by a 6-foot cable or in separate cities connected using modems and a telephone
line.

OTHER PHYSICAL STANDARDS

Many other American and international standards are
commonly used to connect communicating devices at
the physical layer. As we have already mentioned,
the CCITT *V.24* and *V.28* recommendations are equivalent to the EIA RS-232-

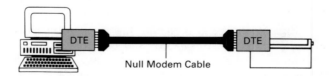

Figure 5.11   Two DTEs can be directly interconnected by using a null modem cable that crosses the appropriate RS-232-C circuits.

BOX 5.4   Alternative physical-layer standards

- **The RS-422 Standard.** The RS-422 standard (also published by the EIA) specifies a more electrically stable method than RS-232-C for generating positive and negative voltages in the range of 2 to 6 volts. The standard states that these techniques can be used to implement equipment capable of transmitting and receiving data at up to 10 Mbps. However, many implementations are limited to speeds much less than this. For example, some Apple Macintosh computers implement a variation of the RS-422 standard in their serial communication ports that are designed for speeds up to about 230,400 bps.

- **CCITT** *Recommendation X.21.* The RS-232-C and RS-422 standards apply mainly to situations where modems are used to transmit data over telephone circuits. There now exist many public data networks that use digital, rather than analog, circuits for data transmission. CCITT *Recommendation X.21* defines the electrical interface between a DTE and a DCE that is used for communication over digital lines.

C standard. Box 5.4 describes the purposes and characteristics of two other important physical-layer standards.

Readers interested in specific details on the many physical-level standards that govern data communication can consult the appropriate parts of the CCITT *Red Book* or *McGraw-Hill's Compilation of Data Communication Standards* (see Chapter 1).

In Chapter 6, we examine the line termination equipment that is used at each end of a communication line to allow terminals and other types of data processing equipment to communicate with one another.

6 MODEMS AND LINE DRIVERS

As we discussed in Chapter 2, an analog communication line requires a modem at each end in order for digital information to be sent over it. Modems are available in a wide range of speeds, generally 300 to 19,200 bps for use with voice-grade channels and up to hundreds of thousands of bits per second for use with wideband leased lines.

We have now seen that the signal we send down a communication line can travel to its destination by a wide variety of means. When it disappears into the wall plaster on its telephone wires we are not necessarily sure how it is going to travel. It may go in solitude on a wire circuit, or it may be huddled with hundreds of other signals on coaxial cable or microwave. It may race 25,000 miles into space to be beamed back by a satellite. However, if a standard telephone channel is used for transmission, we know that the signal must fit with the frequencies that the telephone channel is designed to transmit. Figure 6.1 shows the characteristics of a standard telephone channel. When a terminal screen flashes back a response after a pause of a second or so, its operator does not know how the data was transmitted.

In this chapter, we will explore the different types of *line termination equipment* that can be used for data transmission. As we have already discussed, the most common form of device used at each end of a communication channel is a *modem*. It is the primary function of a modem to convert a binary data signal into a set of frequencies that fit into the transmission space of a standard telephone channel. The need for modems can be eliminated in some cases by using private telecommunication channels rather than those supplied by a common carrier.

IN-PLANT AND OUT-PLANT LINES

Many computer users have privately owned lines on their own premises linking terminals to computers. The term *in-plant* is used for these lines to distin-

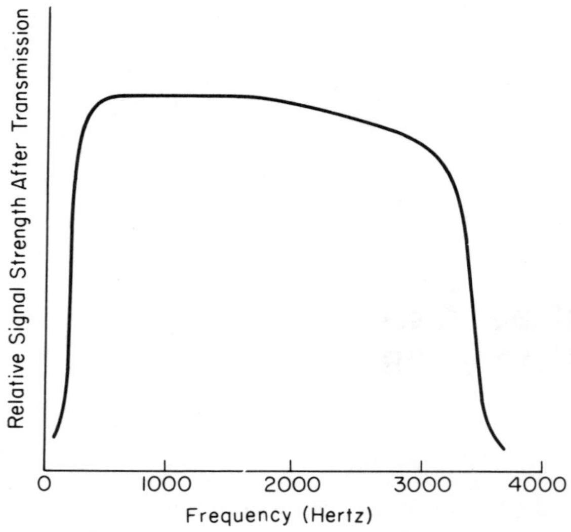

Figure 6.1   Characteristics of a standard telephone channel.

guish them from the *out-plant* lines that are supplied by common carriers. In other words, *out-plant* refers to common carrier lines connecting separate premises, whereas *in-plant* refers to lines or systems within one building or complex of buildings. In-plant lines are most commonly copper wire pairs, but coaxial cables are sometimes used instead. They may be installed by an organization's own engineers or by a telecommunications company.

In many cases, private lines can be specifically engineered to a company's own specifications so that they require no modems for data transmission. They can use baseband digital signaling at speeds ranging from telegraph speeds to several million bits per second. For high speeds, digital repeaters might be used every 1000 feet or so. In-plant lines can be used to handle ordinary data communication. But more often in today's data communication environment, they are used to construct *local area networks* (LANs), in which very high speed transmission facilities connect data processing machines in a flexible way to create *resource sharing networks*. Local area networks are the subject of Chapter 15.

FULL-DUPLEX VERSUS HALF-DUPLEX   Over a given physical line, the line termination equipment must be designed so that it can transmit either in both directions at once—full-duplex transmission—or else in either direction but not both at the same time—half-duplex. Simplex transmission is also possible, but this is rarely used in data transmission because it provides no easy way of controlling the flow of data or requesting retransmission after errors.

A terminal or modem will work somewhat differently depending on which transmission mode is required. Full-duplex transmission can be used either to send data streams in both directions at the same time or to send data in one direction and control signals in the other. The control signals might govern the flow of data and might also be used for error control. Data at the transmitting end might be held until the receiving end indicates that it had been received correctly. Control signals might be used to ensure that no two terminals transmit at once on a line with many terminals and might organize the sequence of transmission.

Simultaneous transmission in both directions can be obtained on a half-duplex line by using two separate frequency bands. One band is used for transmission in the opposite direction. By keeping the signals strictly separated in frequency, they can be prevented from interfering with each other. Many full-duplex modems provide a full-speed data channel in each direction.

FUNCTIONS OF LINE TERMINATION EQUIPMENT

The equipment at the ends of a communication line carries out several functions. In general, this equipment could perform all of the functions listed in Box 6.1. Often, however, the modem or other device car-

BOX 6.1 Modem functions

- Handling the initial setting up of the connection (sometimes called *handshaking*)
- Transmitting and receiving digital bit streams over the physical circuit to which it is attached
- Converting digital signals into a form suitable for transmission over the physical circuit
- Reconverting signals after transmission
- Possibly protecting the transmission facilities from harmful signals or voltages
- Possibly initiating calls by automatically sending dialing pulses and accepting responses to them
- Possibly detecting some forms of data errors and taking action to correct them
- Possibly detecting transmission or equipment failures and diagnosing where they occurred so that action can be taken

ries out only the first four functions listed in the box. Dialing the call may be done by the terminal or computer operator. The protection of the line may be done by an external device, such as the *data access arrangement* (DAA) that was required at one time to connect a device to the telephone network. The error detection is sometimes done by the software that runs above the physical level, in the data link layer. And automatic diagnosis of failures is too often not done at all. The most economical and efficient approach is for all of these functions to be carried out in an integrated fashion ''under the cover'' of the terminal or other data processing device.

MODEM STANDARDS

It is desirable that independent organizations be able to design and manufacture modems and data processing equipment that have modems integrated into them. Various standards exist for modem design that permit modems of different manufacturers to communicate with one another. It is desirable that modem standards be internationally accepted, and they should permit international transmission. The CCITT has published its V series of recommendations for modems. As long as a modem manufacturer conforms to the standards in designing a modem, modems of different manufacturers will be able to communicate with one another over communication channels. An important form of standard, especially in the United States, are ad hoc standards that have arisen simply because certain types of modems have become very popular.

Standards for modems are important at two levels:

- The signals that are used for transmitting data over the physical circuit
- The command set that is used by the data processing machine to control the functions of the modem

Signaling System Standards

Two of the most commonly used modem signaling system standards have been set by AT&T. Almost all the modems used today with personal computers in North America support data transmission at 300 bps using the form of signaling employed by the AT&T Model 103 data set, an obsolete modem that is little used today. Another obsolete AT&T modem, the Model 212A data set, supported data transmission at either 300 bps using the Model 103 signaling system or at 1200 bps using a different signaling system. Modems that are compatible with the two signaling systems of the Model 212A modem are very common. A third type of modem is used for data transmission at 2400 bps. The signaling system most often used by the manufacturers of 2400-bps modems is that described by the CCITT in *Recommendation V.26 bis*. Most 2400-bps modems also support data transmission at 300 and 1200 bps using the two Model 212A signaling systems.

Command Set Standards

A modem manufacturer can employ any desired command set in controlling the modem. Many manufacturers of sophisticated modems use their own command sets to control the unique features of their modems. Users of these modems must employ custom software that makes use of these command sets. Often the modem manufacturer supplies the necessary software. However, most manufacturers of standard modems that communicate at 300, 1200, or 2400 bps using the signaling systems just discussed use the command set that was first introduced by the Hayes Corporation for its 300-bps *Smartmodem*. This command set, generally referred to as the *AT* command set, is now a standard, simply because it has become so widely used. The advantage to using a modem that employs the Hayes AT command set is that almost all general-purpose data communication software that is available for personal computers can work with any modem that employs the Hayes AT command set.

PARALLEL TRANSMISSION

Most modems are designed to transmit information serially, character by character and bit by bit. Some modems, however, send a character at a time, transmitting the bits of each character in parallel. Parallel transmission is usually employed by inexpensive terminals and modems, often for data collection systems in which many terminals are needed and the data flow is in one direction.

The most inexpensive form of data terminal is a simple push-button telephone. Each button pressed transmits a pair of frequencies that travel well within the telephone bandwidth. A computer receiving the data might respond to the telephone user either with tones or with voice answerback. CCITT *Recommendation V.30* documents a system that can be used for parallel transmission over the public telephone network. The signals used in this transmission scheme are shown in Fig. 6.2.

Telephone networks use signaling schemes that employ frequencies inside the telephone bandwidth, and these frequencies must be avoided by multifrequency transmission devices. The frequencies used by push-button telephones are suitable for North America, but telephone networks in many other countries use different signaling frequencies.

ACOUSTICAL COUPLING

Where audible tones are used, there is no need to have a direct wire connection to the communication line. Instead, the modem can use a technique called *acoustical coupling*. With a typical acoustical coupler, the telephone handset fits into a special cradle. The device converts data signals into audible tones that are picked up by the microphone of a telephone handset. The earpiece of the telephone instrument at the other end sends these same tones into another acoustical coupler where the signals are converted back into data signals.

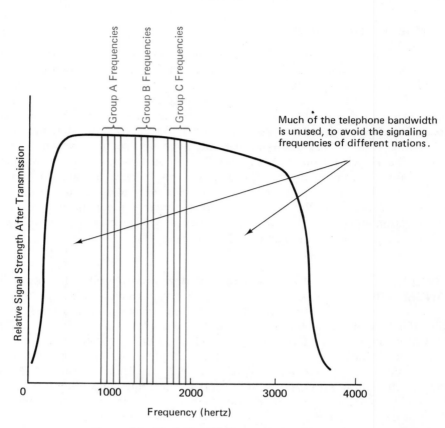

Figure 6.2   Typical parallel transmission frequencies.

An advantage of acoustical coupling is that it allows data transmission to take place anywhere there is a standard telephone. Acoustical couplers were once very widely used but have today fallen out of favor. This method of connection to the public telephone network is somewhat less efficient than a direct wire connection. It is also more expensive and can be used only for transmitting between relatively slow machines. A commonly used speed with acoustical couplers is 300 bps. Some more expensive models allow transmission at 1200 bps. Higher speeds than this are not generally used with acoustical couplers. Today, because of the widespread use of the standard modular telephone jack, it is much easier than in days past to connect a modem directly to the telephone network. Acoustical couplers are most often used today where direct connection to the public telephone network is difficult, such as where data calls must be placed using public call boxes.

HIGH-SPEED LINE TERMINATION

As we saw in Chapter 3, communication lines with a bandwidth much greater than that of a telephone line can be leased. For example, the bandwidth of a *12-channel group* can be leased, giving a bandwidth of 48 kHz instead of the 4 kHz of a standard telephone channel. Channels of even higher bandwidths are routinely used for data transmission. Modems are available from various manufacturers for wideband transmission. CCITT *Recommendation V.35* is for a 48,000-bps modem operating in the 60 to 104 kHz band.

With the spread of digital circuits, it is more common today for high-data-rate links to operate over digital lines and hence not need modems. T1 links are widely used today, both by common carriers for the transmission of telephone signals and by individual users for data transmission. The approach of some common carriers is to provide their customers with an *interface unit* that can contain different facilities depending on the nature of the transmission link. Sometimes it contains a modem; sometimes it contains a digital baseband signaling unit. The customer does not necessarily need to know what it contains. The customer needs to know merely how it interfaces with the data processing equipment.

DIGITAL LINE TERMINATION

As we discussed in Chapter 4, the AT&T Dataphone Digital Service (DDS) provides a digital channel and hence requires no modems. The digital channel operates at speeds of 2400, 4800, 9600, or 56,000 bps using either half-duplex or full-duplex transmission. Instead of a modem, AT&T provides the user with a line termination device called a *data service unit*. The data processing machine passes data to and receives data from this device.

The data service unit is designed so that the user's terminal or data processing equipment connects to it with the same plug that would be used with a modem on an analog line. For transmission at 2400, 4800, or 9600 bps this is the 25-pin plug that conforms to the EIA RS-232-C interface standard. The data service unit used for 56,000-bps transmission uses the 34-pin plug conforming to CCITT *Recommendation V.35* for wideband modems.

In Chapter 7, we discuss the various types of equipment that can be used to create a data communication network and to control the communication lines that implement it.

7 LINE CONTROL EQUIPMENT

At a conference in Europe, I needed to demonstrate some points by accessing a computer in the United States. I used a simple asynchronous terminal and was able to get a dial-up connection to a computer in the United States with no difficulty. At the end of half an hour, I looked at the printout and estimated that a total of no more than 3000 characters had been transmitted in both directions. This is about typical. That voice line was capable of transmitting 4800 bps with a fairly inexpensive modem. So in half an hour, then, it could transmit 8,640,000 bits. In fact, fewer than 21,000 bits were transmitted. We can calculate the efficiency of my use of that line by dividing 21,000 by 8,640,000— about 0.0024. You might say that this was certainly a poor way to use such an expensive facility.

Most telecommunications applications require techniques that permit multiple users to *share* trunks and switches so that the utilization is higher. A variety of techniques exist for sharing the facilities. The purpose of this chapter is to examine the characteristics of equipment that can be used to optimize the use of expensive communication facilities.

POINT-TO-POINT VERSUS MULTIPOINT LINKS

As we have seen, a single data link is made up of one communication channel and the related equipment necessary for transmitting data over it. Data links can be used to interconnect data processing equipment in many ways, each providing a different level of line sharing.

Figure 7.1 shows the first way in which we might implement connections between a group of terminals and a mainframe computer. We are using a separate physical data link for each terminal. The advantage is that each terminal can communicate with the mainframe at any time, but no line sharing is in-

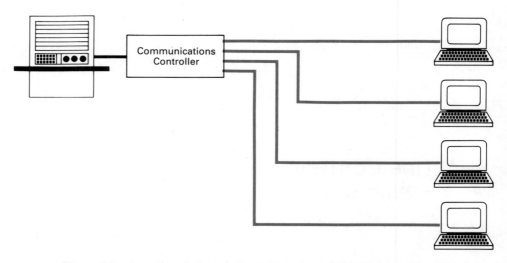

Figure 7.1   A separate point-to-point link can be used to connect each terminal to a computer's communications controller.

volved. This is an expensive way to implement the data links, especially when they are long.

One method to introduce line sharing is to use a single multipoint data link to connect the terminals to the computer. In Fig. 7.2, each terminal can communicate with the computer as long as only one of the terminals transmits or receives at a time. All stations on the data link receive all the messages that are transmitted over it. An addressing scheme must be used to identify the intended recipient of each message, and all the terminals must have enough intelligence to implement the addressing scheme. Also, multipoint data links are not well suited to asynchronous transmission, so the terminals generally should have buffers and be capable of transmitting messages in blocks rather than one character at a time.

A major risk involved with multipoint data links is one of degraded response time. If a terminal wants to transmit to the computer, it must wait until no other terminal is using the data link. Occasionally, and by chance, all the devices may be ready to transmit at once. Then, one terminal will have to wait until all the others have finished, thus making the response time uneven. If every terminal has a buffer, the wait may never be very long. When the terminals do not have buffers and transmit one character at a time, the time it takes to send a message depends on the rate at which the operator types it. For a realtime system in which a fast response time is necessary, unbuffered terminals should not ordinarily be used on a multipoint line.

In addition to the use of multipoint lines, four different categories of equipment can be used in a data communication network to increase the utili-

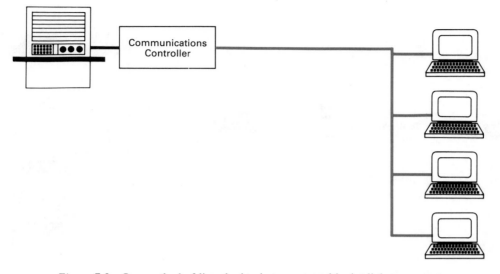

Figure 7.2 One method of line sharing is to use a multipoint link to connect all terminals to the communications controller.

zation of telecommunication lines: multiplexors, concentrators, communications controllers, and switching devices of various types.

MULTIPLEXORS

The simplest type of device for increasing line utilization is the multiplexor. Instead of connecting the terminals to the mainframe using a single multipoint data link, we can use a single high-capacity data link and a multiplexor to provide a separate channel for each terminal. In Fig. 7.3, each terminal has a separate 1200-bps line to the multiplexor. A single 4800-bps data link connects the multiplexor at the terminal's end to another multiplexor at the computer's end. This splits the 4800-bps data link back into the four original 1200-bps channels for input to the computer.

The multiplexor's main job is to combine the data being transmitted over a number of low-bandwidth data links for transmission over one or more channels of higher bandwidth. The net effect here is of a single 1200-bps channel between each terminal and the mainframe. But a single 4800-bps data link is used to implement them. This is especially advantageous if the high-capacity data link is long, say, coast-to-coast, while the low-capacity links are short, say, in the same building. Here we trade the cost of the lines against the cost of the multiplexing equipment. Box 7.1 lists some of the advantages of using multiplexors to increase line utilization.

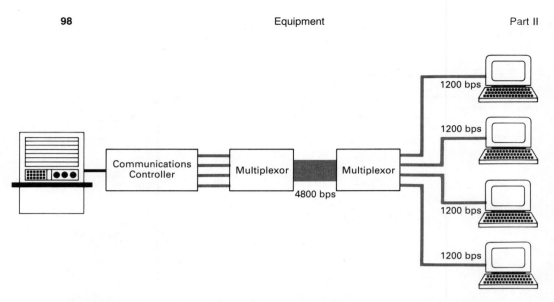

Figure 7.3 A multiplexor allows a single high-capacity link to be divided into several lower-capacity links.

As we mentioned in Chapter 2, two main techniques are used in implementing multiplexors: *frequency-division multiplexing* with analog lines and *time-division multiplexing* with digital lines.

Frequency-Division Multiplexing

With frequency-division multiplexing, a multiplexor at one end of a group of low-capacity lines combines these lines into a single high-bandwidth channel. It does this by assigning a different range of frequencies to each of the incoming signals. Generally, a small portion of the total bandwidth is lost in separating the subchannels. A complementary multiplexor at the other end splits each of these frequency ranges back into the original group of lower-capacity channels. Most frequency-division multiplexors also perform the functions of a modem in addition to carrying out the multiplexing function.

Time-Division Multiplexing

Time-division multiplexing is most often used with digital channels. With this technique, the time available is divided up into small slots, and each of these is occupied by a piece of one of the messages to be sent. The multiplexing apparatus scans the input in a round-robin fashion. Only bits from one of the messages occupies the channel at one instant. It is thus quite different from frequency-division multiplexing, in which all the signals are sent at the same time, each occupying a different frequency band. A time-division multiplexor reads

BOX 7.1 Advantages of multiplexors

- Multiplexors are relatively inexpensive compared to many other devices designed to increase line utilization.

- Multiplexors do not affect the programming in any way and are transparent to the programs that send and receive data and control signals.

- Being relatively simple devices, multiplexors generally have a high reliability.

- If it is desired to send a long continuous stream of data on some of the lines, as in remote batch operation, multiplexors can handle this without interruption of the data stream and without interference with other users.

- The use of multiplexors generally causes no significant increase in response time.

each of the incoming low-speed bit streams and interleaves them to form a single high-speed bit stream. Similar equipment at the other end separates the bits from the high-speed bit stream and re-creates the original lower-speed ones.

CONCENTRATORS With the simple multiplexing techniques just described, *all* the terminals can transmit *all* the time, because each has its own dedicated subchannel. In many systems, terminals do not need this capability. When an operator is carrying on a dialog using a terminal, the data flows in bursts, which are often small compared with the total capacity of the line. Furthermore, when an operator uses a keyboard, the resulting character rate is usually far less than that of the line. An input rate of 3 characters per second would be faster than that of most terminal operators, but this is but a small fraction of the 300- or 1200-bps rate used for many applications.

If advantage is taken of the low character rate, a number of terminals can be handled without the need of a higher-speed line. This can be done with a concentrator. Figure 7.4 shows a system in which each of the terminals is attached to a concentrator. The concentrator is then connected to the main computer, with one or more data links, possibly having the same capacity as those used for the terminals. The concentrator generally has enough intelligence to allow multiple terminals to communicate simultaneously. The concentrator uses buffer storage to store messages for transmission and uses the data link between it and the mainframe more efficiently. All the terminals act as if they have a dedicated circuit to the mainframe. They get acceptable response time as long

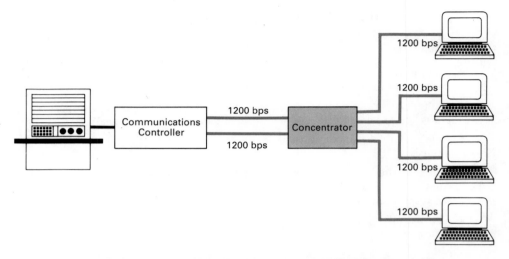

Figure 7.4 A concentrator uses intelligence and buffer storage to achieve better utilization of a communication facility than can be achieved with a multiplexor.

as the combined transmissions of all the terminals do not overload the links between the concentrator and the mainframe.

Concentration functions are often performed in a cluster controller. But concentrators can be used anywhere in a network. In Fig. 7.5, several concentrators, each controlling several terminals, tie into a mid-network concentrator, which in turn ties into a host computer's communications controller.

The operation of a concentrator is rather like people driving to a bus station, one person per car, and all getting into a bus. Both the cars and the bus

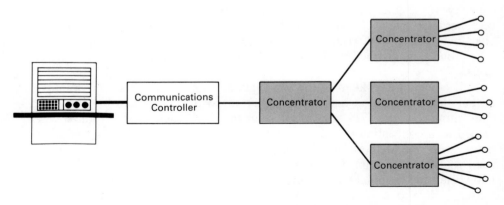

Figure 7.5 Concentrators can be used at any desired point in a data communication network.

use the same road facilities, but the bus uses the road facilities more efficiently than the individual cars.

A system that uses a concentrator may avoid the cost of a high-speed line but is taking a risk that input data will occasionally have to be reentered or that a keyboard will have to be locked because of a temporary overload when all the terminal operators enter data at once.

CONCENTRATOR AND MULTIPLEXOR DIFFERENCES

Multiplexors and concentrators perform similar functions, but the way in which they operate and their real purposes are fundamentally different. The main distinguishing characteristic of a simple multiplexor is that the total bandwidth entering the device is roughly equivalent to the total bandwidth leaving it. All it does is chop up a high-capacity channel into several smaller subchannels. With a concentrator, by contrast, the total bandwidth entering is normally different from the bandwidth leaving it. It uses computer logic and memory to combine several inefficient transmissions into one (or several) more efficient ones. It can give a much better utilization of the available bandwidth than a multiplexor.

Today, devices are available that perform the functions of both concentrators and multiplexors. For example, a device called a *statistical multiplexor* combines several low-speed channels into one or more high-speed channels whose total bandwidth is less than the total of the lines entering it.

CONCENTRATOR AND MULTIPLEXOR COMBINATIONS

In complex networks, various combinations of concentrators and multiplexors can be used to create almost any kind of configuration. In Fig. 7.6, cluster controllers perform concentration functions for small

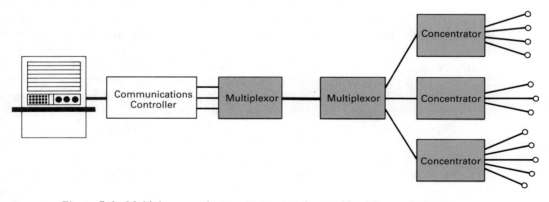

Figure 7.6 Multiplexors and concentrators can be combined in any desired configuration.

groups of terminals. Each of the concentrators ties into a multiplexor at some convenient location for transmission over higher-capacity channels to the location of the computer. Multiplexing equipment there splits out the individual subchannels used by each concentrator.

Multiplexors can also be used to combine computer and noncomputer traffic. Multiplexors can be used to split a single wideband transmission facility into a number of voice channels. Some of the voice channels might be used for data transmission and others for normal voice traffic.

COST TRADE-OFFS If communication lines are long, and therefore expensive, it is generally worthwhile to use elaborate techniques to reduce the number of lines needed. The larger computer networks of today would be unthinkably expensive without the concentrators and multiplexors that they use.

If the lines are short or inexpensive, however, the emphasis should be on reducing terminal and equipment cost rather than line cost. When the lines are very short—for example, all in one plant, in one office building, or on one campus—their cost is of little significance in the design, and we often find their bandwidth being used quite wantonly.

The cost of placing logic and storage (such as buffers) in the peripheral parts of the network is dropping rapidly, largely through the use of microprocessors and other types of integrated circuits. As this happens, an increasing number of systems will use multiplexors, concentrators, and other remote mechanisms for lowering the overall network cost.

COMMUNICATIONS CONTROLLERS A third type of device that is used to perform line control functions in a data transmission system is the *communications controller,* which we have seen in the network examples. The major purpose of a communications controller is not to optimize the use of the transmission facilities but to optimize the use of the host computer to which it is attached. As we have seen, digital information is normally transmitted over communication lines a bit at a time. The messages to be transmitted must therefore be broken into bits, and these bits must be sent at the speed of the line. Similarly, on receiving a message, bits are assembled one at a time into characters, and the characters are assembled into messages. Both characters and messages must be error-checked and the errors corrected, if possible. Suitable control signals must be generated for operating the distant terminals at the correct times. Many of these communication-related functions are best handled by a separate communications controller instead of by the host computer.

The value of a stored-program computer in controlling communication functions lies in its adaptability. It must handle messages of any length; therefore, dynamic memory allocation is desirable. It might control differing numbers of lines with different devices. It will often have to change the sequence in which it accepts messages from terminals, as terminals are shut down and opened up. It may have to dial out to terminals and accept calls dialed in. Diagnostic programs will be run in it to detect network faults and help in terminal checkout.

The communications controller most often has an instruction set that is different from conventional computers and is designed for handling communication functions. It may have the facility to log messages on its own disk drives or magnetic tape units. It may send English-language messages to the terminal operators as part of its control procedures. Because it is a programmable unit, its procedures may be modified as circumstances demand.

An additional function of the communications controller might be code conversion. The transmission line often uses a different means for encoding characters than the main computer. Seven-bit ASCII is a very commonly used code for transmission of data over communication lines, whereas the 8-bit EBCDIC code is used in the internal circuitry of IBM mainframe computers. (These character codes are described in Chapter 8.) Either the communication controller or the main computer may have to translate back and forth between EBCDIC and ASCII. This step is now often done by hardware or microprogramming in the communication controller.

SWITCHING EQUIPMENT

Another category of device that is used in constructing communication networks includes switches of various types. A circuit switch allows an incoming channel to be switched to any one of several outgoing channels. Circuit switches are used in telephone exchanges to switch phone calls from one subscriber to another. Privately installed circuit switches can also be used by the system designer in implementing data communication systems.

Let us suppose that we want to interconnect a great number of intelligent machines so that any machine in the network can establish a logical connection to any other machine. With point-to-point connections, we need a great many data links. To interconnect three machines, three data links are required. But to interconnect eight machines, 28 separate data links are required (see Fig. 7.7). Multiplexors can't help in this situation because all they do is provide a more economical means of implementing individual data links. A concentrator network could be built, but then one of the machines would have to be in charge of the network and handle the setting up of the various logical connections that might be required.

A common technique is to use one or more switches to interconnect the various users. For example, each intelligent machine might be connected to the

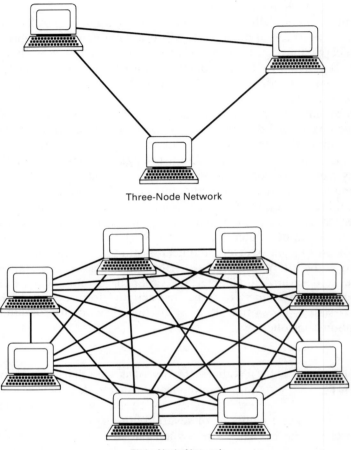

Three-Node Network

Eight-Node Network

Figure 7.7   A great number of point-to-point connections are required to interconnect all nodes directly when there are more than a few nodes.

public telephone system with voice-grade channels, as shown in Fig. 7.8. For any machine to contact any other, all that is needed is the other user's telephone number.

PRIVATE BRANCH EXCHANGES   When an organization has many telephones, it may have its own switching facility that interconnects its telephones with one another and also with the public network. These private switching facilities can also be used for data communication by employing appropriate modems and other line termination equipment.

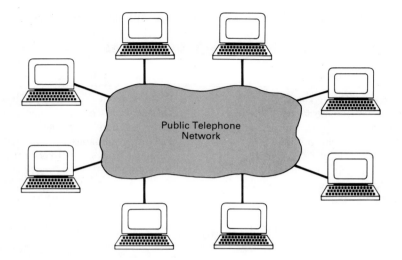

Figure 7.8 The public telephone network can be used to provide the switching capabilities that are required to interconnect all the nodes in a network.

A private switching facility is called a *private branch exchange* (PBX). Today most PBXs are fully automatic rather than manually controlled by operators; an automatic PBX is often referred to by the term *private automatic branch exchange* (PABX). Most large PABXs today are computer-controlled, and each extension attached to the system ordinarily has its own individual telephone number. Some PABXs are specifically designed to support users of data communication services and use digital technology. A digital PABX can often be used to connect data processing equipment directly with digital circuits, thus avoiding the use of modems.

DISADVANTAGES OF CONVENTIONAL SWITCHING

The conventional switching techniques used in the public telephone network and in PBXs are better suited to conventional telephone users than to users of data communication services. Some of the differences between telephone users and data users are listed in Box 7.2.

Perhaps the most important difference in handling telephone traffic versus data traffic is that telephone users talk or listen more or less *continuously,* whereas typical users of data communication transmit and receive *bursts* of data with relatively long periods of silence between the bursts. It is common for a data communication line to be idle a majority of the time.

To overcome these disadvantages a network designed specifically for data transmission should be able to handle sporadic bursts of transmission rather than continuous transmission. The *transmission* facilities in existence for telephone

BOX 7.2   Characteristics of telephone and data users

Telephone Users	Data Users
Fixed channel capacity	Wide range of channel capacities
Two-way conversations	One-way or two-way transmissions
Tolerance to channel noise	Error-free delivery of data
Continuous transmission	Burst or continuous transmission
Immediate delivery of signal	Frequent delays in delivery time
Constant transmission rate	Bursty traffic
Switching in seconds or minutes	Switching in milliseconds
Session switching required	Item switching desirable
Manual dialing	Automatic dialing
Simple compatible instruments	Range of incompatible machines

traffic are well suited to such a network, but the *multiplexing* and *switching* facilities need to be different. Such a network needs *burst multiplexing* and *burst switching* rather than continuous-channel multiplexing and switching.

The continuous-channel switching and multiplexing used for conventional telephone traffic thus has two disadvantages for computer terminals. First, it causes inefficient utilization of the facilities. Second, transmissions are restricted to the maximum speed of the telephone channels when in some cases faster transmission bursts would be beneficial.

SWITCHING TECHNIQUES

In examining the nature of a communication channel, we find that there are basically two methods that can be used for dividing up a channel's capacity. These are shown in Fig. 7.9. The horizontal line represents the traditional methodology; a portion of the bandwidth or capacity is allocated to one user for as long as it is needed. The vertical lines represent burst subdivision. A user is given the whole capacity for a brief period of time whenever it is needed. The two methods of operation apply to both the multiplexing process and the switching. In some cases, these two methods can be used together, as shown in Fig. 7.10. Some networks operate using continuous subchannels that are leased from the telephone companies, but the channels are subdivided using burst multiplexing and burst switching. The two ways of dividing up channel capacities lead to four different methods that can be used for switching:

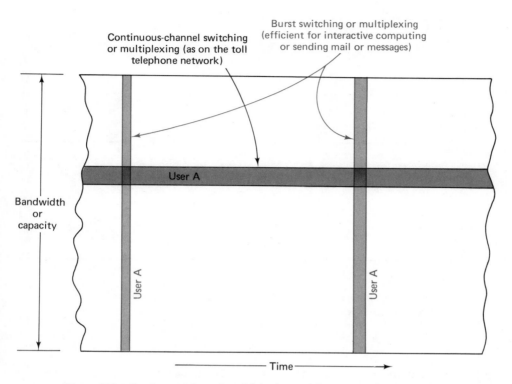

Figure 7.9 Continuous-channel multiplexing and burst multiplexing provide two different methods for dividing up a channel's capacity.

- Conventional circuit switching
- Fast-connect circuit switching
- Message switching
- Packet switching

CONVENTIONAL CIRCUIT SWITCHING

The first switching method is the method we have already discussed. We have seen that conventional circuit switching is wasteful of both switching and transmission capacity when the traffic consists of short or high-speed bursts. It may take many seconds to complete the circuit, but then a data message may take only a few milliseconds to travel to its destination. Because the switching time is so long relative to the transmission time,

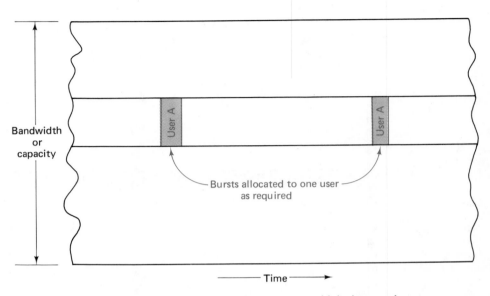

Figure 7.10 Both continuous-channel and burst multiplexing can be combined when required.

the circuit usually remains connected for an entire terminal session. It would be unreasonable to ask terminal operators to dial up the computer each time they press the ENTER key.

FAST-CONNECT CIRCUIT SWITCHING

Fast-connect circuit switching is a form of burst switching that is more efficient with sporadic traffic. Since the circuit is connected very fast (in a few milliseconds), it is feasible to establish a new connection each time there is new data to transmit. Since the circuits remain connected only briefly, busy signals occur rarely. A terminal connected to a fast-connect circuit switching network might be programmed to dial the appropriate computer automatically each time the ENTER key is pressed.

Public data networks that use fast-connect circuit switching have been implemented, and they solve many of the problems associated with conventional switching. However, experience has shown that the two other switching methods—message switching and packet switching—are better suited to handling large volumes of data traffic on complex networks.

MESSAGE SWITCHING

Message switching and packet switching represent a fundamentally different type of switching than the two types of circuit switching just discussed. With circuit switching, the physical transmission path is switched; with message switching and packet switching, circuits remain permanently connected and the messages themselves are switched. The user of a data network would like to tie into the network and have a simple way of sending a message to another network user. In the ideal situation, the user should not have to know any of the details of how the network is implemented. The message should contain the network address of the destination user, and the network should take care of delivering it.

With a typical message switching system, terminals are connected to a central computer that performs the message storage and message switching functions, as in Fig. 7.11. The central computer accepts messages coming into the network from network users, examines their destination addresses, and sees that they are properly delivered to the appropriate user at the other end. Figure 7.12 shows a large message switching system that uses a mesh-structured rather than a star-structured network. Each node in the network may implement storage in which messages are retained for a period of time.

Message switching networks can give better line utilization than the same network operated with circuit switching. Although the cost of the message switching computers is often higher than conventional circuit switches, the total line cost is lower, since a greater degree of sharing can be achieved. Message switching therefore tends to be economical on a large network with long lines and many terminals.

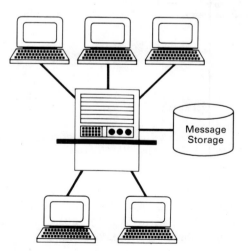

Figure 7.11 In addition to providing message delivery services, a message switching system typically maintains messages in storage.

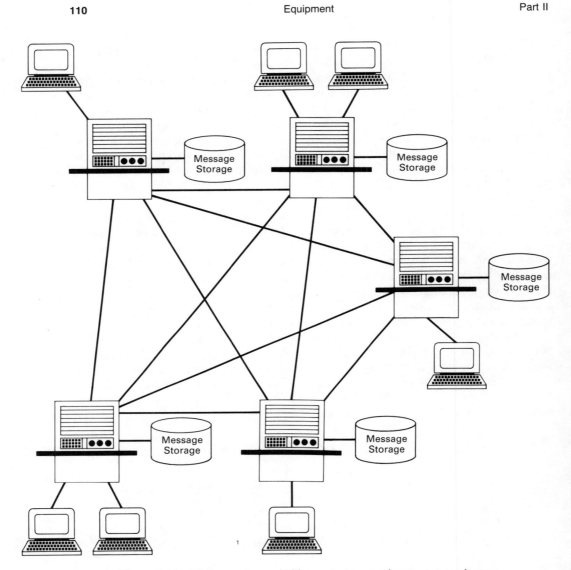

Figure 7.12 Large message switching systems sometimes use a mesh-structured network with many message switching computers.

A message switching computer carries on three functions continuously: It receives messages, stores them, and sends them to their destinations. Message switching can form a "nonblocking" network that never fails to accept traffic unless there is a breakdown. The *risk* with message switching is not of busy signals, as with circuit switching, but of a lengthened delivery time.

Message switching systems have traditionally been used to relay messages that need to get to their destinations in perhaps a few seconds or even a few minutes. When faster delivery times are essential, a special form of message switching called *packet switching* is typically used.

PACKET
SWITCHING

Most of today's public data networks use packet switching techniques. In a packet switching network, the terminals or computers are linked to the network via *interface computers* that are designed to work with small units of data, called *packets,* that are no larger than some fixed maximum size. As shown in Fig. 7.13, a packet switching network is similar to a mesh-structured message switching network. What is different is that the terminals and computers that are connected to a packet switching network must have enough intelligence to break long messages into *packets* for transmission through the network. The packets are given to the interface computers for transmission to their final destinations. The computer or terminal at the destination then reassembles the individual packets into copies of the original messages. Less capable terminals can be attached to a packet switching network through an intermediary device that implements a *packet assembly and disassembly* (PAD) function. The device

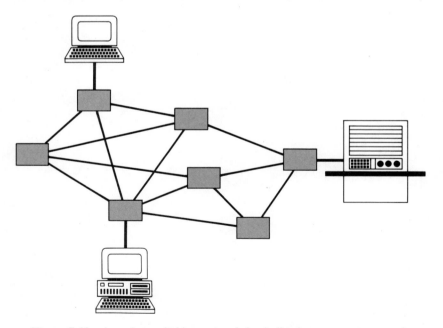

Figure 7.13 A packet switching network is similar in structure to a mesh-structured message switching system.

that performs the PAD function can be supplied by the user and can be on the user's premises, or it can be supplied by the network operator and can be installed at the location of a network interface computer.

High-speed communication links (56,000 bps and higher) are normally used to interconnect the interface computers. The network is usually designed so that if one of the lines fails, there is always an alternate path to the destination. The interface computers determine the routing for the packets, and the packets are passed very quickly from one node to another. Typical packet switching networks do not retain the packets or messages once they have been delivered correctly. The network acts simply as a mail service. A message switching network, by contrast, generally *files* messages for possible retrieval later.

A widely used standard for packet switching networks is documented in CCITT *Recommendation X.25,* which describes the way in which a data terminal interfaces with a packet switching network. Chapter 14 discusses packet switching and *X.25* in detail and shows how packet switching is used in implementing public data networks.

Part III of this book examines the programming used in constructing data communication networks. Chapter 8 begins Part III by describing the techniques that are used in controlling transmission on a data link.

PART **III** PROGRAMMING

8 CONTROLLING TRANSMISSION

When data transmission devices send data to each other, a variety of control signals must pass to and fro between the devices to ensure that they are working in step with each other. Throughout the transmission, exact synchronization must also be maintained, and slippages in synchronization must be corrected. An important set of standards, called *data link protocols,* govern the way in which communicating machines interact at the data link level. We look at some specific data link protocols in Chapter 9. In this chapter, we discuss the general characteristics of data links and examine the types of functions most data link protocols must perform.

For the stations on a data link to communicate successfully, they must all agree on a common data code to be used. We begin by examining two commonly used data codes.

DATA CODES

It is desirable to have internationally agreed-on codes for the transmission of data so that computers and terminals from different manufacturers can intercommunicate. During the 1960s, an alarming proliferation of data transmission codes developed. Some of these codes have now dropped into disuse, and two codes predominate:

- **International Alphabet No. 5.** This is a widely accepted 7-bit code that permits minor national variations. In the International Alphabet No. 5, ten characters can be varied to produce *versions* or *dialects* of the code. Figure 8.1 shows the United States national version of International Alphabet No. 5, which is commonly called *ASCII (American Standard Code for Information Interchange)*. ASCII is the most widely used code for data transmission and telegraphy in North America.

- **EBCDIC.** A great many people who work with IBM equipment are familiar with *EBCDIC (Extended Binary Coded Decimal Interchange Code)*. EBCDIC

Bit positions 5, 6, 7:

Bit positions 1, 2, 3, 4:		000 / 0	100 / 1	010 / 2	110 / 3	001 / 4	101 / 5	011 / 6	111 / 7
0000	0	NUL	TC_7 (DLE)	SP	0	@	P	`	p
1000	1	TC_1 (SOH)	DC_1	!	1	A	Q	a	q
0100	2	TC_2 (STX)	DC	''	2	B	R	b	r
1100	3	TC_3 (ETX)	DC_3	#	3	C	S	c	s
0010	4	TC_4 (EOT)	DC_4	¤	4	D	T	d	t
1010	5	TC_5 (ENQ)	TC_8 (NAK)	%	5	E	U	e	u
0110	6	TC_6 (ACK)	TC_9 (SYN)	&	6	F	V	f	v
1110	7	BEL	TC_{10} (ETB)	'	7	G	W	g	w
0001	8	FE_0 (BS)	CAN	(	8	H	X	h	x
1001	9	FE_1 (HT)	EM	)	9	I	Y	i	y
0101	10	FE_2 (LF)	SUB	*	:	J	Z	j	z
1101	11	FE_3 (VT)	ESC	+	;	K	[	k	{
0011	12	FE_4 (FF)	IS_4 (FS)	,	<	L	\	l	|
1011	13	FE_5 (CR)	IS_3 (GS)	–	=	M	]	m	}
0111	14	SO	IS_2 (RS)	.	>	N	^	n	–
1111	15	SI	IS_1 (US)	/	?	O	_	o	DEL

Figure 8.1 The ASCII code.

is an 8-bit code that was introduced by IBM in the 1960s with the System/360 computing system and is used internally in much of IBM's computing equipment. In many cases, a computing system may use the EBCDIC code internally but will have equipment that automatically translates between EBCDIC and ASCII for data transmission. Some systems use the EBCDIC code directly for data transmission. A code chart for the EBCDIC code is shown in Fig. 8.2. Notice that the EBCDIC code provides for more control functions than the International Alphabet No. 5. The EBCDIC code is used less often for data transmission than ASCII, but it is nonetheless an important character code due to the widespread use of IBM equipment.

DATA LINK CONFIGURATIONS

We use the term *data link* to describe a *physical* connection between two hardware components. A data link consists of a communication channel and the

Bit Positions 0.1	00				01				10				11			
Bit Positions 2, 3	00	01	10	11	00	01	10	11	00	01	10	11	00	01	10	11
First Hexadecimal Digit	0	1	2	3	4	5	6	7	8	9	A	B	C	D	E	F
0000 0	NUL	DLE	DS		SP	&	–						{	}	\	0
0001 1	SOH	DC1	SOS		RSP		/		a	i	~		A	J	NSP	1
0010 2	STX	DC2	FS	SYN					b	k	s		B	K	S	2
0011 3	ETX	DC3	WUS	IR					c	l	t		C	L	T	3
0100 4	SEL	RES/ENP	BYP/INP	PP					d	m	u		D	M	U	4
0101 5	HT	NL	LF	TRN					e	n	v		E	N	V	5
0110 6	RNL	BS	ETB	NBS					f	o	w		F	O	W	6
0111 7	DEL	POC	ESC	EOT					g	p	x		G	P	X	7
1000 8	GE	CAN	SA	SBS					h	q	y		H	Q	Y	8
1001 9	SPS	EM	SFE	IT				\	i	r	z		I	R	Z	9
1010 A	RPT	UBS	SM/SW	RFF	¢	!	¦	:					SHY			
1011 B	VT	CU1	CSP	CU3	.	$	,	#								
1100 C	FF	IFS	MFA	DC4	<	*	%	@								
1101 D	CR	IGS	ENQ	NAK	(	)	_	'								
1110 E	SO	IRS	ACK		+	;	>	=								
1111 F	SI	IUS/ITB	BEL	SUB	|	¬	?	"								EO

Figure 8.2   The EBCDIC code.

hardware needed to transmit data over it. Three data link configurations are in common use: *point-to-point, multipoint,* and *loop.*

POINT-TO-POINT CONFIGURATION

A point-to-point data link, shown in Fig. 8.3, is the simplest and easiest to control. When one station transmits, the station at the other end of the link receives. Since no other stations are attached to the data link, there are no problems associated with determining for whom a message is intended. In some systems that use point-to-point links, one station on the link is designated as the *primary* station (often a computer), and the other is designated as the *secondary* station (often a terminal). In a system in which a primary/secondary relationship exists, only the primary station is capable of originating an exchange of messages; the secondary station can transmit only after the primary station has given it permission. In other systems, the two stations are *peers,* and either can initiate an exchange of messages.

MULTIPOINT CONFIGURATION

When the communication lines used to implement a data transmission system are expensive and the terminals are in use only a fraction of the time, several terminals are often attached to the same data link. A data link that has more than one station attached to it is called a *multipoint* data link, as shown in Fig. 8.4. The terminals might be all in one location, or the communication line might wander in a zigzag fashion from one to another.

In most cases, one of the stations on a multipoint data link is designated as the primary or master station (often a computer) and the others as secondary stations (often terminals). In most cases, the primary station can send a message to any of the secondary stations, but each secondary station can send messages only to the primary station; secondary stations cannot communicate with one another directly.

Controlling Transmission

In Chapter 2, we used a fire hose analogy to describe data flowing along a communication line. By carrying the analogy a step further, we can see that if

Figure 8.3   A point-to-point data link is the simplest and easiest to control.

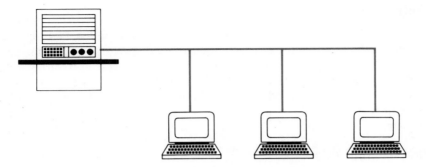

Figure 8.4 A multipoint data link has a primary station and two or more secondary stations.

our espionage firefighter had several agents connected to the fire hose over which data was being sent, only one of them could be transmitting at once. In fact, the espionage agent must have some way of maintaining discipline over the other agents. When the agent sends a pulse down a multipoint fire hose, it will be detected by all the agents connected to that hose. They must have a carefully worked out procedure for determining who transmits when and for whom a particular message is meant. Discipline is needed on multipoint data links for the same reason.

Equally important, each terminal must have a means of recognizing which signals are meant for *it;* otherwise, it will react to the messages that are sent to and from the other terminals on the data link. If a message is sent from the computer to a terminal, the message might contain the address of the terminal for which the message is destined. The terminal whose address this is recognizes it and takes appropriate action. All the other terminals on the data link ignore it. In addition to having the ability to address one terminal, some systems also have *group* codes that allow selected sets of terminals to receive messages and a *broadcast* code that can cause a message to be accepted by all terminals.

In order to recognize its address and carry out the various line control functions needed, each terminal must contain some logic capability. This logic is built into some terminals; in others, it resides in a terminal control unit. These logic circuits make the terminal somewhat more expensive than otherwise. A terminal without the required logic circuits cannot be used on a multipoint data link.

To control transmission on a multipoint data link, various characters or sequences of characters sometimes have special meanings during transmission. In some systems, certain characters are reserved as control characters. A variety of these are seen in the ASCII and EBCDIC codes. Special characters or character sequences can also be used for terminal addressing. An address must be specified when the master station is sending a message to an individual secondary station.

Contention Techniques

One method that can be used for controlling a multipoint data link is called *contention*. When the contention technique is used for controlling transmission, any station on the data link is free to make a request to transmit. If the data link is available, transmission proceeds. If the data link is in use, the station must wait. When contention is used, queues of contention requests are normally built up. This queue is then scanned by the master station. The queue can be scanned in a prearranged sequence or in the sequence in which the requests were made.

Polling Techniques

Far more common than contention are various *polling* techniques. The simplest form of polling is called *roll-call polling*. With roll-call polling, the master station asks the secondary stations, one by one, whether they have anything to transmit. The master station sends a polling message down the line to one of the secondary stations asking, ''Terminal X, have you anything to transmit? If so, go ahead.'' If terminal X has nothing to send, it may send a negative reply and the next polling message will be sent: ''Terminal Y, have you anything to transmit? If so, go ahead.''

Normally the master station consists of a computer, or its communications controller, that organizes the polling; the secondary stations may consist of ter-

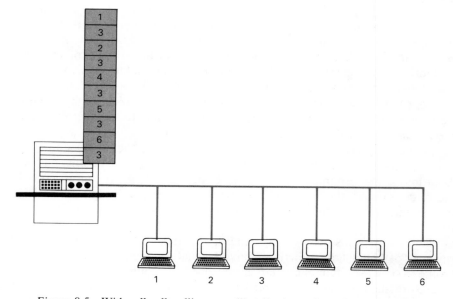

Figure 8.5 With roll-call polling, a polling list is used to control the order in which the secondary stations are polled.

minals. The master station might have in its storage a polling list indicating the sequence in which the secondary stations should be polled (see Fig. 8.5). The polling list and its use determine the priorities with which the secondary stations are scanned. Certain important stations may have their address more than once on the polling list so that they are polled more frequently than the others. Once a polling message has established an interconnection between a secondary station and the master station, the transmission can proceed much like point-to-point transmission.

LOOP CONFIGURATION

Some systems allow devices to be connected in the form of a loop. This technique often uses a high-speed pulse stream, traveling in a constant and unbroken fashion, over links that are generally installed on the user's premises. Loops are not generally used with systems that use common carrier facilities for data communication. The loop configuration has the advantage that both the terminals and the communication links can be relatively inexpensive. Bits can be carried at a very high rate over a simple pair of wires if regenerative digital repeaters are used with sufficiently close spacing. As with multipoint data links, the loop configuration requires that each terminal implement the procedures that are used to control transmission on the loop.

In a typical low-cost loop implementation, each secondary station on the loop examines the address of every frame and captures frames that are addressed to it. When a station originates a frame, it briefly suspends its repeater function and transmits its frame. A station is permitted to do this only after it receives a special "go-ahead" bit pattern. The primary station, usually a computer or communications controller, begins a cycle by transmitting a go-ahead pattern around the loop. If no terminal wants to transmit, the go-ahead pattern eventually arrives back at the primary station. It then transmits another go-ahead pattern.

When a station that wants to transmit receives the go-ahead pattern, it changes the go-ahead pattern to a starting-flag pattern that it uses as the beginning of the frame it transmits. It then follows the frame that it transmits by sending another go-ahead pattern. When that go-ahead pattern reaches the primary station, the cycle starts again. In this way the go-ahead patterns keep the terminals from interfering with one another's transmissions.

MODES OF TRANSMISSION

A variety of techniques can be used for transmitting data over a given data link. Each technique uses a different method for organizing the signals sent so that they convey the information in question. Families of devices are built to operate using each transmission technique. We will next discuss some of the modes of transmission that can be used in implementing data links.

HALF-DUPLEX VERSUS FULL-DUPLEX

We have already seen that a given physical transmission facility supports either half-duplex or full-duplex transmission. Three interrelated factors determine the transmission mode of the data link itself: the transmission mode that the communication line itself supports, the transmission mode supported by the line termination devices used in implementing the link, and the data link protocol used by the terminals and other devices that use the data link.

- **Communication Line Transmission Mode.** A communication channel that is either built by the organization that will use it or leased from a common carrier can be either half-duplex or full-duplex. A full-duplex circuit, however, is not required to implement a full-duplex data link. It is possible for full-duplex transmission to take place over a half-duplex communication channel if appropriate modems are used.

- **Line Termination Device Transmission Mode.** In order for full-duplex transmission to take place over an analog circuit, modems or other types of line termination devices specifically designed to transmit in both directions at once must be employed.

- **Data Link Protocol Transmission Mode.** Over a given data link, the terminal equipment may be designed so that it uses a data link protocol that supports either full-duplex or half-duplex transmission. The type of transmission supported by the data link protocol determines the transmission mode of the data link. Some data link protocols are inherently half-duplex and support only half-duplex transmission, no matter what type of communication line or modem is used. Others support full-duplex transmission if the appropriate communication line and line termination devices are available.

PARALLEL VERSUS SERIAL TRANSMISSION

Another way to classify data links is by whether data is transmitted over the link in a parallel or a serial fashion. As we have seen, one of the functions of a terminal is to convert messages into bit streams for transmission over a communication channel. It is not always necessary in all cases to transmit the data serially, bit by bit. Though most data transmission is done on a serial basis, digital data can be sent over a data link in a parallel fashion. The stream of data is often divided into characters, the characters being composed of bits. This stream may be sent either serially by character and serially by bit or serially by character and parallelly by bit.

One type of data link that transmits data in a parallel fashion uses a protocol called the *Centronics interface* (named for the company that first standardized it). The Centronics interface is often used to connect printers to personal computers. Box 8.1 shows the circuits that are used to control data transmission when the Centronics interface is used to implement a data link.

BOX 8.1   The Centronics interface

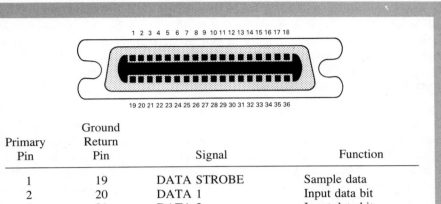

Primary Pin	Ground Return Pin	Signal	Function
1	19	DATA STROBE	Sample data
2	20	DATA 1	Input data bit
3	21	DATA 2	Input data bit
4	22	DATA 3	Input data bit
5	23	DATA 4	Input data bit
6	24	DATA 5	Input data bit
7	25	DATA 6	Input data bit
8	26	DATA 7	Input data bit
9	27	DATA 8	Input data bit
10	28	ACKNOWLEDGE	Character received
11	29	BUSY	Device busy
12		PE	Paper out error
13		SELECT	Device online
14		TEST	Used in device testing
15		—	Unassigned
16		—	Unassigned
17		CHASSIS GROUND	Chassis ground
18		+5 VDC	+5 volts DC
19		LOGIC GND	Logic ground
31		INIT	Initialize device
32		FAULT	Fault
33		—	Unassigned
34		—	Unassigned
35		—	Unassigned
36		SELECT IN	Select device

SYNCHRONOUS VERSUS ASYNCHRONOUS TRANSMISSION

Data transmission can be either *asynchronous* or *synchronous*. With an asynchronous protocol, sometimes called *start-stop* transmission, one character is sent at a time. Relatively simple equipment can be used, because the two stations must be in synchronization only for the time it takes to transmit and receive a single character. With synchronous transmission, characters are sent in blocks. A block of perhaps 100 characters or more can be sent at one time, and for the duration of the entire block's transmission the receiving terminal must be exactly in synchronization with the transmitting terminal.

Asynchronous Transmission

Asynchronous transmission is usually used with slow-speed devices, for example, terminals that do not have a buffer and with which the operator sends characters along the line at more or less random intervals. Each transmitted character begins with a *start* bit and ends with one or more *stop* bits. The start bit indicates the beginning of a transmission, and there can be an indeterminate interval between transmitted characters. Characters are transmitted when the operator's fingers press the keys.

The receiving machine has a clocking device that starts when the start bit is detected and operates for as many bits as there are in a character. With this, the receiving machine can distinguish which bit is which. In many cases, two stop bits are used at the end of each character in case the receiver's clock was not operating at quite the same speed as the transmitter's.

Synchronous Transmission

When machines transmit to each other continuously, with regular timing, *synchronous* transmission can give much more efficient data link utilization. Here the bits of one character are followed immediately by those of the next. Between characters, there are no start or stop bits and no pauses. The stream of characters is divided into blocks called *frames*. The transmitting and receiving machines must be exactly in synchronization during the time it takes to transmit a complete frame. To permit synchronous transmission, terminals must have buffers, and thus synchronous terminals are more expensive than asynchronous devices.

The synchronization of the transmitting and receiving machines on many systems is controlled by oscillators. Before a frame is sent, the oscillator of the receiving machine must be brought exactly into phase with the oscillator of the transmitting machine. This is done by sending a synchronization pattern at the start of the frame. If this were not done, the receiving device would not be able to tell which bit received was the first bit in a character, which the second, and so on.

Synchronous transmission can give better protection from errors than asynchronous. Transmitted at the end of each frame is an error-checking sequence that is constructed by putting the data bits in the frame through an algorithm. The algorithm selected for generating the error-checking sequence is chosen to provide a high degree of error detection.

ERROR DETECTION AND CORRECTION

Transmission errors invariably occur when data is transmitted over telecommunications channels. Noise on the lines can destroy bits or switch a one bit to a zero or vice versa. In addition to the continuing background of thermal noise, there are sharp noise *impulses,* occasionally of high magnitude. They are caused by ill-protected switching equipment, crosstalk, pickup from electrical cables, and atmospheric static, among other factors. If you listen down a telephone line when nobody is talking, you can occasionally hear crackles, hums, clicks, and whistles. I once heard violin music. These stray noises are usually of low intensity but occasionally are loud enough to damage the data being sent.

NUMBERS OF ERRORS

On a good-quality telephone line with conservatively designed modems, a typical error rate is one bit incorrect in 100,000. If the modems are designed to maximize the data rate, the receiving machine has to recognize smaller changes in signal condition and so is more prone to misinterpret noise conditions and cause errors. When communication lines are constructed especially for data, much lower error rates than these can be achieved. One error in 10 million bits or 100 million bits is more common for digital circuits. Unfortunately, many of our systems today must be connected using data links that were not designed with the transmission of computer data in mind. The high error rate is part of the price we pay for the compromise of using lines intended for something else. However, there are steps that we can take to make the communication channel *appear to the user* as error-free as we like. All data link protocols use one or more of these methods to transform the error-prone communication channel into an essentially error-free virtual channel between users.

A number of approaches can be used to deal with noise on transmission lines. All the approaches that we will discuss here are in current use with data transmission systems.

IGNORING ERRORS

The first, and easiest, approach is to ignore the errors. Surprisingly, this is often done. The majority of telegraph links in operation, for example, have no error-checking facilities at all. Part of the reason is that they normally transmit English-language text that will be read by human beings. Errors in ordinary text caused by the changing of a few bits are usually obvious to the human eye, and we correct them in the mind as we read the material. Telegrams that have figures as well as text in them commonly repeat the figures or spell them out. This inexpensive approach is also taken on computer systems where the transmission handles ordinary text. If the text turns out to be unintelligible, the user can always ask for a retransmission.

DETECTING ERRORS

To *detect* communication errors, we must build some degree of redundancy into the messages transmitted. In other words, more bits must be sent than need be sent for the coding of the data alone. Redundancy can be built into individual characters or into an entire transmitted block. The two forms of redundancy that are commonly used in error detection are vertical redundancy checking (also called parity checking) and longitudinal redundancy checking. Both forms of error checking are described in Box 8.2.

It is possible to devise a coding scheme that gives any desired level of protection. In fact, there are coding schemes that give an undetected error rate

BOX 8.2 Two forms of error detection

Vertical Redundancy Checking

Some data transmission systems use *vertical redundancy checking* (VRC), in which each transmitted character is accompanied by a *parity bit*. If odd parity is used, the transmitter sets the parity bit to either 0 or 1 in order to make the total number of one bits between the start and stop bits an odd number. With even parity, an even number of one bits is required. If the receiver detects a parity error in a received character, it knows that a transmission error has occurred. A parity check is not very useful for detecting transmission errors, especially at high transmission speeds, because it is likely that when an error occurs, many adjacent bits will be changed and many errors will not be detected.

Longitudinal Redundancy Checking

When a *longitudinal redundancy checking* (LRC) method is employed, redundant bits are used to check the accuracy of an entire transmitted frame. In this form of error detection, the transmitter passes the entire message through an arithmetic algorithm to generate a number that is sent with the message. When the receiver receives the message, it passes the message through the same algorithm and compares its generated value with the value received with the message. If the two values match, the receiver assumes that the message is correct. If the two values do not match, the receiver assumes that a transmission error has occurred. In most systems that use longitudinal error checking, frames that are found to be in error are retransmitted.

as low as one bit in 10^{14}. The error-correcting coding scheme used to store data on the CD/ROM optical disks that are based on compact audio disk technology gives an undetected error rate that is less than one incorrect bit in 10^{13}. This corresponds to one single bit error in about 2000 CD/ROM disks, each of which stores up to 600 megabytes of data. And this low error rate is achieved using a physical medium that is very error-prone (microscopic pits on an imperfect plastic surface).

An error detection rate of one bit in 10^{13} or 10^{14} is much better than is needed for most practical purposes in data transmission systems. For example, if one had been transmitting using an error rate of one error in 10^{14} bits over a voice line at 2400 bps for a normal working week (no vacations) since the time of Christ, one would probably not have had an error yet! By using sufficiently powerful error-detecting codes, virtually any measure of protection from transmission errors can be achieved.

CORRECTING ERRORS

Once the errors have been detected, the question arises: What should the system do about them? It is generally desirable that it should take some automatic action to correct the fault. Some data transmission systems, however, do not do so and leave the fault to be corrected later by human means. For example, some early systems that transmitted data to be punched into cards caused a card to be sent to a different stacker when an error was detected. The cards in the error stacker were later picked out by the operator, who then arranged for retransmission.

In some systems, automatic retransmission has not been used because it is easy for the terminal operator to reenter a message or request retransmission. In general, it is much better to have some means of automatic retransmission rather than a manual procedure, and it is usually less expensive than employing an operator for this purpose. Most modern data transmission systems do cause messages in error to be retransmitted. This is an automatic function of all modern data link protocols.

FORWARD ERROR CORRECTION

Automatic error correction can take a number of forms. First, sufficient redundancy can be built into the transmission code so that the code itself permits *automatic error correction* as well as detection. As no return path is needed, this is sometimes referred to as *forward error correction*. To do this effectively in the presence of *bursts* of noise can require a large proportion of redundant bits. Codes that give safe forward error correction are therefore inefficient in their use of communication line capacity. It is interesting to note that the coding scheme used with CD/ROM disks does handle automatic error correction. The physical medium is very error-prone, and once the data is stored, there is no opportunity for repeating it. So the system is designed with the assumption that a great many errors will have to be corrected automatically if the storage system is to have the required degree of reliability.

If a communication line permitted the transfer of information in one direction only, forward error correction techniques, such as those used with CD/ROMs, would be extremely valuable. However, a typical transmission channel supports transmission in both directions and retransmission is possible. In general, error-*correcting* codes alone on voice-grade lines do not give us as good value for money, or value for bandwidth, as error-*detecting* codes coupled with the ability automatically to retransmit data that is found to contain an error.

In some special cases, for example, with some high-speed modems, forward error correction is handled in the modems themselves. But this is generally backed up by the normal error-handling methods used by the data link protocol. When this is done, the transmission errors that are corrected by the modems are transparent to the data link protocol. Any errors that get by the modems are handled by the error detection and automatic transmission procedures of the data link protocol. This results in less data having to be retransmitted.

RETRANSMISSION OF DATA IN ERROR   Many different forms of error *detection* and *retransmission* are built into data-handling equipment. Systems differ in how much they require to be retransmitted when an error is detected. Some retransmit only one character when a character error is found. Others retransmit many characters or even many messages. There are two possible advantages in retransmitting a *small* quantity of data. First, it saves time. It is quicker to retransmit 5 characters than 500 when an error is found. However, if the error rate is one character error in 100,000 (a typical figure for telephone lines), the percentage loss in speed does not differ greatly between these two cases. It *would* be significant if a block of 5000 had to be retransmitted.

Second, when a large block is retransmitted, it has to be stored somewhere until the receiving machine has confirmed that the transmission was correct. With transmission from a keyboard, for example, a buffer is needed if there is a chance that the message may have to be retransmitted automatically. In some cases, several input devices may share a common control unit, and this contains the buffer storage.

The *disadvantages* of using small blocks for retransmission are, first, that the error detection codes can be more efficient on a large block of data. In other words, the ratio of the number of error detection bits to the number of the data bits is smaller for a given degree of protection if the quantity of data is large. Second, where blocks of data are sent synchronously, a period of time is taken up between acknowledgments in control characters and line turnaround procedures. The more data transmitted between acknowledgments, the less significant is this wasted time. The well-designed transmission system achieves the best compromise between these factors.

TRANSMISSION ERROR CONTROL

In order to govern the automatic retransmission of data in which an error has been detected, control characters are sometimes used. For example, with some data link protocols, characters representing a positive acknowledgment are sent by the receiver to signal the transmitter that a frame has been received correctly. Similarly, codes representing a negative acknowledgment are often sent by the receiving terminal to tell the transmitter that a frame received had an error in it. When the transmitter sends a frame on many systems, it waits before it sends the next one until the acknowledgment control characters are received from the transmitter. If a positive acknowledgment is received, the transmitter proceeds normally; if the acknowledgment is negative, it resends the frame in error.

In more sophisticated protocols, entire frames flow back and forth between the communicating stations to control error procedures. In some cases, normal data frames can carry control bits that allow them to be used as positive acknowledgments. In this way, when a positive acknowledgment is required, a normal data frame is used for this purpose, thus reducing the amount of overhead transmission that is required when no errors have occurred.

It is possible that the control characters or control frames themselves or the end-of-transmission characters could be invalidated by a noise error. If this happens, there is a danger that a complete transmission frame might be lost or two frames inadvertently joined together. It is possible that during the automatic retransmission process a frame could be erroneously sent twice. To prevent these errors, an odd-even count is sometimes kept of the records transmitted. With some protocols, a control character that indicates whether this is an odd-numbered or even-numbered block is sent.

It is improbable that two blocks could be lost together or that two blocks are transmitted twice in such a manner that an odd-even count would not detect the error. However, to avoid this possibility, most modern protocols use a *sequence number* instead of an odd-even count to check that this has not happened. In addition to providing better protection against lost or duplicated frames, these sequence numbers also allow more data to be sent before an acknowledgment is required.

Now that we have introduced the general characteristics of data links and the procedures that are used to control transmission over them, Chapter 9 examines three specific categories of data link protocols in common use: *asynchronous protocols,* the *binary-synchronous protocol,* and *bit-oriented protocols.*

9 DATA LINK PROTOCOLS

The station at one end of a physical link must follow a specific set of rules in converting a message into a serial bit stream and transmitting it over a channel. The station at the other end must follow a similar set of rules in correctly reconverting the bit stream into a copy of the original message. If the two communicating devices do not follow the same rules, communication is not possible. The rules that the communicating stations follow are called *data link protocols*. The functions of data link protocols are listed in Box 9.1.

CATEGORIES OF DATA LINK PROTOCOLS

In this chapter, we will examine three major categories of data link protocols: *asynchronous protocols,* the *binary-synchronous protocol,* and *bit-oriented protocols*. The asynchronous protocol and the binary-synchronous protocol are both *character-oriented* protocols. A character-oriented protocol uses a particular code set for transmission, with some of the characters in the code set reserved for control functions. Special provision must be made with these protocols for messages that contain, in their text, characters ordinarily reserved for control functions. Bit-oriented protocols are more modern protocols and are used in implementing today's computer networks. Bit-oriented protocols share a common set of characteristics and are more flexible and efficient than character-oriented protocols. A bit-oriented protocol is independent of any particular code set, and no character codes are reserved for control functions. Messages consist simply of bit streams, and no special significance is attached by the data link protocol to any of the bit configurations in the message.

BOX 9.1   Data link protocol functions

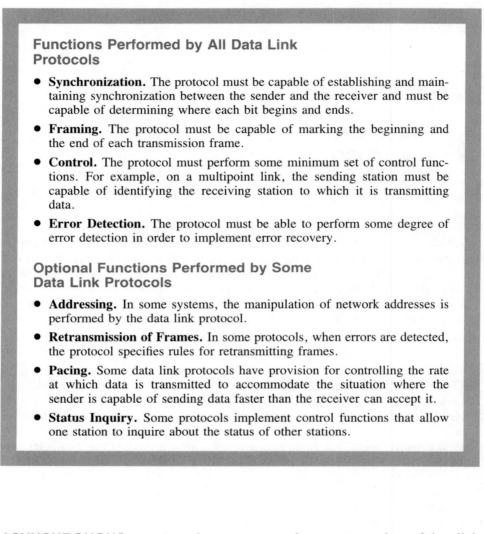

Functions Performed by All Data Link Protocols

- **Synchronization.** The protocol must be capable of establishing and maintaining synchronization between the sender and the receiver and must be capable of determining where each bit begins and ends.

- **Framing.** The protocol must be capable of marking the beginning and the end of each transmission frame.

- **Control.** The protocol must perform some minimum set of control functions. For example, on a multipoint link, the sending station must be capable of identifying the receiving station to which it is transmitting data.

- **Error Detection.** The protocol must be able to perform some degree of error detection in order to implement error recovery.

Optional Functions Performed by Some Data Link Protocols

- **Addressing.** In some systems, the manipulation of network addresses is performed by the data link protocol.

- **Retransmission of Frames.** In some protocols, when errors are detected, the protocol specifies rules for retransmitting frames.

- **Pacing.** Some data link protocols have provision for controlling the rate at which data is transmitted to accommodate the situation where the sender is capable of sending data faster than the receiver can accept it.

- **Status Inquiry.** Some protocols implement control functions that allow one station to inquire about the status of other stations.

ASYNCHRONOUS PROTOCOLS   *Asynchronous protocols* represent a class of data link protocols that use asynchronous techniques for coordinating transmission. As we have seen, asynchronous transmission is commonly used for slow-speed applications. There are many protocols that use asynchronous transmission, all of which use similar techniques. They differ in the character code that is used, the number of stop bits, whether or not parity bits are sent, the specific interpretation of control characters, and a number of other factors.

With one commonly used asynchronous protocol, the data link is in either of two conditions, which are represented by the binary values 0 and 1. A typical character transmitted using this protocol is illustrated in Fig. 9.1. When no data is being transmitted, the data link is in the 1 condition. Data is sent over the data link one 7-bit character at a time. When the sending machine has a character to send, it starts by transmitting a zero bit (the *start* bit). Then comes the 7 bits that make up the character, followed by a parity bit. Finally come 2 one bits (the *stop* bits) to signal the end of the character. If there is an interval between characters, the line remains in the 1 condition.

The receiving machine has a clocking mechanism that starts when the line's condition changes to 0 and counts the number of bits that follow. After the 11 bits arrive, the receiving machine waits for the next zero bit, which signals the beginning of the next character.

ASYNCHRONOUS TRANSMISSION CONVENTIONS

There is very little standardization in the specific details concerning asynchronous transmission. For the most part, all aspects of asynchronous line control are determined by the design of specific terminal equipment. For example, when using an asynchronous protocol, the communication circuitry in the terminal and the computer must both be in agreement on the following:

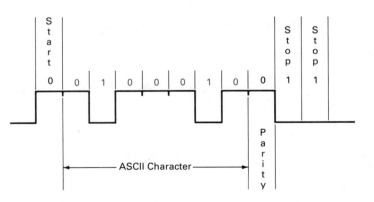

Figure 9.1 An ASCII character transmitted using a typical asynchronous data link protocol.

- The line status that indicates an idle condition
- The line status that indicates a zero bit and the line status that indicates a one bit
- The amount of time that elapses in transmitting a single bit
- The number of bits that make up a single character
- Whether one or two stop bits are used to indicate the end of a transmitted character

Note that none of the above factors are standardized for asynchronous protocols; all that is required is that both the sender and the receiver use the *same* conventions.

RS-232-C TRANSMISSION

As we have shown, asynchronous line control is a general method that is used to control transmission. Many protocols employ asynchronous techniques for delimiting the beginning and end of each transmitted character and for controlling each character's transmission and receipt. Box 9.2 lists the conventions that might be followed by a typical asynchronous protocol that employs an RS-232-C link at the physical level.

Figure 9.2 illustrates how a single character is transmitted over the physical RS-232-C connection when the conventions listed in Box 9.2 are used. The sender begins with the line set at a negative voltage (mark condition), indicating that the line is in an idling condition. To send a character, the sender changes

BOX 9.2   Typical asynchronous protocol conventions

- A negative current on the line between transmitted characters indicates an idle condition.
- During data transmission, a negative voltage indicates a one bit, and a positive voltage indicates a zero bit.
- Data is sent at 2400 bps, indicating that a single bit is transmitted in approximately 0.0004166 second.
- The ASCII code is used, with each transmitted character consisting of 7 data bits followed by a parity bit.
- One stop bit is transmitted at the end of each transmitted character.

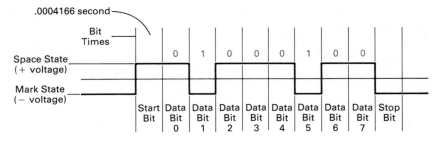

Figure 9.2 Asynchronous transmission of an ASCII character at 2400 bps over a physical link that conforms to the RS-232-C interface.

the line to a positive voltage (space condition) for one bit time to send the start bit. Immediately following the start bit, the sender transmits the 8 bits that make up a character. To transmit a zero bit, the sender sets the line to a positive voltage (spacing condition); to transmit a one bit, the sender sets the line to a negative voltage (marking condition). The sender has a clock that allows it to change the line condition at the appropriate times.

If the sender is transmitting at 2400 bps, each bit time is approximately 0.0004166 second. The receiver knows where each bit begins and ends because it also has a clock that tells it when to sample the line condition to interpret each bit. When the line is in the marking condition for a bit time, the receiver interprets this as a one bit; when the line is in the spacing condition for a bit time, the receiver interprets this as a zero bit. The sender's and receiver's clocks need only stay in synchronization for the duration of a single character because the start bit allows the receiver to be resynchronized with the sender at the beginning of each character.

Finally, after all the bits that make up a character have been transmitted, the transmitter places the line back into a marking condition for at least one bit time. The one bit that follows the bits of data is called a stop bit because it marks the end of a transmitted character. After transmitting the stop bit, the sender keeps the line in the marking condition until the next character is ready to be sent.

ASYNCHRONOUS MESSAGE EXCHANGES

In a typical asynchronous protocol, certain characters from the character set that is used by the communicating devices are reserved for data link control functions. The particular characters that are used to implement each function must be agreed on by convention between the communicating stations. Since these codes perform control functions, they must not appear in the text of any message that is sent.

Boxes 9.3, 9.4, and 9.5 illustrate some message flows that might occur over data links that use asynchronous transmission. Keep in mind as you examine these message flows that they are meant as examples only; each asynchronous data link protocol uses its own conventions for control functions. Each implementation of asynchronous transmission uses its own control procedures.

THE BINARY-SYNCHRONOUS PROTOCOL

Asynchronous protocols are protocols in which synchronization must be established by the sending and receiving stations before each character is transmitted. The start and stop bits are the mechanism by which this synchronization is established. The *binary-synchronous* (BSC) protocol is different from the asynchronous protocol in that bit synchronization is established for a much longer duration, usually for the time it takes to transmit several thousand bits. Figure 9.3 illustrates the synchronization process. The following are the steps that take place to bring two communicating stations into synchronization:

1. **Bit Synchronization.** To achieve synchronization, two characters called PAD characters are sent before each message to ensure that the sending and receiving stations are in bit synchronization before transmission begins. The PAD characters consist of sequences that contain alternating zero and one bits: hexadecimal AA (10101010) or hexadecimal 55 (01010101).

2. **Character Synchronization.** After the PAD characters are sent, a sequence of two characters called SYN characters (hexadecimal 3232) are sent to establish character synchronization between the sending and receiving stations.

3. **Frame Transmission.** After the two SYN characters are sent, the sending station transmits the frame itself.

4. **Synchronization Maintenance.** During the transmission of a long frame, the sending station maintains synchronization with the receiving station by inserting an additional SYN pattern into the data stream approximately every second.

5. **Frame End.** After the frame is transmitted, two more PAD characters are sent.

BOX 9.3 Point-to-point asynchronous message flow

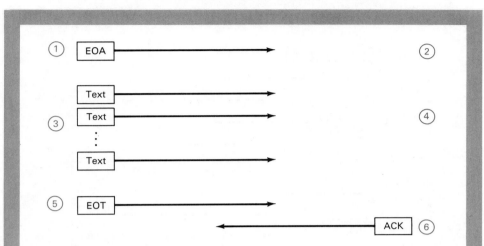

The simplest type of data link consists of a point-to-point connection between two stations. With this type of connection, the requirement for control functions is minimal.

1. The computer begins by transmitting an end-of-addressing (EOA) command to the terminal.

2. The terminal receives the EOA command.

3. The host computer transmits the characters that make up a message, one character at a time.

4. The terminal receives each character of the message and performs a parity check as it receives each character.

5. The computer transmits an end-of-transmission (EOT) command, indicating the end of the message.

6. The terminal receives the EOT command, performs LRC error checking on the received message, and finds the message to have been received correctly. The terminal then transmits an ACK command back to the host and waits for the next control character from the computer.

BOX 9.4   Multipoint asynchronous message flow

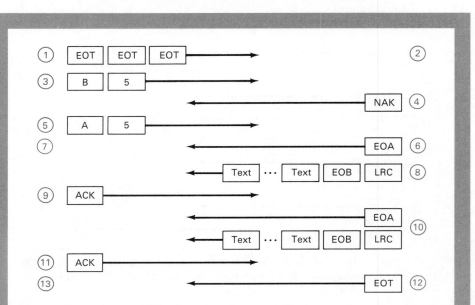

Each device attached to a multipoint data link has an address. In this example, each station address has two parts: a station identifier (A or B) and a device number (1, 3, or 5). In this message exchange, the communication controller in the primary station asks one of the devices on a secondary station if it has any data to send.

1. The communication controller attached to the host computer sends a sequence of three EOT commands.

2. All devices on the data link receive the EOT commands.

3. The host communication controller transmits a B followed by a 5. These two address characters constitute a *poll* sequence that asks if device 5 on station B has any data to send.

4. All devices other than device 5 on station B ignore the poll. Device 5 on station B accepts the poll and transmits a negative acknowledgment (NAK) command back to the communication controller.

5. The communication controller receives the NAK command, which tells it that device 5 on station B has no data to send. The host communication controller then consults its polling list and transmits an A followed by a 5 to poll the next device on its list (in this case, device 5 on station A).

BOX 9.4 *(Continued)*

6. Device 5 on station A has data to send, so it transmits an EOA command.

7. The communication controller receives the EOA command.

8. Device 5 on station A transmits its message text and then sends an end-of-block (EOB) command and an LRC character for error checking.

9. The communication controller receives the message. The EOB command marks the end of the message and indicates that the next character contains the LRC value. The communication controller computes an LRC value using the received text and compares the received LRC value against the value that it computes. In this example, it determines that the message was received correctly. It then transmits a positive acknowledgment (ACK) command.

10. Device 5 now transmits a second message back to the communication controller using the same sequence of events.

11. The communication controller attached to the host again receives the message correctly and responds with an ACK.

12. Device 5 transmits an EOT indicating that it has no more data to send.

13. All devices on the data link receive the EOT command. The host communications controller is now ready to issue the next poll sequence.

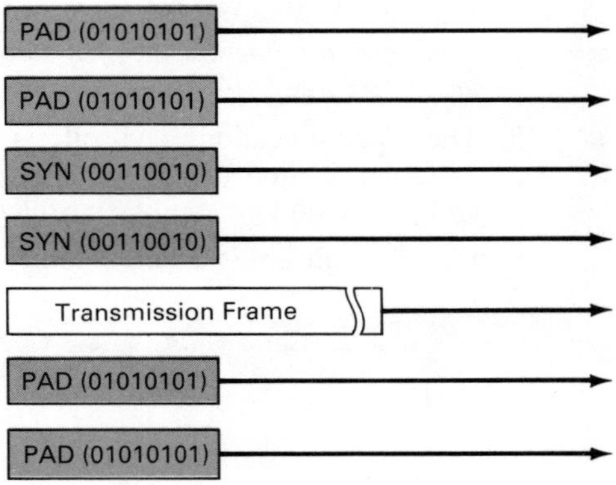

Figure 9.3 At the beginning of each binary-synchronous transmission frame, two PAD characters are sent to achieve bit synchronization followed by two SYN characters to achieve character synchronization.

BOX 9.5 Transmission error in asynchronous message flow

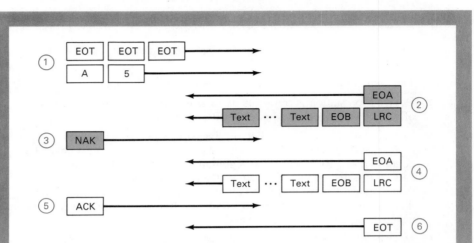

In this message exchange, a transmission error occurs and the receiving station detects a mismatch between the LRC value it receives and the LRC value it generates.

1. The host communications controller sends a sequence of three EOT commands following by the A5 address characters.

2. Device 5 on station A has data to send, so it sends an EOA command, the message text, an EOB command, and an LRC character. A transmission error occurs during the sending of the message text.

3. The communication controller receives the message, performs the LRC computation, and finds that its computed LRC value does not match the value in the LRC character that it received. The communications controller transmits a NAK command, which constitutes a negative acknowledgment to the message.

4. Device 5 retransmits the original message, including another EOB and an LRC value.

5. The communications controller receives the message and performs the LRC verification procedure. This time the message is received correctly and the communications controller transmits an ACK.

6. Device 5 transmits an EOT indicating that it has no more data to send.

Control Code Function	BSC Mnemonic	EBCDIC Code	ASCII Code
Start of Heading	SOH	SOH	SOH
Start of Text	STX	STX	STX
End of Transmission Block	ETB	ETB	ETB
End of Text	ETX	ETX	ETX
End of Transmission	EOT	EOT	EOT
Enquiry	ENQ	ENQ	ENQ
Negative Acknowledge	NAK	NAK	NAK
Synchronous Idle	SYN	SYN	SYN
Data Link Escape	DLE	DLE	DLE
Intermediate Block Character	ITB	IUS	US
Even Acknowledge	ACK0	DLE (70)	DLE 0
Odd Acknowledge	ACK1	DLE /	DLE 1
Wait Before Transmit	WACK	DLE ,	DLE ;
Mandatory Disconnect	DISC	DLE EOT	DLE EOT
Reverse Interrupt	RVI	DLE @	DLE <
Temporary Text Delay	TTD	STX ENQ	STX ENQ

Figure 9.4   Binary-synchronous control codes in ASCII and EBCDIC.

LINE CONTROL CHARACTERS

Figure 9.4 lists some of the codes that are used to control binary-synchronous transmission. The codes in the column labeled "BSC Mnemonic" are the mnemonic codes used to identify each line control function. Each mnemonic represents a general binary-synchronous function that is implemented differently depending on the character code that is being used.

In some cases, a particular character code, such as ASCII, uses the same mnemonic as the corresponding binary-synchronous mnemonic to implement a particular function. For example, the binary-synchronous *Start of Text* function has the binary-synchronous mnemonic STX. This is implemented in both the EBCDIC and ASCII character sets by the STX code.

In many cases, a particular binary-synchronous mnemonic has no corresponding mnemonic in the particular character code being used. For example, the binary-synchronous function *Intermediate Block Character* has the binary-synchronous mnemonic ITB. There is no ITB mnemonic in either the ASCII or EBCDIC code charts. In EBCDIC, the ITB function is represented by the IUS code (hexadecimal 1F). In ASCII, the ITB function is represented by the code US (also hexadecimal 1F).

Figure 9.5   Binary-synchronous transmission frame format.

Some of the binary-synchronous functions are represented by a combination of two characters. For example, the binary-synchronous protocol uses two ACK functions: ACK0 *(Even Acknowledge)* and ACK1 *(Odd Acknowledge)*. Neither of these binary-synchronous functions uses the ACK codes that are included in both EBCDIC and ASCII. ACK0 is implemented in ASCII by the DLE character followed by the digit 0; ACK0 is implemented in EBCDIC by a DLE character followed by a byte containing hexadecimal 70.

Throughout this section, we will reference binary-synchronous control functions using binary-synchronous function names and/or binary-synchronous mnemonics.

BINARY-SYNCHRONOUS TRANSMISSION FRAME

Figure 9.5 shows the format of a typical frame transmitted using the binary-synchronous protocol. Note that the protocol supports variable-length frames of any size. However, a specific implementation of the binary-synchronous protocol may limit frame length based on a variety of factors, including the availability of buffer storage. A primary reason for limiting frame length to a reasonable value is that the longer the frame, the higher the chance that an error will occur in transmitting it.

ERROR CHECKING

Each binary-synchronous transmission frame contains a BCC sequence that is used by the receiving station to verify that the frame was received correctly. To generate the 1- or 2-byte BCC sequence, the sending station passes the entire binary-synchronous frame through an arithmetic algorithm. (The details of the specific algorithms used to generate BCC sequences are beyond the scope of this book.)

After all the bytes have been examined, the result of the BCC algorithm is a value that is sent with the frame in the BCC sequence. On the receiving end, the frame being received is passed through an identical algorithm to generate a corresponding value. The receiving station compares the generated BCC value to the value contained in the received BCC sequence. If the two values are the same, it is likely that the frame was received correctly. If the two values are different, one or more of the received bytes are not the same as the bytes that were transmitted, and the receiver then requests that the frame be retransmitted.

BINARY-SYNCHRONOUS MESSAGE EXCHANGES

When two stations are connected by a point-to-point connection, the configuration is called a *point-to-point contention* link. Box 9.6 shows a simple binary-synchronous message exchange over a point-to-point contention link. Box 9.7 shows the message exchange that occurs when a transmission error occurs in sending data from station 1 to station 2.

TRANSPARENT TEXT TRANSFER

In ordinary message exchanges, a number of the codes from the character set being used are used to control the flow of messages between the two stations. To enable the communicating stations to interpret control codes correctly, it is important that the text that makes up the message or block being transmitted not contain any of the codes that are used to control transmission. For example, if the text of a message contains an ETX code, the message will be terminated prematurely and the 2 bytes that follow the stray ETX will be interpreted as the BCC sequence.

BOX 9.6   Point-to-point binary-synchronous message flow

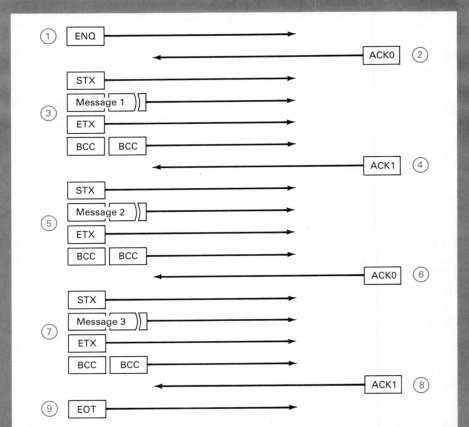

Between data transfers, the line is in an idle condition. To begin data transmission, one of the two stations on the line must initiate a bid procedure. This type of message exchange takes place between two stations over a point-to-point contention link in initiating a bid and in completing a normal transfer of data.

BOX 9.6 *(Continued)*

1. Station 1 indicates to station 2 that it has data to send by transmitting an *Enquiry* (ENQ) code. The ENQ in effect asks station 2 if it is ready to receive a message.

2. Station 2 responds to the ENQ by transmitting an *Even Acknowledge* (ACK0) code. This informs station 1 that station 2 is ready to receive the message.

3. Station 1 sends a complete message in a single frame across the data link. The message begins with a *Start of Text* (STX) code and is followed by the text of the message. The end of the text of the message is marked by an *End of Text* (ETX) code and is followed by the 2 *block check character* (BCC) bytes.

4. After the message has been received, station 2 passes the text of the message through its CRC algorithm and compares the computed value with the value contained in the 2 BCC bytes it received. If the values are the same, station 2 assumes it has received the frame correctly and transmits a positive acknowledgment. Since the positive acknowledgment code that it used previously was an *Even Acknowledge* (ACK0), it transmits an *Odd Acknowledge* (ACK1) code this time.

5. The receipt of the positive acknowledgment indicates to station 1 that it can now send the second message.

6. Station 2 receives the message correctly and transmits an ACK0.

7. Station 1 transmits the third message.

8. Station 2 responds positively with an ACK1.

9. Station 1 signifies that it has finished sending data by transmitting an *End of Transmission* (EOT) code. At this point the line reverts to an idle condition and either station is free to send an ENQ code to initiate another message transfer sequence.

BOX 9.7   Transmission error in binary-synchronous message flow

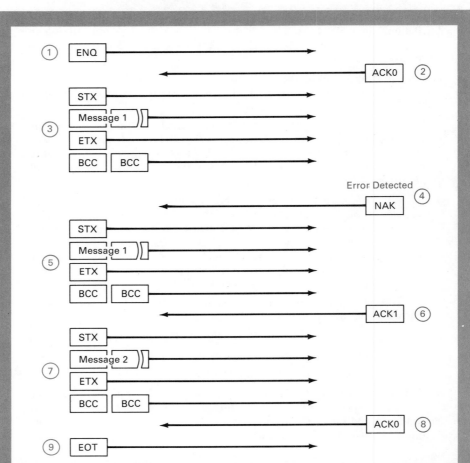

Each transmission frame is accompanied by a 2-byte BCC sequence generated by putting the message text through a CRC algorithm. The receiving station puts the text of each message it receives through an identical CRC algorithm and then compares the calculated value with the received value. If the values do not match, retransmission is requested.

BOX 9.7 *(Continued)*

1. Station 1 initiates a bid by transmitting an *Enquiry* (ENQ) code.

2. Station 2 responds to the ENQ by transmitting an *Even Acknowledge* (ACK0) code.

3. Station 1 sends a complete message across the data link. A transmission error occurs during transmission of the message text.

4. Station 2 performs its CRC calculation, compares the resulting value with the value contained in the BCC bytes it received, and finds that the values do not match. Station 2 assumes that a transmission error occurred and transmits a *Negative Acknowledge* (NAK) code.

5. The receipt of the negative acknowledgment indicates to station 1 that it should retransmit the original message.

6. Station 2 receives the message correctly and this time responds positively with a positive acknowledgment (ACK1).

7. Station 1 transmits the next message.

8. Station 2 responds positively with an ACK0.

9. Station 1 ends the transmission by sending an *End of Transmission* (EOT) code.

In some applications, however, such as in the transmission of executable code, it is desirable to be able to send sequences of bytes containing any bit configuration. To permit this, the binary-synchronous protocol has a mode, supported by some implementations, called *transparent text* mode. Transparent text mode allows a station to send a message whose text can consist of any sequence of bits, including bit sequences that contain the same bit patterns as binary-synchronous control codes. Box 9.8 shows a message exchange involving transparent text transfer.

The technique used by the binary-synchronous protocol to implement transparent text is called *character stuffing*. The receiver must be able to recognize that the 2-byte sequence DLE ETX (or some other combination, such as DLE ETB) at the end of the message is in fact a control sequence rather than data. Remember, true transparency must allow the data portion of the message to contain sequences of DLE ETX, DLE ETB, or any other combination of

BOX 9.8   Binary-synchronous transparent text transfer

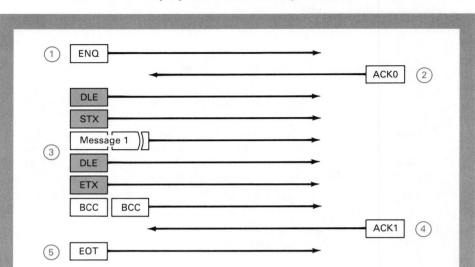

Once transparent text mode has been entered, the receiving station does not interpret as control functions bytes in the message text that contain binary-synchronous control codes; it interprets them instead as ordinary data. Transparent text mode is terminated when station 1 sends the 2-byte sequence DLE ETX (or something similar, such as DLE ETB).

1. Station 1 initiates a bid by transmitting an *Enquiry* (ENQ) code.

2. Station 2 responds to the ENQ by transmitting an *Even Acknowledge* (ACK0) code.

3. Station 1 indicates that it is going into transparent text mode by starting message transmission with a 2-byte sequence consisting of *Data Link Escape* (DLE) followed by *Start of Text* (STX). The message that follows can now consist of bytes that contain any desired bit configuration.

4. Station 2 responds positively with an *Odd Acknowledge* (ACK1) code.

5. Station 1 ends the transmission by sending an *End of Transmission* (EOT) code.

characters. To handle this, whenever the transmitting station detects a DLE character in the text stream, it sends a sequence of two DLE characters instead of only one. Then, when the receiving station receives a sequence of two DLE characters, it discards one of them.

Because of character stuffing, a sequence of DLE ETX that is embedded in the text is sent as DLE DLE ETX. Only when the receiving station receives an actual DLE ETX rather than DLE DLE ETX does it determine that transparent text mode has ended and that the DLE ETX sequence is in fact a control sequence indicating the end of the message text.

MULTIPOINT LINES AND POLLING

When implementing the binary-synchronous protocol with multipoint lines, one station is known as the *control station;* the other stations on the line are called *tributary stations*. With multipoint lines, mechanisms implemented in the control station are required for *polling* the tributary stations on the line and for *selecting* a tributary station to which a message is being sent. Corresponding mechanisms are implemented in the tributary stations for responding to polling and selection sequences. Box 9.9 shows a polling sequence on a multipoint line.

BIT-ORIENTED PROTOCOLS

All modern network architectures use *bit-oriented* protocols for data link control procedures. Bit-oriented data link protocols have evolved to overcome some of the inherent deficiencies of the two classes of character-oriented protocols. Box 9.10 describes the major bit-oriented protocols in use today. They are all similar, differing only in small details; the principles described here apply to all the bit-oriented protocols listed in Box 9.10.

Standardization of the bit-oriented protocols began in 1968 with the development of ADCCP by ISO and of HDLC by the CCITT. Many major computer manufacturers worked closely with the CCITT in the development of HDLC; as a result, IBM's SDLC, first described in 1973, is today a compatible subset of HDLC.

Bit-oriented protocols provide for a number of operating modes, only some of which may be supported by a specific protocol:

- **Normal Response Mode (NRM).** A secondary station cannot initiate transmission without first receiving permission from the primary station.

- **Asynchronous Response Mode (ARM).** A secondary station can initiate transmission without receiving permission from the primary station.

BOX 9.9 Binary-synchronous multipoint polling

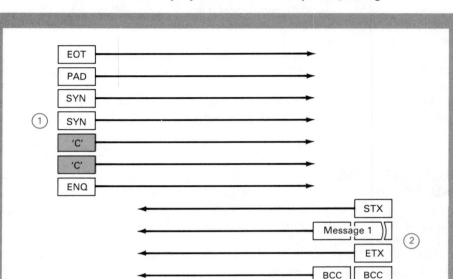

On a multipoint line, the control station sends a polling sequence to determine if a particular tributary station on the line has a message to send back to the control station. The number of addressing characters used and the interpretation of the addressing characters is implementation-dependent.

1. The control station on the multipoint line polls the station whose address is "C" by sending an *End of Transmission* (EOT) code, followed by a PAD SYN SYN sequence, followed by two addressing characters, finally followed by an *Enquiry* (ENQ) code.

2. Station C responds positively to the poll by transmitting a message back to the control station.

- **Asynchronous Balanced Mode (ABM).** There is no distinction between primary and secondary station, and each station is capable of initializing and disconnecting the data link and recovering from error conditions.

The most commonly used operating mode, supported by all the bit-oriented protocols, is *normal response mode*. When a data link operates in normal response mode, there are two types of link stations: *primary stations* and *secondary stations:*

BOX 9.10 . Bit-oriented protocols

- **High-Level Data Link Control (HDLC).** The standard for HDLC was developed by the International Standards Association (ISO) and is documented in ISO Standards 3309 and 4335.

- **Link Access Protocol (LAP) and Link Access Protocol—Balanced (LAPB).** The protocols for LAP and LAPB document the data link–layer functions of CCITT *Recommendation X.25*. LAP and LAPB are compatible subsets of ISO's HDLC.

- **Synchronous Data Link Control (SDLC).** SDLC is the main data link protocol used to implement SNA networks. SDLC is a compatible subset of ISO's HDLC and is similar to the LAP protocol of the CCITT.

- **Advanced Data Communication Control Procedures (ADCCP).** The standard for ADCCP was developed by the American National Standards Association (ANSI) and is documented in ANSI Standard X3.66 and in Federal Standard 1003. ADCCP is similar to HDLC.

- **Primary Station.** This is the station that initiates a data transfer and is in control during the exchange of messages. It notifies each secondary link station when it can transmit data and when it should expect to receive data.

- **Secondary Station.** This is a station that is contacted by the primary station and is controlled by the primary station during the exchange of data.

The three configurations that can be used to connect a primary station and one or more secondary stations are point-to-point, multipoint, and loop. There can be only one primary station on a data link at a given time; however, with multipoint and loop configurations, there can be multiple secondary stations. All communication on a link takes place between the primary station and a secondary station; secondary link stations cannot communicate directly with each other. A secondary link station is able to send data to the primary link station only after it receives notification from the primary station that it is allowed to send.

LINK STATION ADDRESSES
Each secondary link station has associated with it a set of *receive addresses* and a single *send address*. When the primary link station sends data, an address is included as part of the message. If that address is included in the receive address set of a particular secondary link station, that station recognizes and

accepts the message. Allowing each secondary link station to have a set of receive addresses allows a primary station to send messages to a group of secondary stations on the data link. Broadcast addresses can also be implemented to allow the primary station to send a message to all the secondary stations on the link.

TRANSMISSION STATES

A data link connection can be in one of four *transmission states* at any given time. The following are brief descriptions of these transmission states:

- **Active.** In the *active* state, control bits or bits representing message text are actively flowing between the primary and a secondary station on the link connection.

- **Idle.** In the *idle* state, no information is being transmitted. A continuous sequence of one bits is transmitted when the line is in the idling condition.

- **Transient.** The *transient* state represents the transition that takes place between the time that the primary station transmits a message unit to a secondary station and the time that the secondary station transmits a message unit back to the primary station.

- **Disconnected.** The line is in the *disconnected* state when the secondary station is physically disconnected from the primary station, as when a secondary station connected to a switched line is *on hook*.

TRANSMISSION FRAMES

The message unit that is transmitted over a data link is normally called a *frame*. Some frames are originated by the data link–level software or firmware and are used to control the operation of the data link. Other frames consist of data or control information that is passed down from a higher software layer. As shown in Fig. 9.6, each frame is divided into three major parts: a header, a variable-length information field, and a trailer. Control information is carried in the header and the trailer. Frames originated by the data link–level software sometimes use the variable-length information field in the frame to contain control information. Other frames use the information field to carry messages that are passed down from higher-level software layers. Box 9.11 provides brief descriptions of the fields that make up a transmission frame.

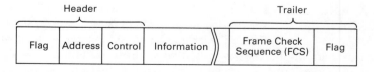

Figure 9.6   Bit-oriented protocol transmission frame format.

BOX 9.11 Transmission frame fields

- **Beginning Flag Field.** A frame begins with a flag field, consisting of a single byte that contains the bit configuration 0111 1110. A *bit-stuffing* technique guarantees that the only place where six consecutive one bits will occur is in a flag field.

- **Address Field.** The field that follows the flag field, normally a single byte in length, is interpreted as the data link address. The address field contains the link address of the secondary station that is sending or receiving the frame.

- **Control Field.** The control field, normally a single byte in length, defines the type of information that is carried by the frame. This byte determines the type of frame being transmitted, conveys information necessary for the proper sequencing of frames, and carries control and polling information. Extensions to most bit-oriented protocols allow for frames that have 2-byte control fields.

- **Information Field.** A variable-length information field is used to carry the data portion of the frame. It consists either of control information or of a message that has been passed from a higher-level software layer. Some frames that are originated by the data link–level software or firmware do not use an information field. There are no minimum or maximum length restrictions on information fields, but IBM's SDLC does require that the length be some multiple of 8 bits; with other bit-oriented protocols, the information field can be any number of bits in length. The receiving station knows where the first byte of the information field begins because it always immediately follows the control field.

- **Frame Check Sequence (FCS) Field.** The frame check sequence contains a 16-bit *cyclic redundancy check* (CRC) value that is used for error detection. The transmitting station generates the CRC value by placing the frame's contents through an algorithm. An identical algorithm is used by the receiving station to verify the frame's content.

- **Ending Flag Field.** Another flag field (0111 1110) terminates each transmission frame.

Notice that a single byte is normally used to contain the address in a frame. This address field always contains the address of a secondary station. Since all communication on the link takes place between a primary and a secondary station, the address of the secondary station is all that is needed to identify the source and destination of a frame; the address of the primary station is always implied. When the primary station is transmitting, the address field defines the address of the secondary station that is to receive the message. When a secondary station is transmitting, the address field contains the address of the secondary station that originated the message.

Transmission frames can be divided into two major categories: *commands* and *responses*. A *command* is a frame that flows from the primary station to one or more secondary stations. A *response* is a frame that flows from a secondary station to the primary station. Normally, when the primary station sends a command, it expects a response or string of responses in reply. Some commands and responses are used to carry data; others are used to perform control functions.

TRANSPARENT OPERATION

Bit-oriented protocols always operate in *transparent mode,* meaning that any desired bit configurations can be carried in the frame's information field. Transparency is easier to achieve with bit-oriented protocols than with character-oriented protocols because the bit configurations for control functions always appear in a fixed place in the frame. Therefore, any desired bit configuration can appear in any of the fields of the frame without confusion. The only requirement for achieving full transparency is to ensure that flag bytes do not occur in any part of the frame other than in the beginning and ending flag field positions. If a flag field appeared anywhere else in the frame, stations would have no way of knowing where a frame begins and ends. If the protocol is to be fully transparent, however, frames must be capable of containing sequences of any desired bit configuration, including bytes that contain the flag configuration (0111 1110). To handle data streams that contain any desired bit configuration, a technique called *zero-bit insertion* (sometimes called *bit stuffing*) is used.

ZERO-BIT INSERTION

In transmitting the data between a beginning and ending flag, the transmitter inserts an extra zero bit into the data stream each time it detects a sequence of 5 one bits. The transmitter turns off the zero-bit insertion mechanism when it transmits an actual beginning or ending flag. In this way, no consecutive sequence of 6 one bits is ever transmitted except when an actual flag is sent over the link.

A complementary technique called *zero-bit deletion* is used by the receiver in removing the extra zero bits. Whenever the receiver detects 5 one bits followed by a zero bit, it discards the zero bit, thus restoring the bit stream to its original value. The bit-stuffing technique ensures that 6 one bits in a row will never occur except in a flag field. When the receiver detects 6 consecutive one bits, it knows that it has received an actual flag field.

FRAME AND CONTROL FIELD FORMATS

There are three types of transmission frames. These have the same general configuration, but three format variations allow them to be used for different purposes. Box 9.12 describes each frame type.

Each frame ordinarily carries a 1-byte control field, as shown in Box 9.12. Most bit-oriented protocols also define an optional mode that supports 2-byte control fields. This mode is hardware-defined, and both the transmitting station and the receiving station must be operating in this mode in order for frame control fields to be properly formatted and interpreted. With 2-byte control fields, 7 bits are used for count fields rather than 3, and up to 127 frames can be sent before the transmitting station must wait for an acknowledgment. Two-byte control fields are often used over channels with long propagation delays, such as satellite links.

BOX 9.12   Bit-oriented protocol frame types

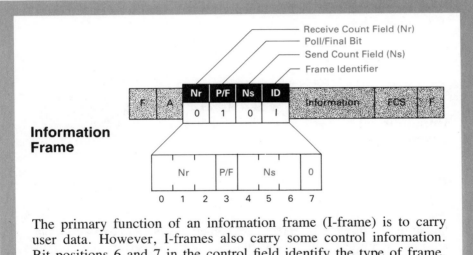

Information Frame

The primary function of an information frame (I-frame) is to carry user data. However, I-frames also carry some control information. Bit positions 6 and 7 in the control field identify the type of frame. An I-frame always has a 0 in bit position 7. The two 3-bit count fields allow up to seven frames to be sent between acknowledgments. A primary station turns on the poll/final bit to indicate that the primary station is *polling* the addressed secondary station. A secondary station turns on the poll/final bit to indicate that the frame is the *last frame* it intends to transmit back to the primary station.

(Continued)

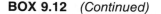

BOX 9.12   *(Continued)*

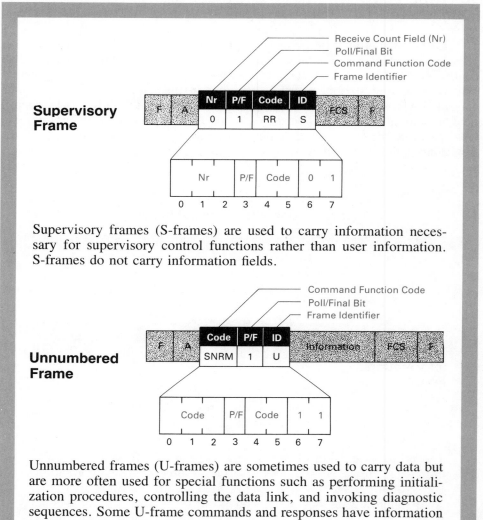

Supervisory frames (S-frames) are used to carry information necessary for supervisory control functions rather than user information. S-frames do not carry information fields.

Unnumbered frames (U-frames) are sometimes used to carry data but are more often used for special functions such as performing initialization procedures, controlling the data link, and invoking diagnostic sequences. Some U-frame commands and responses have information fields; others do not.

ACKNOWLEDGMENTS   One of the primary responsibilities of any data link protocol is to detect errors and, when an error is detected, to cause retransmission of the affected frames. To achieve this, frames that are transmitted require acknowledgments from the receiving station indicat-

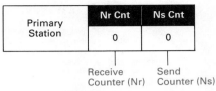

Figure 9.7 With a bit-oriented protocol, each link station maintains two counters to control frame sequencing.

ing whether or not frames were received correctly. In many earlier data link protocols, a sending machine needed to receive an acknowledgment for each frame it transmitted before it could send the next one. In today's data communication environment, with more extensive use of high-performance links, it is desirable to avoid frame-by-frame acknowledgment. The capability for transmitting multiple frames before requiring an acknowledgment is one of the primary reasons that bit-oriented protocols can achieve higher throughput than earlier protocols, such as binary-synchronous.

FRAME SEQUENCE NUMBERS   To ensure that no frames are lost and that all frames are properly acknowledged during a transmission, a system of *sequence numbering* is employed to control frame transmission. All link stations maintain counters that keep track of two counts: a *send count* (Ns) and a *receive count* (Nr) (see Fig. 9.7). These two internal counters are used to update the count fields in the control byte of the I-frames and S-frames that the station transmits. Figure 9.8 shows the format of

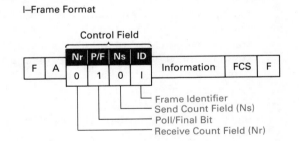

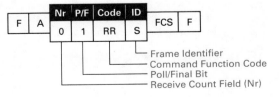

Figure 9.8 Bit-oriented protocol I-frame and S-frame formats.

BOX 9.13   Bit-oriented protocols: sequence numbers

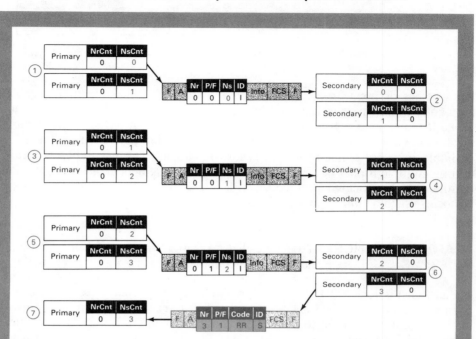

This frame exchange demonstrates how a sequence of I-frames can be sent with an acknowledgment requested only after the entire sequence is sent. The primary station sends a sequence of three I-frames, only the last of which has the poll/final bit set. The secondary station replies with an S-frame only after the third I-frame is received. This frame exchange assumes that the FCS field value is correct after each frame is received. Notice again that the Nr count in the primary station and the Ns count in the secondary station remain unchanged, since no I-frames are flowing from the secondary station back to the primary.

1. The primary station formats an I-frame by setting the Ns field to the current value of its Ns counter and turning off the poll/final bit. It then transmits frame 0 to the secondary station and updates its Ns count.

2. The secondary station receives the I-frame and compares the Ns field value to its Nr count. Since they are both 0, frame sequencing is correct. Since the poll/final bit was off, the secondary station simply updates its internal Nr counter and waits for the next frame.

BOX 9.13 *(Continued)*

3. The primary station formats frame 1 and sends it, again with the poll/final bit off, and updates its Ns count.

4. The secondary station receives frame 1 and compares the Ns field value with its internal Nr counter value. Since they are now both 1, frame sequencing is again correct. The poll/final bit was off, so the secondary station updates its Nr counter and waits for the next frame.

5. The primary station formats frame 2, sends it, and updates its Ns count. This time it turns on the poll/final bit, requesting a response from the secondary station.

6. The secondary station receives frame 2, verifies the Ns field value, updates its Nr counter, and examines the poll/final bit. Since the poll/final bit is on, the secondary station sends an S-frame acknowledgment back to the secondary station.

7. The primary station receives the S-frame acknowledgment and compares the received S-frame Nr field value with the value contained in its internal Ns count. Since they both contain the value 3, the primary station assumes that frame sequencing is correct and that the three frames it sent were all successfully received by the secondary station.

an I-frame and an S-frame with some sample control field contents. I-frames carry both an Ns and an Nr field; S-frames carry only an Nr field. The transmitter always keeps track of how many frames it has sent, and the receiver keeps track of how many frames it has received. The use of sequence numbers is illustrated in the frame exchange shown in Box 9.13.

POLLING AND LOOP OPERATION

On a multipoint data link, the primary station normally sends a poll request to each secondary station, asking whether that station has something to send. Box 9.14 shows an example of a typical polling frame exchange. The process illustrated in the box is likely to be repeated over and over again. The primary will continue to poll the other stations in sequence, and when it completes the circuit and returns to the secondary station that has sent I-frames, it will acknowledge those frames and poll the station for more frames. The polling sequence can be set by the primary link station with information gathered from a polling list maintained in its storage.

BOX 9.14   Bit-oriented protocols: polling

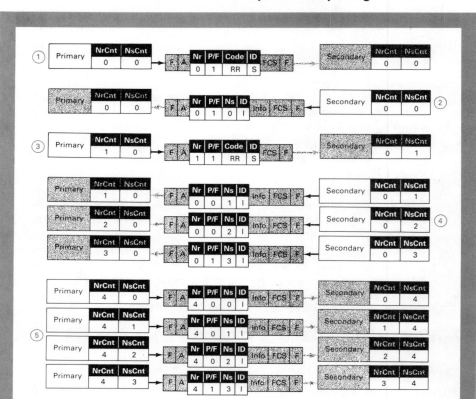

This frame exchange illustrates how polling is used to initiate several frame exchanges.

1. The primary station sends an S-frame RR command to the secondary station asking if it has data to send. Notice that the poll/final bit is on, indicating that this is a poll.

2. The secondary station has a single I-frame of data to send, so it transmits it back to the primary station. Notice that the poll/final bit is on, indicating that this is the last I-frame the secondary station wishes to send.

3. The primary station acknowledges the receipt of the single I-frame and sends another S-frame RR command. Again, the poll/final bit is on, asking the secondary station if it has any more data to send.

BOX 9.14 *(Continued)*

4. The secondary station this time responds by transmitting a sequence of three I-frames. Notice that the poll/final bit is on only in the last of the three I-frames. Also notice that the Ns count is updated after each frame is transmitted to control frame sequencing.

5. The primary station this time has data of its own to send, and it responds by transmitting four I-frames. Again, the poll/final bit is on only in the last frame sent, which serves the same purpose as the S-frame RR command poll and asks the secondary station if it has any data to send.

On multipoint lines, it is sometimes advantageous to interleave transmissions to several secondary stations. When this occurs, a primary station does not send a whole group of frames to one secondary station before sending another group to a different secondary station. Rather, the primary station may send the first frame in a group to one secondary station, then the first frame in another group to a second secondary, and so on until parts of several frame groups are sent to several secondary stations. The primary might then proceed to send subsequent frames to each of the secondary stations in turn. This practice is particularly helpful when the speed of the secondary machines is considerably lower than that of either the primary station or the physical link. On a multipoint link that uses full-duplex lines, interleaved transmissions in both directions can occur simultaneously.

TRANSMISSION ERROR   In our sample frame exchange, we assumed that the CRC value contained in the FCS field of each received frame matches the calculated CRC value that the receiving station generates. When transmission errors occur while a frame is being sent, these values will not match. The receiving station must ask for that frame, and any sent after it, to be retransmitted. A typical frame exchange associated with this type of error situation is illustrated in Box 9.15.

LOOP OPERATION   Some bit-oriented protocols support operation over data links that are configured as loops. The loop configuration described here is a loop that operates using IBM's SDLC protocol in an SNA environment. In an SNA loop configuration, only the primary station

BOX 9.15   Bit-oriented protocols: transmission error

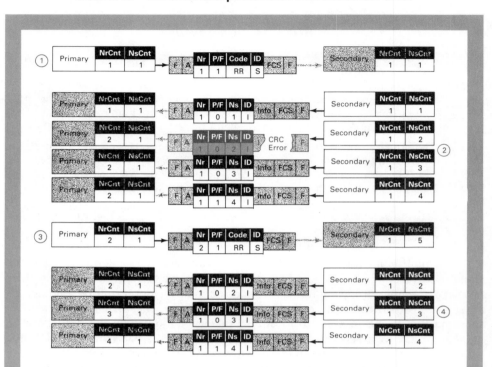

In this frame exchange, a transmission error occurs while the secondary station is transmitting I-frames to the primary station. After the complete sequence of frames has been received, the primary station sends an RR S-frame poll that indicates the number of the frame with which the secondary station should begin retransmission.

1. The primary station initiates a poll by transmitting an RR S-frame to the secondary station.

2. The secondary station transmits a sequence of four I-frames back to the primary station. In this particular case, a transmission error occurs during the transmission of the second frame (frame 2).

3. The primary station detects a CRC error in frame 2 when it compares the value it generates by putting the frame through the CRC algorithm against the value contained in the FCS bytes received with the frame. It then stops updating its Nr count value for that and all subsequent I-frames. After it receives the final frame from the secondary station (frame 4, which has the poll/final bit on), it sends an RR S-frame to the secondary station indicating that the next frame it expects to receive is frame 2.

4. The secondary station compares the value in the Nr count in the received frame with the value in its own internal Ns counter. Since these do not match, the secondary station resets its Ns counter to 2 and retransmits frame 2, 3, and 4.

or one of the secondary stations transmits at any one time. The secondary stations transmit sequentially, as required, according to their physical sequence on the data link.

When the primary station transmits on the loop, it sends command frames that are directed at an individual secondary station or any group of secondary stations on the loop. Each frame transmitted by the primary station carries in its address field the address of the secondary station or stations to which the command is directed. When the primary station finishes transmitting, it begins transmitting a continuous sequence of one bits, which constitute a go-ahead signal.

Each secondary station on the loop receives each frame transmitted by the primary station. Each station decodes the address field in the frame and accepts only commands intended for it. Each secondary station also serves as a repeater to relay each frame to the next station on the loop. All frames are relayed to the next station on the loop, including commands that are accepted by the station and those that are not.

Before a secondary station can transmit on the loop, it must have received a frame intended for itself that constitutes a poll (poll/final bit on). It then formats its response and waits for the go-ahead signal from the primary station (continuous one bits). When the first secondary station on the loop that has a response detects the go-ahead signal, it converts the seventh of a sequence of 7 one bits to a zero bit, thus creating a flag. It then sends its response down the loop to the next station, where it will eventually be relayed to the primary station.

The secondary station that sent the response then begins relaying the go-ahead signal down the loop to the next station. Other secondary stations down the loop each get a similar opportunity to send a response to the primary station. When the primary station receives frames from all the secondary stations on the loop that responded and again detects the go-ahead signal, it then transmits its next frame to one or more secondary stations.

Chapter 10 discusses two categories of data communication software that are important in data transmission systems: telecommunications access methods and teleprocessing monitors.

10 ACCESS METHODS AND TP MONITORS

Two general-purpose software entities that operate in the host computer are especially important in today's data communication systems: *telecommunications access methods* and *teleprocessing monitors*.

Telecommunications access methods make up a software layer that operates above the level of the operating system in the host computer. The functions provided by telecommunications access methods can be accessed directly, if desired, by application programs. Such applications are generally complex programs that are typically written in assembler language.

More commonly, the functions performed by telecommunications access methods are accessed by intermediary software subsystems called teleprocessing monitors (TP monitors). Application programs, written in any desired language, make high-level requests of the TP monitor, which in turn request telecommunications access method services as required. These software subsystem relationships are summarized in Fig. 10.1.

TELECOMMUNICATIONS ACCESS METHODS

The fundamental purpose of a telecommunications access method is to give application programs, or teleprocessing monitor programs, direct access to the messages that are going out or coming in over communication lines. The access method performs polling functions and provides READ- and WRITE-level support for communication functions.

Reading from Communication Lines

Coding a READ instruction in an application program results in a linkage to an access method routine, which may address the indicated communication line or

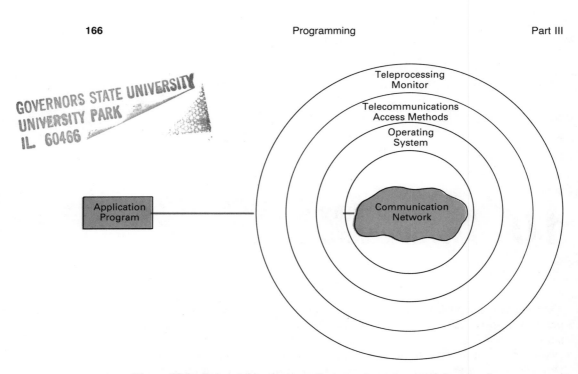

Figure 10.1 Relationships between the operating system and the two classes of data communication software subsystems.

network node and start the transmission of data. After the READ instruction has been executed, the application program can continue if desired with other processing. Eventually the program reaches a point where it can go no further until the message is read in. At this point, a WAIT request can be issued. When the conditions of the WAIT are satisfied—in other words, when the message has been read in and is ready to be processed—control is passed back to the waiting application program. This type of facility gives the programmer complete control over communication functions. However, as indicated earlier, the programs that issue the READ and WAIT instructions tend to be complex and are generally written in assembler language.

Polling

If the terminal is on a polled line, the READ instruction may result in the line's being polled, and when a terminal indicates that it has a message, this message is read. To do so, the application program may have a polling list telling it the addresses of the terminals and the sequence in which they must be polled.

Writing to Communication Lines

An application programmer can send a message to a terminal by means of a WRITE instruction. As with READ, the initial WRITE instruction initiates the write operation. A WAIT instruction can be used at the point in the program where the write operation must be completed.

Handling Transmission Errors

When error-detecting codes are used, with automatic retransmission of erroneous messages, the access method code may ensure that retransmission is initiated when necessary. In many cases, the code that implements the data link protocol, which operates at a lower level than the access method software, may handle error detection and retransmission. If correct transmission has not been accomplished after a specified number of retries, the access method code may notify the application program so that it can take appropriate action.

Organizing Buffer Pools

A telecommunications access method normally allocates blocks of buffers dynamically as required. If a message is being received and fills the block allocated to it, another block will be chained to the first. This chaining process continues until the entire message is received. The converse process takes place on output. As soon as a block is no longer needed, it is made free again in the pool of available blocks.

Dialing and Answering Calls

When the terminal is on a dial-up line, a WRITE instruction can cause the access method code to carry out the dialing operation. One form of WRITE instruction might cause the computer to dial a terminal, establish a connection, and transmit a message. Another form of WRITE might cause it to transmit the data without dialing, because the connection is already established. When a busy signal is obtained for a terminal that is dialed, the access method code may notify the application program.

　　Similarly, a READ instruction may dial a terminal to see whether it has anything to send. In some cases, a dialing list will be given to the access method software, which will then dial the terminals on the list, as in a polling operation. When a terminal user dials the computer, the telecommunications access method can be set up to accept the call, establish contact with the terminal, and notify the application program that the call has been received.

　　Telecommunications access methods perform a number of additional functions. Box 10.1 describes some of them.

HIGHER-LEVEL FUNCTIONS

Some of today's advanced telecommunications access methods provide additional facilities over and above the basic functions discussed above and in Box 10.1. For example, some access methods maintain queues of messages that al-

BOX 10.1   Additional access method functions

- **Converting Character Codes.** Telecommunications access methods normally provide a translation routine and a set of translation tables that convert between the codes employed by the computer and the various codes employed by terminals. The user may be able to define new sets of terminal codes and give these translation tables to the access method routines.

- **Keeping Error Statistics.** Telecommunications access methods generally maintain statistics regarding transmission errors that are detected. This aids in evaluating the performance of the communication network. Often, application systems contain special programs that are designed to organize, display, and evaluate error statistics.

- **Providing Testing Facilities.** Telecommunications access method software sometimes provides online diagnostics that facilitate the testing of terminal equipment. These facilities are helpful in the maintenance of the communication network.

- **Performing Initialization Procedures.** Telecommunications access methods generally allow programmers to use instructions such as OPEN to activate a communication path. This must be done before any message can be sent or received. Similarly, a CLOSE instruction shuts down a path.

low higher-level requests, such as GET and PUT, to be made instead of the more basic READ and WRITE facilities. No WAIT instructions are necessary when using GET- and PUT-level support.

An advanced telecommunications access method may also implement its own *message control program,* which schedules the traffic-handling operations. Interrupts and instructions in the calling programs cause control to be given to the message control program at appropriate times. The message control program generally resides in one region or address space in the system and is executed as one of the high-priority tasks.

Application programs and the teleprocessing monitor are normally executed as lower-priority tasks. Messages reaching the message control program are routed by it to the requisite destination, which may be a terminal, some other device in the network, or an application program. Often the required communication line or program will be occupied, and so the message control program organizes queues of items waiting for these facilities.

Message Switching

An advanced telecommunications access method may have the capability of handling some incoming messages by itself without needing to pass them to an application program or to the TP monitor. Such is the case when the message is merely to be routed to another terminal or computer, as in a message switching system. An advanced telecommunications access method may in fact carry out by itself all the functions that would be found in a message switching system.

Data Collection

Similarly, some advanced telecommunications access methods are able to carry out data collection functions without requiring application programs. Terminal operators might key in data that is to be collected for subsequent batch processing. The access method might either store the data in a queue for a particular application program or else write it in secondary storage independently of an application program. In the latter case, the data may be read for batch processing at some later time by data management software unrelated to the telecommunications access method. The message control program thus serves as an intermediary between application programs and terminals, between network devices and other network devices, and sometimes between network devices and secondary storage devices.

Message Routing

Because of the different routing possibilities, some messages need to have a *header* that the message control program uses in directing the message to appropriate destinations. Many systems do not use a header at all on the incoming messages because all messages are destined for the same application program. In others, a destination address or transaction code may be used to select the appropriate application program.

Queuing

Messages often arrive at random times. They are sometimes not processed immediately because the computing system is occupied. When they have been processed, a response may not be sent immediately because the line is occupied. The message control program, attempting to maintain high utilization of both the computing system and the lines, may build queues of items waiting for these facilities. The queues can be either in the computer's main memory or in secondary storage.

IBM TELECOMMUNICATIONS ACCESS METHODS

Because of the dominance of IBM equipment in the mainframe computing environment, it is useful to examine the telecommunications access methods that are provided to support data transmission on IBM mainframes. Three IBM telecommunications access methods are used most often in the mainframe environment. All conform to the SNA network architecture.

- **ACF/TCAM**—Advanced Communications Function for the Telecommunications Access Method
- **ACF/VTAM**—Advanced Communications Function for the Virtual Telecommunications Access Method
- **ACF/VTAME**—Advanced Communications Function for the Virtual Telecommunications Access Method—Entry

Each of these access methods performs similar functions. ACF/TCAM and ACF/VTAM (often called simply TCAM and VTAM) are designed to be run under the control of an MVS-type operating system; ACF/VTAME (often called VTAME) is the VSE counterpart of ACF/VTAM. ACF/TCAM supports a number of advanced features that are not provided by either ACF/VTAM or ACF/VTAME.

The predecessor to VTAM and VTAME was a system called BTAM, which stands for *Basic Telecommunications Access Method*. BTAM was used with the nonvirtual storage systems, such as MVT and MFT. The predecessor to TCAM was QTAM, for *Queued Telecommunications Access Method*. Neither BTAM nor QTAM is used with today's virtual storage operating systems.

TELEPROCESSING MONITORS

As we discussed earlier in this chapter, most application programs do not request the services of a telecommunications access method directly. Instead they make requests of an intermediary software system called a *teleprocessing monitor* (TP monitor). Examples of teleprocessing monitors are IBM's CICS and IMS/DC and Cullinet Software's IDMS/DC. Application programs that use TP monitors are often written in high-level languages, such as COBOL or PL/I. Some of today's fourth-generation languages also contain interfaces to popular TP monitors, thus allowing the traditional programming process to be bypassed in many cases.

TELEPROCESSING MONITOR FUNCTIONS

The specific functions of each teleprocessing monitor are different, and the way in which they are used varies, but they all provide similar services. In general, a system programmer describes to the TP monitor the communication network environment, including the communication lines and the terminals attached to them. The system programmer also describes the application environment by assigning symbolic names to all the transaction types that the system uses and giving names to the application programs that process them. Some TP monitors also allow the system programmer to describe the file or database environment.

The teleprocessing monitor performs all the functions of sending and receiving messages over the communication network by requesting the services of the underlying telecommunications access method software. Three major functions are performed by a TP monitor in handling the communication-related aspects of the application systems under its control:

- Monitoring the communication network and using telecommunications access method software to read messages coming into the system

- Scheduling the appropriate application programs that are required to process input messages based on control information included in each message

- Accepting output messages from application programs and using telecommunications access method software to transmit them to their destinations

TP monitors operate in either of two ways. Some TP monitors read in each message and then immediately run the application program that is required to process it. Cullinet's IDMS/DC is an example of a TP monitor that normally operates in this manner. Other TP monitors store messages in queues that they maintain. Another task that operates concurrently with the message reading task then selects messages from the queues based on a priority scheme and runs the appropriate application program to process each message. IBM's IMS/DC is an example of a TP monitor that uses message queues. Many TP monitors perform functions in addition to those we have described. For example, IBM's CICS provides functions that are related to the formatting of screens that are displayed on terminals. Box 10.2 briefly describes the two major TP monitor software subsystems that are available from IBM. Many software vendors supply TP monitors that perform services similar to those provided by IBM's TP monitor software.

IMS/DC

The remainder of this chapter examines the characteristics of a typical TP monitor. The one we use as an example is the particularly powerful IMS/DC TP monitor marketed by IBM. As mentioned, IMS/DC is a TP monitor that uses a queuing scheme to separate the functions of reading transactions from terminals and selecting transactions for processing by application programs.

BOX 10.2   IBM teleprocessing monitors

IMS/DC

IMS (for *Information Management System*) is a family of software components whose main purpose is to provide database management services. However, one independent subsystem of IMS, called IMS/DC (for *IMS/Data Communication*) is designed to provide teleprocessing monitor support. Although IMS/DC is designed to be run in conjunction with the database portions of the IMS software, either the database portion, sometimes referred to as IMS/DB, or the data communication portion can be run separately. Each component is priced separately by IBM. IMS/DC operates under the control of any of the MVS-type operating systems; there is no VSE version of IMS/DC.

CICS

CICS (for *Customer Information Control System*) is another IBM teleprocessing monitor. It provides roughly the same types of services as IMS/DC, although there is little compatibility between the two subsystems. The CICS software provides no direct database support but does provide support for file operations on application files that are defined to the software; an interface allows access to IMS databases. Like IMS/DC, CICS uses the services of a telecommunications access method in working with the communication-related resources of the system. Versions of CICS are available for both the MVS and VSE environments.

IMS/DC RESOURCES
In the IMS/DC environment, all resources under the control of the IMS/DC software must be defined during system definition. Two main categories of system resources must be defined to IMS/DC: *application resources* and *data communication resources*. Application resources are system resources related to application programs that operate in the IMS/DC system. Specifically, these resources consist of *message processing programs* and *transactions*.

- **Message Processing Programs.** *Message processing programs* (MP programs) are application programs that run under the control of IMS/DC and are automatically loaded by IMS/DC at the appropriate time. Each MP program is assigned a unique name.

- **Transactions.** A *transaction* is a message that has an MP program as its destination. Transactions can be sent to MP programs either from remote terminals or from other programs. Each transaction is assigned a unique transaction code.

During IMS/DC system definition, each transaction code is associated with an MP program. Only one program can be assigned to process a given transaction; however, a given program can process more than one type of transaction.

A second category of resource that must be defined during IMS/DC system definition includes the data transmission equipment in the network. The following entities define the network to the IMS/DC software:

- **Communication Lines.** In an IMS/DC network, a single communication line can handle one or more remote terminals of a particular type. A line can be switched or nonswitched. Lines that connect terminals of a similar type can be collected into *line groups*.

- **Physical Terminals.** One or more physical terminals can be connected to each communication line through one or more levels of controllers. In a switched line network, each terminal can be connected to any one of several lines. In a nonswitched network, a terminal is always connected to the same line.

- **Logical Terminals.** MP programs do not communicate directly with physical terminals. Instead, messages that are destined for remote terminals include a logical terminal name. When a logical terminal name message is sent, the physical terminal currently assigned to that logical terminal name receives the message. The system operator has commands that can be used to change the logical and physical terminal assignments at any time.

MESSAGE QUEUES

All messages that flow through IMS/DC are stored in *message queues*. IMS/DC maintains a separate message queue for each transaction code and for each logical terminal. As shown in Fig. 10.2, a separate task running in the IMS/DC region or address space

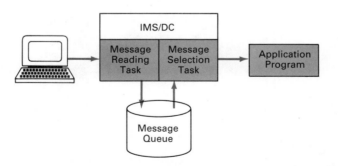

Figure 10.2   IMS/DC maintains a message queue for each transaction code and for each logical terminal.

selects transactions from the message queues for processing by MP programs. Because the queues often contain more transactions than can be processed at one time, a priority scheme is used in determining which transaction to select first from the various queues. Messages destined for logical terminals are also selected from the appropriate message queues and transmitted to the appropriate physical terminal at appropriate times.

OPERATING ENVIRONMENT Multiple operating system regions or address spaces are normally used for running the IMS/DC software and the various MP programs. IMS/DC supports three region types: the IMS control region, MP regions, and BMP regions. Figure 10.3 shows a typical IMS/DC region configuration.

IMS Control Region

The IMS control region handles all communication between IMS/DC and remote terminals and contains the IMS/DC software. The software running in the IMS control region controls the allocation of the various MP regions in the system. The IMS control region also contains the database management system software if the DBMS portion of IMS is also being used.

Message Processing Regions

The scheduling of MP programs into the MP regions is handled by the IMS/DC software. Each of the transaction codes defined to IMS/DC is assigned to a

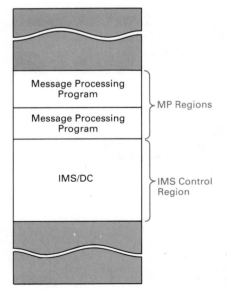

Figure 10.3 The IMS control region controls the way in which MP programs are executed in the MP regions.

transaction class identified with a number from 1 to 255. Each MP region is set up to process transactions from up to four transaction classes. Each time an MP region becomes available, IMS/DC checks the message queues to see if a transaction of the appropriate class is available. If none is available, the region remains idle. If there are many transactions to choose from, IMS/DC uses a priority scheme to select the highest-priority transaction.

Batch Message Processing Regions

A *batch message processing program* (BMP program) is a special type of message processing program designed to operate in the batch mode. The system operator must initiate a BMP program in an available BMP region; IMS/DC does not automatically start BMP programs. A BMP program might be used when each transaction of a particular type requires substantial processing. Normally, MP programs are designed so that they occupy a message processing region for as short a time as possible. In cases that require lengthy processing times but not immediate responses, a BMP program might better suit the application requirements. Batch message processing programs are often used when it is desirable to submit input from a terminal but an immediate response back to the terminal is not required.

MESSAGE PROCESSING
IMS/DC messages can be divided into segments. As shown in Fig. 10.4, the text of a message segment is preceded by a 2-byte length field and 2 bytes of control information. In many cases, a message segment consists of a particular line of the total message. For example, if a terminal operator is required to send a message that consists of five individual lines, that message might consist of five segments. In order for a program to send a message consisting of seven lines of data to a terminal or remote printer, the message might contain seven segments.

When a message processing program is loaded into a message processing region and control is passed to the MP program, a transaction will be waiting in the message queue with one of that program's assigned transaction codes. An MP program normally begins its processing by reading the first segment of the waiting message.

An MP program retrieves message segments by issuing CALL statements in a conventional programming language such as COBOL, PL/I, or assembler language. Calls to IMS/DC reference a number of parameters that describe the

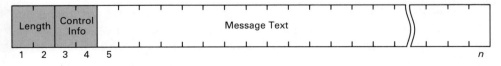

Figure 10.4   IMS/DC message segment format.

BOX 10.3   IMS/DC MP program calls

- **Get-Unique (GU).** Used to retrieve the first segment of a message from the message queue.
- **Get-Next (GN).** Used to retrieve the second and all subsequent message segments from the message queue.
- **Insert (ISRT).** Used to send a message to a logical terminal or to another MP program.
- **Purge (PURG).** Used to establish a synchronization point from which restart can begin should a system failure later occur.

function to be performed. Among these parameters is a 4-character *function code* that describes the type of service desired. Box 10.3 lists four IMS/DC services, with their associated function codes, that are commonly used in writing MP programs that send and receive messages.

The interface between the MP program and IMS/DC is designed so that the message queue behaves in a similar manner to a sequential file. Each message retrieval CALL statement reads a new message segment until no more segments in the message queue are available for that message. A status code value returned by IMS/DC tells the program when the end of the message has been reached.

Box 10.4 shows the sequence of events within the system after a terminal operator enters a message at a terminal.

IMS/DC MESSAGE SCHEDULING   As discussed earlier, messages from terminals are placed into message queues before they are passed to MP programs. During IMS/DC system definition, transactions are normally separated into classes based on their response-time requirements. For example, a particular application system may have a particular transaction type that occurs very frequently and must be given a fast response time. One or more MP regions might be set aside for that transaction type only. The MP regions are set up according to the requirements of the individual MP programs that run in the system.

IMS/DC attempts to select a transaction for each of the message processing regions currently in operation. Each transaction type has two priorities associated with it: a *normal priority* and a *limit priority*. In addition, each transaction has a *limit count*.

Within each message queue, messages are queued serially by transaction

BOX 10.4   IMS/DC processing

Message Input. The terminal operator sends a message by entering it at the terminal and pressing the ENTER key. Software running in the IMS control region works with the telecommunications access method to handle the transmission of the message from the remote terminal to the central computing system. Each received message is accompanied by a transaction code and possibly a password. The transaction code and password are entered by the terminal operator or are supplied by software running either in the terminal equipment or in the central computing system. After the message is received, the control region checks the transaction code against a list to see if the transaction code is valid; if required, it also verifies the password. If the transaction code and the password are valid, the message is stored in the appropriate message queue. Each transaction code and logical terminal name has its own message queue.

Message Selection. Another task running in the IMS control region selects messages from the message queues. When this task selects a message, it consults an internal list to see which MP program is associated with the message's transaction code. It then schedules that MP program for loading into an available MP region.

Message Processing. Once a message processing program is loaded into an MP region, a task is created, and control is passed to the MP program. The MP program then competes for system resources with all other tasks running in the system. The MP program begins by issuing a CALL statement to IMS/DC to retrieve the first message segment. The program then processes the data in that message segment, which may require making one or more file or database accesses. If the message consists of more than one segment, the program issues additional CALL statements to IMS/DC to retrieve the remaining message segments.

Message Output. If an MP program determines that a reply is necessary, the MP program issues CALL statements to IMS/DC to send one or more messages back to the originating terminal. Optionally, the program can send messages to other terminals and can also put messages back into the message queues to be read by other MP or BMP programs.

code. When an MP region becomes available, IMS/DC examines the message queues to determine which messages can be handled by the available region. It then selects the transaction having the highest priority. To determine whether to use the normal priority or the limit priority, IMS/DC looks at the number of transactions with each transaction code stored in each message queue. If the number of transactions in a particular queue is greater than or equal to that transaction code's limit count, the limit priority is used. If the number of messages queued is less than the limit count, the normal priority is used.

MESSAGE FORMAT SERVICE

Message Format Service (MFS) is a powerful screen formatting facility that is part of the IMS/DC software. Messages to be sent to an MP program from a terminal often consist of entire screens of information. These screens often contain descriptive information that helps make the screen readable. When MFS is used, the MP program works only with certain predefined data fields. MFS inserts and removes fixed text, filler characters, and control codes that are required to format a screen at the terminal. MFS provides two control blocks, set up by macros, to separate out information of direct interest to the MP or BMP program.

One control block, called the *Message Input Descriptor* (MID), is used to describe an input message as the program would like to see it. The MID describes only fields on the screen in which the program is interested. Another control block, called the *Device Input Format* (DIF), describes the screen format as the terminal operator formats it.

Two other MFS control blocks are used to help format screens that will be transmitted from an MP program to a terminal. The *Message Output Descriptor* (MOD) describes the message as the program formats it. Another control block, *Device Output Format* (DOF), describes the screen format as it will appear at the terminal. MFS uses a MOD and a DOF to translate the data fields that the program places in the output message into a complete screen format as it will appear on the display screen.

MFS allows IMS/DC application programs to work with information on the data field level, avoiding concern over where on the screen the information is stored or should appear. It allows complex screen formats to be used without tying the MP program to the screen location where the pertinent information is stored.

In this chapter, we discussed software that runs in the host processor in mainframe-based data communication systems. The personal computer is playing an ever-increasing role in today's data processing environment. The hardware and software that is used to support data communication using personal computers is the subject of Chapter 11.

11 PERSONAL COMPUTERS

Personal computers of all types are today performing many tasks that required more specialized hardware in days past. For example, the personal computer has become a widely used terminal device in many of today's data transmission systems. In this chapter, we see how personal computers can be used to perform data communication functions.

PARALLEL COMMUNICATION

The simplest application of data communication with personal computers involves parallel communication between the personal computer and a printer using the parallel communication port implemented in many personal computers. This port is sometimes installed on the circuit board that is used to control the personal computer's display screen. The standard parallel port normally implements a form of parallel interface that was standardized a number of years ago by the Centronics Corporation, a supplier of computer printers.

ASYNCHRONOUS COMMUNICATION ADAPTERS

Parallel communication is used most often for attaching a printer to a personal computer, but most other data communication applications use serial communication. For example, serial communication is used most often for connecting a personal computer to a remote mainframe using modems.

The simplest type of data communication functions generally require the use of an *asynchronous communications adapter*. These adapters generally implement the RS-232-C interface introduced in Chapter 5. Many personal computers have such an adapter installed as original equipment. For example, many Macintosh computers from Apple Computer include serial communication ports that can be used for asynchronous communication. Many IBM and IBM-compatible computers also have serial adapters installed as standard equipment. Computers that do not have standard asynchronous communication capabilities can generally be upgraded through the addition of an inexpensive add-on circuit board.

The asynchronous communications adapter allows the user to attach the personal computer to all types of devices that support asynchronous communication. Common examples of such equipment are serial printers and modems.

DTE VERSUS DCE

Most asynchronous communications adapters are wired as DTEs, which allows them to be connected with a standard RS-232-C cable to any device that is wired as a DCE, such as a modem. [The distinction between *data terminal equipment* (DTE) and *data circuit–terminating equipment* (DCE) was introduced in Chapter 5.] Many adapters provide jumper wires or internal switches that allow the adapter to be configured as a DCE instead of a DTE. Configuring the adapter as a DCE allows it to be connected with a standard cable to a device that is configured as a DTE, such as a printer or a display terminal.

If it is necessary to connect an asynchronous adapter that is configured as a DTE to a device that is also configured as a DTE, as when connecting two personal computers, a special cable called a *null modem* can be used. The null modem cable simply crosses the appropriate circuits to simulate the presence of two modems between the DTEs. Various types of null modem cable adapters that cross the appropriate circuits are commercially available. If you are interested in learning more about the RS-232-C interface and the types of connections that are used for various applications, consult *Data Communication Technology* by James Martin and Joe Leben (Englewood Cliffs, N.J.: Prentice Hall, 1988).

CONNECTING COMPUTERS

A common application of asynchronous communications adapters and null modem cables is to connect two personal computers, possibly for transferring data from one computer to the other. When the two computers are located in the same place, a simple RS-232-C cable can be used to connect the asynchronous adapter in one personal computer to the adapter in the other computer using a null modem cable.

An ordinary RS-232-C null modem cable can be used over distances up to about 50 feet. If a longer cable is required, simple, short-distance modems can be used to transmit the data over privately installed cables up to a mile or so in length. If the two computers are widely separated, a conventional modem can be used at each location to connect the computers via the telephone network. (See Fig. 11.1 for examples of these configurations.)

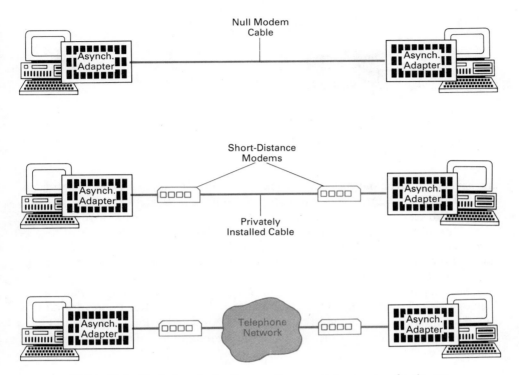

Figure 11.1 Typical methods of connecting personal computers for the purpose of file transfers.

INTERNAL MODEMS

The connection to communication facilities can be simplified by using an internal modem instead of an asynchronous communications adapter and an external modem. An internal modem contains circuitry that performs the functions of both an asynchronous communications adapter and a modem, all on the same circuit card. The interface between the adapter and the modem is implemented directly on the circuit board itself, and the circuit board terminates in a standard modular telephone jack that can be connected directly to the telephone network (see Fig. 11.2).

ASYNCHRONOUS TERMINAL EMULATION

The most common use of a personal computer and a modem is to emulate an asynchronous terminal. Such a hardware configuration is combined with a software package that makes the personal computer appear to the device to which it is attached as if it were a simple asynchronous terminal. The simplest such software simply monitors the personal computer keyboard

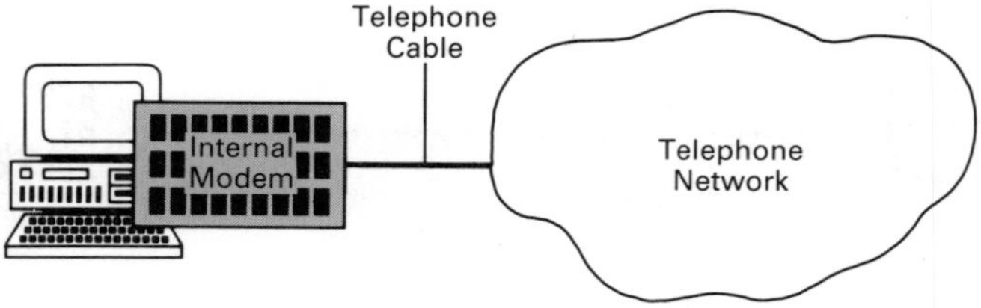

Telephone
Cable

Internal
Modem

Telephone
Network

Figure 11.2   An internal modem can be installed in a personal computer for direct connection to the telephone network.

and sends out over the modem the character corresponding to each key that is pressed. The software also monitors the communication line and displays on the screen each character that is received by the modem (see Fig. 11.3).

The software may also interpret control sequences that are received to perform certain terminal control functions, such as clearing the screen and moving the display cursor. Many commercially available terminal emulation software packages also often support additional functions that use the personal computer's memory and disk storage to perform many of the functions normally associated with intelligent terminals. Terminal emulation functions and file transfer functions are often combined in the same data communication software package. Some of the functions performed by terminal emulation software packages are listed in Box 11.1.

FILE TRANSFERS   A particularly useful function, performed by almost all asynchronous terminal emulation packages, is to transfer files between two personal computers or between a personal computer and a larger processor. In the mid-1970s, Ward Christensen, an early microcomputer user, developed a simple protocol to support file transfers, which he placed into the public domain. This protocol has become known as the *XMODEM* protocol, after the original program that supported it. Over the years, the XMODEM protocol has become widely used, and most commercial software

Figure 11.3   Terminal emulation software makes it appear to the device to which it is attached as if it were an asynchronous terminal.

BOX 11.1   Terminal emulation software functions

- **Asynchronous Terminal Emulation.** All asynchronous terminal emulation packages perform the simple input and output functions that are handled by an asynchronous terminal.

- **Automatic Dialing.** The program may store a telephone number list and allow the user to automatically dial up a time-sharing service or computer utility.

- **Capture to Memory or Disk.** The program may allow the user to automatically capture for later use all the data that flows back and forth between the personal computer and the computer to which it is connected. The data can be captured in memory and then later stored into a disk file, or it can be captured directly to disk.

- **Script Facility.** The program might implement some type of script facility that allows the user to create sequences of commands that are sent out automatically over the communication line. These scripts can be used to perform any type of processing, including automatic log-on sequences.

- **File Transfers.** The program might perform the error checking necessary to permit files to be transferred between computer systems.

- **Uploading Capabilities.** The program might allow the user to change the input source from the keyboard to a file in the midst of an interactive session. The computer to which the user is connected then accepts data from the file as if it were being keyed in by the user. This is useful in electronic mail applications where the user wishes to compose an electronic mail message offline before logging onto the electronic mail service.

packages that perform file transfer operations support the XMODEM protocol. Even though more efficient and reliable protocols exist for file transfers, the XMODEM protocol has become something of a de facto standard for personal computers.

SYNCHRONOUS COMMUNICATIONS ADAPTERS

Although most data communication applications of personal computers use an asynchronous protocol for communication, a synchronous protocol is sometimes used for higher-performance applications. IBM offers two communications adapters that support synchronous communication; other vendors supply similar add-on circuit cards. The IBM *Binary Synchronous Communications Adapter* uses the binary-synchronous protocol for communicating with devices that use this line control procedure. The IBM *Synchronous Data Link Control (SDLC) Communications Adapter* uses the SDLC protocol for communicating with devices in the SNA environment (see Chapter 9).

3270 EMULATION

As we mentioned in Chapter 5, a widely used terminal is the IBM 3270 display station. More data communication applications in the IBM mainframe environment have been written for this terminal than for any other. Since many people that may require access to mainframe applications already have personal computers on their desks, it is common to use these same personal computers to emulate the functions of 3270 display stations. As with asynchronous terminal emulation, a combination of a circuit board and a software package is required for this type of terminal emulation.

A widely used communications adapter for 3270 emulation is the *IRMA* board marketed by Digital Communications Associates, 1000 Alderman Drive, Alpharetta, GA 30201. The IRMA board plugs into the personal computer in the same manner as an asynchronous adapter and is supplied with software that handles all standard 3270 terminal functions. The IRMA board circuitry terminates with a standard 3270 coaxial cable connector that allows the adapter to be attached to a 3270 cluster controller in the same manner as an ordinary 3270 terminal (see Fig. 11.4).

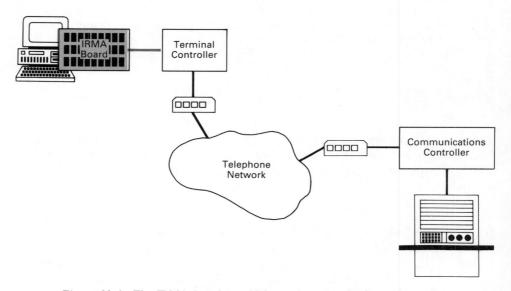

Figure 11.4 The IRMA board, a widely used communications adapter for 3270 terminal emulation, allows the personal computer to be attached to a 3270 terminal controller.

Another method of handling 3270 terminal emulation is through the use of a protocol converter. For example, IBM markets a device called the *3708 protocol converter,* to which one or more personal computers can be attached via conventional asynchronous communications adapters. The 3708 in turn communicates with a host communications controller using a synchronous protocol as if it were a 3270 cluster controller (see Fig. 11.5). Other vendors also supply devices that perform concentration and protocol conversion functions.

Software that performs 3270 terminal emulation performs many of the same functions described earlier for asynchronous terminal emulation. Synchronous terminal emulation programs are generally supplied with the communications adapters that are designed to emulate certain types of synchronous terminals. For example, the IRMA card comes with a software package that allows the personal computer to perform all the functions normally associated with a synchronous 3270-type terminal.

In many types of applications where mainframe programs must communicate with programs running in personal computers or where personal computers must communicate with one another, 3270 terminal emulation techniques are used to handle communication. This is because the protocols involved in communicating with 3270 terminals are widely used and well understood. In the

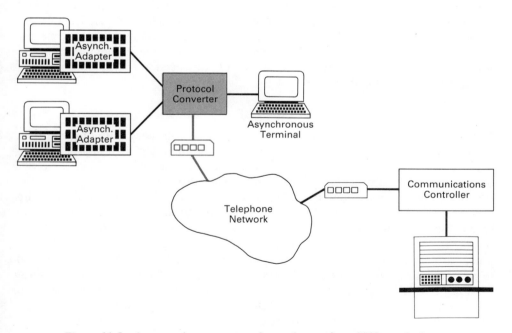

Figure 11.5   A protocol converter can be used to perform 3270 terminal emulation functions.

future, it is likely that protocols better suited to program-to-program communication will become more prevalent and will replace these more cumbersome terminal emulation techniques.

MICRO-MAINFRAME LINK SOFTWARE

Many software packages perform more advanced functions than simple terminal emulation and file transfers. These packages are generally referred to as *micro-mainframe link* packages. Unfortunately, the term *micro-mainframe link* has been much overused, to the point where it has now become almost meaningless. Today, nearly any vendor who has software that allows a personal computer to be connected to a larger system refers to that software as a micro-mainframe link. This often includes the simplest terminal emulation and file transfer software.

We feel that for a package to be called a micro-mainframe link, it should perform advanced functions over and above terminal emulation and file transfers. For example, some true micro-mainframe link packages allow virtual disk drives to be created on the mainframe. The personal computer user is allowed to access the virtual disk on the mainframe as if it were a disk drive attached directly to the personal computer. With a virtual disk, the communication functions that take place in moving data to and from the mainframe are transparent to the user. Another advanced function might be extracting selected data from a mainframe database and converting it to the personal computer format necessary for manipulating the data with conventional personal computer software, such as a spreadsheet program. Many other advanced micro-mainframe link functions are also possible.

INTEGRATED SOFTWARE

Much more can be done with personal computer data communication software than terminal emulation, file transfers, and simple micro-mainframe links. In order to perform truly advanced functions, it is necessary to coordinate closely the functions that are performed by the personal computer and the functions that are performed by the software that runs in the mainframe or other processor to which the personal computer is attached. Figure 11.6 shows a hardware environment that is becoming commonplace. In this configuration, personal computers are attached directly to a host mainframe, which may itself be connected to a complex network of other mainframes. Figure 11.7 shows a second configuration in which a group of personal computers is connected to a departmental minicomputer, which is in turn connected to a larger mainframe network.

While it is possible today to create all manner of distributed data processing configurations, the software to support such complex environments lags far behind the hardware. What is needed in complex environments that have mul-

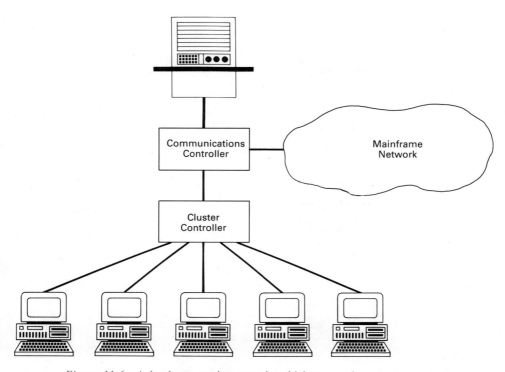

Figure 11.6 A hardware environment in which personal computers are attached to a mainframe that is connected to a network of other mainframes.

tiple levels of processors is *seamless integration* of functions. This seamless integration is extremely difficult to achieve.

For a personal computer user to employ a distributed system effectively, the system must operate simply. For example, for electronic mail, the user should be required simply to compose a message, indicate the user ID or network address of the destination user, and send the message on its way. The user of the personal computer should have one software package, with a simple user interface, that handles the interactions that are required with all the higher levels of hardware and software. Unfortunately, many of today's distributed systems are not simple; they are instead quite difficult to use. Users are often required to negotiate several complex layers of software and are required to memorize a different command syntax at each level. Nontechnical users tend to avoid using this type of system and instead find other ways to accomplish their tasks.

One tool that is being used to provide the required integration in a distributed environment is the *Advanced Program-to-Program Communication* (APPC) facility that is provided in the SNA environment (see Chapter 13). APPC provides application developers on mainframes, minicomputers, and personal computers with a standard protocol that can be used in transferring mes-

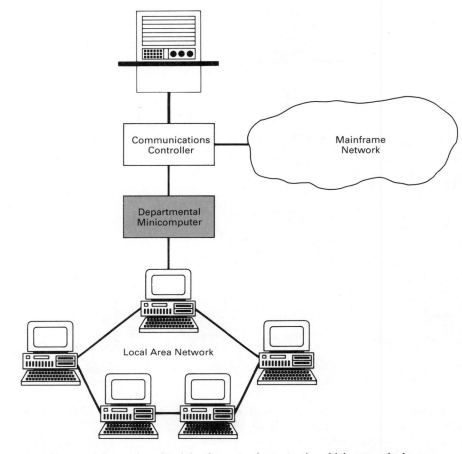

Figure 11.7 A three-level hardware environment in which networked personal computers are attached to a departmental minicomputer, which is in turn connected to a mainframe network.

sages between intelligent machines. The APPC protocols have been adopted as one of the standards for the higher-level layers of the OSI Reference Model (see Chapter 12). Acceptance of the APPC protocols as an international standard makes it more likely that the machines of different vendors will be able to communicate in a compatible manner. IBM's *Systems Application Architecture* (SAA), which defines common programming interfaces for all types of IBM processors, also helps in the creation of easy-to-use integrated software.

Part IV of this book discusses computer networks and network architectures. Chapter 12 begins Part IV by examining the Reference Model for Open Systems Interconnection, a network architecture under development by the International Standards Organization.

PART **IV** NETWORKS

12 OPEN SYSTEMS INTERCONNECT (OSI) MODEL

All advanced computer systems have software that has grown up in layers rather like the skins of an onion. Different layers relate to different types of functions and services. This applies to operating systems, to database software, and also to data transmission software. Each layer that is added is an attempt to increase the usefulness of the underlying hardware or to introduce modularity by dividing the complex set of functions into discrete layers.

When data is transmitted over a communication line or is stored in a storage unit, it becomes a serial stream of bits. In both cases, layers of software exist between the user program and the physical storage unit or transmission system. Conversion between the data the user perceives and what is physically transmitted or stored ranges from simple to complex, depending on the sophistication of the system. Figure 12.1 shows the layers used in implementing database management systems. The layers closest to the user process provide user services and represent data in the form most useful to the user. As we move to the layers that are closer to the computer (the central layer), the data becomes more abstract.

For advanced data communication systems, layers of software (or hardware or microcode) are also needed around the telecommunications links to make these more useful, to hide the complexity from the system's users, and to separate the functions into more manageable pieces.

THE OPEN SYSTEMS INTERCONNECT (OSI) MODEL

Given the immense proliferation of machines now occurring, one of the activities most important to the future of data processing is the setting of standards for the various software layers to enable machines of different manufacturers and different countries to communicate. As a start in the setting of such standards, the *International Stan-*

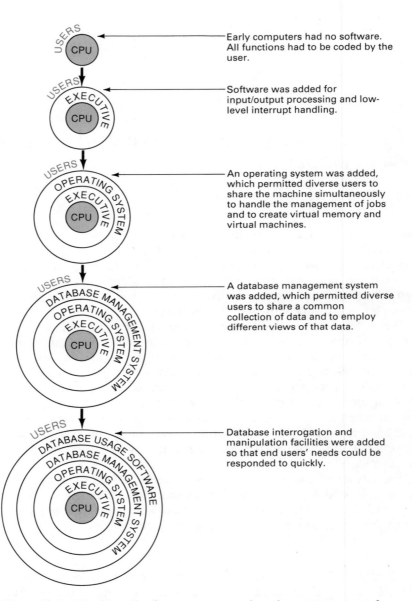

Early computers had no software. All functions had to be coded by the user.

Software was added for input/output processing and low-level interrupt handling.

An operating system was added, which permitted diverse users to share the machine simultaneously to handle the management of jobs and to create virtual memory and virtual machines.

A database management system was added, which permitted diverse users to share a common collection of data and to employ different views of that data.

Database interrogation and manipulation facilities were added so that end users' needs could be responded to quickly.

Figure 12.1 All advanced software systems, such as data management software, have layers that increase the usefulness of the underlying hardware.

dards Organization (ISO), in Geneva, Switzerland, has defined a seven-layer architecture. The seven ISO layers define a generalized architecture called the *Reference Model of Open Systems Interconnection* (OSI Reference Model or OSI model). The seven OSI layers are shown in Fig. 12.2.

ISO International Standard 7498 is the original source of documentation of the OSI Reference Model. The OSI Reference Model is also now documented in the CCITT X.200 series of recommendations. The ISO and CCITT descriptions of the OSI model are essentially identical. The primary purpose of the OSI model is to provide a basis for coordinating the development of standards that relate to the flexible interconnection of systems using data communication facilities. It is the plan of the CCITT, for example, to document in its X series of recommendations comprehensive standards and protocols for each of the seven OSI model layers.

CORPORATION FOR OPEN SYSTEMS

Many computer manufacturers, software companies, and telecommunications vendors are actively involved in the development of standards that conform to the OSI model. In 1985, an organization called the Corporation for Open Systems (COS) was formed in the United States under the auspices of the Computer and Communications Industry Association. A number of large organizations, including IBM and many other computer manufacturers, have joined the COS. The COS was chartered to monitor OSI and *Integrated Services Digital Network* (ISDN) standards development. ISDN standards have to do with the combining of all types of traffic, including voice, data, and images, over the same communication facilities (see Chapter 20).

INTERCONNECTION OF SYSTEMS

The OSI model is concerned with the *interconnection* of systems—the way systems exchange information—and not the *internal functions* performed by a given system. The OSI model provides a generalized view of a layered architecture that can apply to a very simple system, such as the connection of a terminal

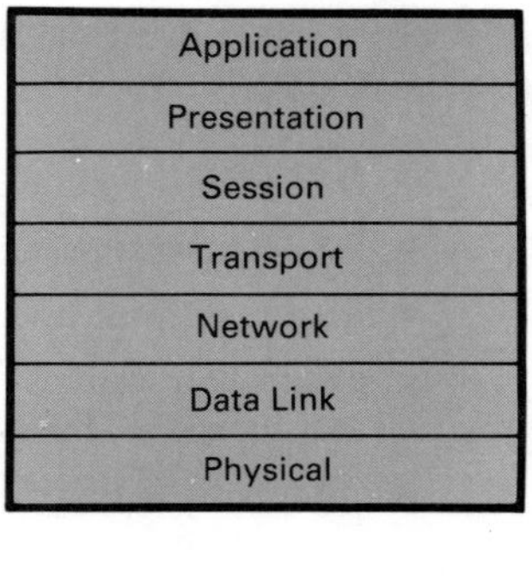

| Application |
| Presentation |
| Session |
| Transport |
| Network |
| Data Link |
| Physical |

Figure 12.2 The Reference Model for Open Systems Interconnection (OSI model) defines seven functional layers.

to a computer, or to a very complex system, such as the interconnection of two entire computer networks. The development of the OSI model is still in progress. For some areas, specific standards have been defined in support of the model; in other areas, standards still need to be developed.

We will next examine each of the seven OSI layers and introduce the functions that each layer performs.

THE PHYSICAL LAYER

The physical layer is responsible for the transmission of bits across a particular physical transmission medium. It involves a connection between two machines that allows electrical signals to be exchanged between them. Typically, the hardware consists of a cable, appropriate connectors, and two communicating devices that are capable of both generating and detecting voltages on the connecting cables.

Standards are also important for the simple software, or firmware, that runs in the physical layer. For example, the firmware that runs in the two communicating devices must agree as to how long in duration each bit should be and how to tell the difference between a one bit and a zero bit. The physical layer must deliver bits in the same sequence they are submitted and must notify the next higher layer of any faults that are detected.

The physical layer performs the following functions:

- Activates and deactivates physical connections upon request from the data link layer
- Transmits bits over a physical connection
- Handles physical-layer management activities, including activation and error control

THE DATA LINK LAYER

The data link layer is responsible for providing reliable data transmission from one network node to another and for isolating higher layers from any concerns about the physical transmission medium. The data link layer is concerned with the error-free transmission of frames of data. The data link layer performs the following functions:

- Determines where each frame starts and ends
- Detects transmission errors
- Recovers from transmission errors to give the appearance of an error-free link
- Controls transmission when several machines share the same physical circuit so that their transmissions do not overlap and become jumbled
- Addresses a frame to one of several machines

- Establishes and releases data link connections for use by the network layer
- Builds a data link connection using one or more physical connections
- Synchronizes the receipt of data that has been split over several physical connections
- Provides flow control, including dynamically altering the rate at which frames are accepted, and temporarily stops transmission to a particular receiving station upon request

THE NETWORK LAYER

The network layer relates to *virtual circuits*. The path between computers may, at any one instant, be via a number of physical communication links, as shown in Fig. 12.3. Each physical link spans two network machines, which must use at least the physical- and data link-layer procedures to exchange data. The users at either end of the network do not need to know over what route the data travels or how many physical links it travels over. The user machines perceive a simple interface that takes the form of a virtual circuit. The network layer creates the virtual circuit and provides the higher levels with an interface with it.

On some systems, the route over which data travels between two user machines varies from one instant to another. The network machine may require that messages be divided into slices, called *packets,* no greater than a certain length. The packets are then reassembled into messages after transmission. There are many such complications in the implementation and operation of a virtual circuit. The network layer provides a standard interface with the virtual circuit and, as far as possible, hides the complex mechanisms of its operation from the higher layers of software.

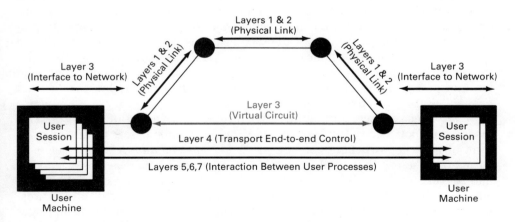

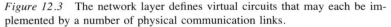

Figure 12.3   The network layer defines virtual circuits that may each be implemented by a number of physical communication links.

The network layer performs the following functions:

- Determines an optimum routing through the network and relays packets over the various data links that make up that route
- Provides a network connection between two transport entities and transfers data over the network connection in a transparent fashion
- Multiplexes numerous network connections onto a single data link connection in order to optimize its use
- Segments and/or blocks packets for the purposes of facilitating the transfer of packets over network connections
- Detects errors and recovers from them
- Selects an appropriate quality of service and maintains this quality of service even when a network connection spans subnetworks of dissimilar quality
- Handles network-layer management activities, including activation and error control

THE TRANSPORT LAYER

The lowest three layers of Fig. 12.2 represent a common network that many machines can share, independent of one another, just as many independent users share the postal service. It is possible that a postal service might occasionally lose a letter. To ensure that this has not happened, two users of the postal service might apply their own end-to-end controls, such as sequentially numbering their letters. The transport layer is concerned with similar end-to-end controls of the transmission between two users that are conducting a session.

Figure 12.3 illustrates that whereas the network layer is concerned with the interface between the user machine and the network, the transport layer is concerned with the end-to-end interaction between user processes. The functions executed in the transport layer may include end-to-end integrity controls to prevent loss or double processing of transactions, flow control of transactions, and addressing of end-user machines or processes. The transport layer, together with the three layers below it, provide a *transport* service. They are concerned with the transport of messages from one user process to another, but they do not manipulate the data contained in the messages.

The transport service may be implemented in a variety of ways; the OSI model does not specify implementation details. In some cases, it may take the form of a packet switching network using *Recommendation X.25* for layers 1, 2, and 3. When *X.25* is used, the transport layer must break each user message into packets for transmission through the network. In other cases, point-to-point circuits will be used, possibly with circuit switching, and in still other cases, satellite circuits might be employed. When these techniques are used, messages may not have to be broken up into packets for transmission. The interface from higher layers or from user machines to the transport layer is intended to provide a standard interface to users of the transport service independent of what network type is used.

The transport layer performs the following functions:

- Converts transport addresses into network addresses. Multiple transport addresses can be associated with the same network entity, and thus multiple transport addresses might be mapped onto a single network address.

- Multiplexes multiple transport connections onto a single network connection or splits a transport connection over multiple network connections as needed to optimize use of network connections

- Sequences messages transferred in order to ensure that they are delivered in the same sequence in which they were sent

- Detects and recovers from errors

- Segments, blocks, and concatenates messages

- Controls data flow to prevent overloading of network resources

- Handles transport-layer supervisory activities

- Provides for expedited transfer of messages between session entities

THE SESSION LAYER

The task of setting up a session between user processes can be complex because there are so many different ways in which machines can cooperate. Like two businessmen agreeing to a joint venture, they must agree in advance on the rules of the game. In effect, they sign a contract stating the manner in which they will cooperate. The session layer standardizes the process of establishing a session and of terminating it. If something goes wrong in mid-session, the session layer must restore the session without loss of data, or, if this is not possible, it must terminate the session in an orderly fashion. Error checking and recovery procedures are thus functions that are carried out in this layer.

In some types of sessions, a dialog takes place between machines, and a protocol must regulate who speaks when and for how long. In some cases, the two machines transmit alternately. In others, one machine may send many messages before the other replies. In some sessions, one machine may interrupt the other; in other cases not. The rules for how the dialog is conducted need to be agreed on when the session is set up.

There can be several concurrent session connections between a given pair of entities. A session connection can be mapped onto transport connections in a variety of ways. In the simplest case, a session connection uses a single transport connection. In more complex situations, one session might use a series of transport connections if, for example, a transport connection has to be terminated because of errors or failures. In other cases, a series of consecutive session connections might use the same transport connection.

The session layer performs the following functions:

- Provides a one-to-one mapping between a session connection and a presentation connection at any given instant. Over time, however, a transport connection can use several consecutive session connections, and several consecutive transport connections might use a single session connection.

- Prevents a presentation entity from being overloaded with data by using transport flow control (There is no explicit flow control in the session layer.)

- Reestablishes a transport connection to support a session connection in the event of a reported failure of the underlying transport connection

- Handles session-layer management activities

THE PRESENTATION LAYER

The presentation layer performs functions relating to the character code that is used and to the way data is displayed on a screen or printer. A stream of characters reaching a terminal will result in certain actions that result in a meaningful display or printout. The character stream may contain characters that cause editing of the data, line skipping, tabbing to position the data in columns, adding fixed column headings, highlighting certain fields, appropriate use of color, and so on. Formats may be displayed into which an operator enters data, and then only the entered data is transmitted. A coded number sent to an intelligent terminal may cause it to select a panel for display and enter variable data into that display. These are only a few of the many possible functions concerned with the presentation of data.

In some cases, network users and application programmers perceive a *virtual terminal or virtual display space*. Input/output statements relate to this make-believe facility, and the presentation-layer software must do the conversion between the virtual facility and the physical terminal being used. It is desirable that devices that use different character sets be able to communicate. Conversion of character streams may therefore be a concern of the presentation layer. The character stream may also be compacted in order to save transmission costs, and encryption and decryption for security reasons may be performed.

The presentation layer performs the following functions:

- Issues a request to the session layer for the establishment of a session
- Initiates data transfer from one user to another
- Negotiates and renegotiates the choice of a syntax to be used in the data transfer
- Performs any required data transformation or conversion
- Issues a request to the session layer for the termination of a session

THE APPLICATION LAYER

The application layer is concerned with higher-level functions that provide support to the application or system activities. These might include operator support, the use of remote data, file transfer control, distributed database activities, and higher-level dialog functions. The extent to which these are supported in the network architecture and in the software external to the network architecture, such as database software, will differ from one system to another.

When distributed files and databases are used, various controls are needed to prevent integrity problems or deadlocks. Some of the types of controls for this are strongly related to networking, for example, the time stamping of transactions and delivery of transactions in time-stamp sequence (sometimes called *pipelining*). Pacing is necessary with some processes so that the transmitting machine can send records continuously without flooding the receiving machine or so that an application can keep a distant printer going at maximum speed.

The application layer provides application processes with a point of access to the data communication system. The application layer provides a means for application processes to access the system interconnection facilities in order to exchange information. It provides all functions related to communication between systems that are not provided by the lower layers. These functions include those performed by people as well as those performed by application programs.

The application layer provides management services related to management of both the application processes and the systems being interconnected. Management of application processes includes initializing, maintaining, and terminating the processes, allocating and deallocating resources, detecting and preventing deadlocks, and providing integrity, commitment control, security, checkpoint, and recovery control. Again, this list is not exhaustive. Management of systems might include activating, maintaining, and deactivating various system resources; program loading; monitoring and reporting status and statistics; error detection, diagnosis, and recovery; and reconfiguration and restart.

The OSI model divides the possible functions that can be performed by the application layer into the following two broad categories:

- *Common application functions* that provide capabilities useful to many applications
- *Specific application functions* that are required to service the needs of a particular application

MESSAGE HEADERS

As data flows down through the various OSI layers, headers are added by each layer to the original message that enters the system at the application layer. The data link layer typically adds a trailer as well as a header. These headers and trailers contain control information that the system at the opposite end uses

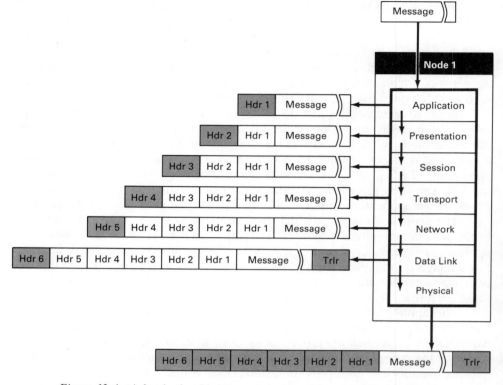

Figure 12.4 A header is added to a user message by each functional layer.
The data link layer adds a trailer as well.

in interpreting the information found in the transmission frame. This is shown
in Fig. 12.4.

The final transmission frame transmitted over the physical circuit thus contains many more bits than the original message. As the message moves up
through the layers at the opposite end, each layer strips off its corresponding
header and uses the information contained in it to handle the message properly
(see Fig. 12.5). The content of the headers and trailers must be rigidly defined
by the standards that document the functions performed by each layer.

OTHER NETWORK ARCHITECTURES

There are many similarities between the OSI model
and the network architectures that have been defined
by computer manufacturers. The architectures for
distributed processing from the various mainframe and minicomputer manufacturers perform all or most of the functions that are performed by the seven OSI

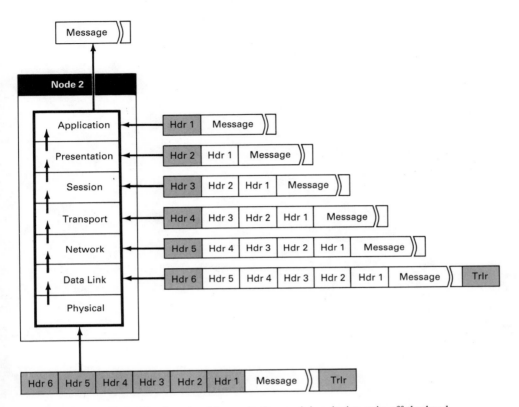

Figure 12.5 The functional layers in the receiving device strip off the headers and the trailer as the message moves up through the layers to the receiving user.

layers we have described. The functions of layers 1, 2, and 3 are usually clearly distinguished in most network architectures, but the functions of layers 4, 5, 6, and 7 may be intermixed and often do not correspond exactly to the layers specified in the OSI model.

As the various architectures evolve, the compatibility between manufacturers' architectures and the OSI Reference Model is likely to increase. For example, the Digital Equipment Corporation has stated that DEC's long-term intention for its DECNET architecture is to come into complete conformance with the OSI model. And the protocols for IBM's Advanced Program-to-Program Communications (APPC) SNA functions have been accepted as an international standard for the high-level layers of the OSI model (see Chapter 13).

Chapter 13 examines Systems Network Architecture (SNA), the network architecture defined by IBM for the interconnection of its own computing equipment.

13 IBM'S SYSTEMS NETWORK ARCHITECTURE

During the mid-1970s, several of the major computer manufacturers perceived that a large part of their future market was to come from distributed data processing. A wide range of machines would be hooked together into all manner of configurations. A user or application program at one machine would want to employ the facilities, data, or processing power of another, easily and inexpensively. For widely varying devices to be linked together, the hardware and software of those devices would have to be compatible; if compatibility was not achieved, complex interfaces would have to be built for meaningful communication to take place. To facilitate this compatibility, hardware manufacturers developed *network architectures* that allow complex networks to be built using a variety of equipment. The most widely used of these manufacturers' architectures is IBM's *Systems Network Architecture* (SNA).

SNA USERS   To understand SNA, it is necessary to have a clear idea of what IBM means by the term *SNA user*. An SNA user, or simply a *user*, is either a person or an application program that uses the SNA network to communicate with some other user. *People* use networks to send or receive information, and thus the person interacting with the network through a terminal is considered to be a user of the network. Often, however, a person does not interact directly with the network, but rather works through or with an *application program*. Application programs that employ an SNA network are also considered users of the network. These application programs may be located at different points within the network; for example, they may be located in a terminal, in a terminal controller, or in a host computer. These application programs may in turn provide services either to people or to other application programs; but whenever they draw on the services of the SNA network, they are considered SNA users. Figure 13.1 illustrates this concept,

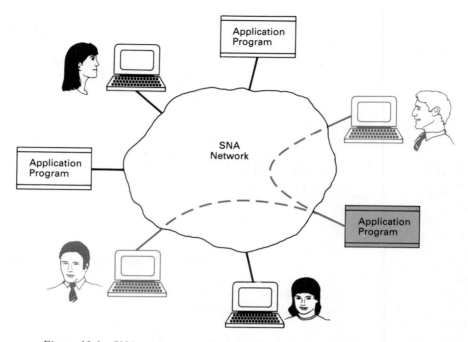

Figure 13.1 SNA users are people or application programs that use the services of an SNA network.

with the dotted lines representing logical interconnections that are implemented by the network between various network users.

LOGICAL UNITS

The primary purpose of an SNA network is to implement logical paths between users so that they can communicate with one another. To establish a virtual or logical connection with another user, each user must gain access to the SNA network. SNA defines *logical units* (LUs) that provide points of access through which users interact with the SNA network. A logical unit can be thought of as a *port* or *socket* into which a user plugs. An LU is not a *physical* port or plug but a *logical* one. SNA defines several logical unit types; each one provides *transmission capabilities* and a set of *services* that are related to a particular type of user.

Logical units are implemented in the form of software or microcode and reside in the various devices that make up an SNA network. Each logical unit type is identified by a number. Currently, seven major LU types are supported, identified by the numbers 0 through 7. (There is currently no type 5 logical unit.) The type 2 logical unit, for example, is designated as LU type 2, or simply as LU 2.

As the functions performed by the various logical units evolve, new versions of the supporting software are often released. For example, the capabilities of LU 6 have been enhanced over time, and its latest version is now known as LU 6.2. LU 6.2 is the logical unit type that currently has the most comprehensive set of defined capabilities; it is used to implement a set of functions collectively called *Advanced Program-to-Program Communication* (APPC). Figure 13.2 shows the relationship of network users to logical units. Logical units provide one user with the ability to communicate with another user without the two users having to know detailed information about each other's characteristics.

PHYSICAL UNITS

An SNA network consists physically of various types of devices and the communication links that connect them. The devices that typically make up a network are computing systems, various types of controllers, and terminal devices. Just as SNA users (people or programs) that use the network are not part of the architectural definition of SNA, neither are the actual devices and communication links that are used to implement the network. Instead SNA uses *physical units* (PUs) to *represent* actual devices. A physical unit provides the services needed to manage and use a particular type of device and to handle any physical resources, such as com-

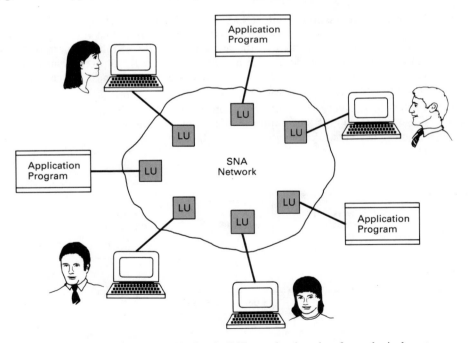

Figure 13.2   An SNA logical unit (LU) can be thought of as a logical port or socket into which a user plugs.

munication links, that may be associated with it. A physical unit is implemented with some combination of hardware, software, and microcode within the particular device that the physical unit represents.

**SYSTEM SERVICE
CONTROL POINTS**
In addition to logical units and physical units, an SNA network also has entities called *system service control points* (SSCPs). A system service control point provides the services needed to *manage* an SNA network (or some portion of it) and to establish and control the interconnections that are necessary to allow network users to communicate with one another. Thus an SSCP has a broader function than a logical unit, which represents a single user, or a physical unit, which represents a physical device and its associated resources.

SNA COMPONENTS
The components that make up an SNA network can be divided into two major categories, each of which consists of hardware, software, and microcode contained within the devices that make up the network. Figure 13.3 shows the relationships between these two major categories:

- **Network Addressable Units (NAUs).** An NAU consists of all the logical units, physical units, and system service control points that reside in a single network device. NAUs provide the services necessary to move data through the network from one user to another and to allow the network to be controlled and managed. Each network addressable unit has a *network address* that identifies it to the other NAUs in the network.
- **Path Control Network.** The path control network consists of lower-level components that control the routing and the flow of data through the network and handles the physical transmission of data from one device in the network to another.

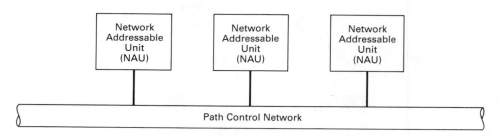

Figure 13.3 The components that make up an SNA network can be divided into two major categories: network addressable units (NAUs) and the path control network.

SNA NODES   An *SNA node* is a device that contains one or more network components. An SNA node contains an SNA physical unit to represent the node to the network. If the node has application programs or terminal devices that offer users access to the network, the node also contains one or more logical units that represent those programs or terminals. At least one SNA node in the network must contain an SSCP. If a node does not contain an SSCP, it contains a *physical unit control point* (PUCP). A PUCP implements a subset of SSCP functions that are needed to activate or deactivate the node. Each node also contains path control network components that provide the services needed to enable the node to link to and communicate with other nodes. Figure 13.4 shows the relationship between SNA nodes and the various SNA components.

Each terminal, controller, or computing system that conforms to SNA specifications and contains SNA components can be a node in an SNA network. These nodes, along with the transmission links that connect them and any peripheral devices attached to them, are the *physical building blocks* of SNA. They contain the network service and control capabilities required both to operate the network and to handle information exchange between network users. An SNA network can contain several types of nodes, which can be divided into two major categories: *peripheral nodes* and *subarea nodes*. Figure 13.5 shows these two major node types.

Peripheral Nodes

A peripheral node communicates directly only with the subarea node to which it is attached. For example, the two peripheral nodes attached to subarea node A in Fig. 13.5 cannot communicate directly with each other, nor can they communicate directly with other subarea or peripheral nodes in the network; they

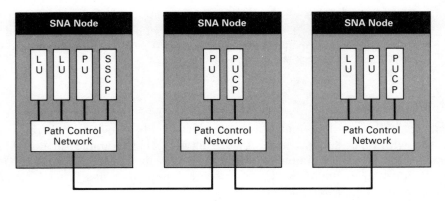

Figure 13.4   Each SNA node can contain various SNA components: logical units (LU), physical units (PU), system service control points (SSCP), and physical unit control points (PUCP).

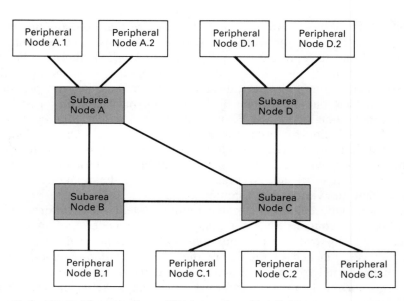

Figure 13.5 The nodes in an SNA network can be divided into two categories: subarea nodes and peripheral nodes.

can exchange data directly only with subarea node A. In order for a peripheral node to exchange data with other nodes in the network, it must do so through its subarea node. Peripheral nodes often take the form of *cluster controllers*. There are two types of peripheral nodes:

- **Type 2 Nodes.** Type 2 nodes have greater processing capabilities than type 1 nodes and are typically user-programmable. Most of IBM's newer terminal systems are implemented as type 2 nodes.

- **Type 1 Nodes.** Type 1 nodes have fewer capabilities than type 2 nodes and are typically not user-programmable. Many of IBM's older and less powerful terminals and controllers are implemented as type 1 nodes.

Subarea Nodes

A subarea node is a node that can communicate with its own peripheral nodes and also with other subarea nodes in the network. For example, in Fig. 13.5, subarea node A can communicate directly with subarea node B and subarea node C. It can also communicate with subarea node D by going through subarea node C. Subarea nodes are also of two types:

- **Type 5 Nodes.** A type 5 node is a subarea node that contains an SSCP. A type 5 node is often a mainframe computer and is sometimes called a *host node*.

- **Type 4 Nodes.** A type 4 node is a subarea node that does not contain an SSCP. A type 4 node is typically a communications controller and is often called a *communications controller node*.

Physical Unit Type

An SNA node contains a physical unit that represents the device and its resources to the network. A physical unit is given the same *type designation* as its corresponding node type. Thus each physical unit in the network is one of four possible types:

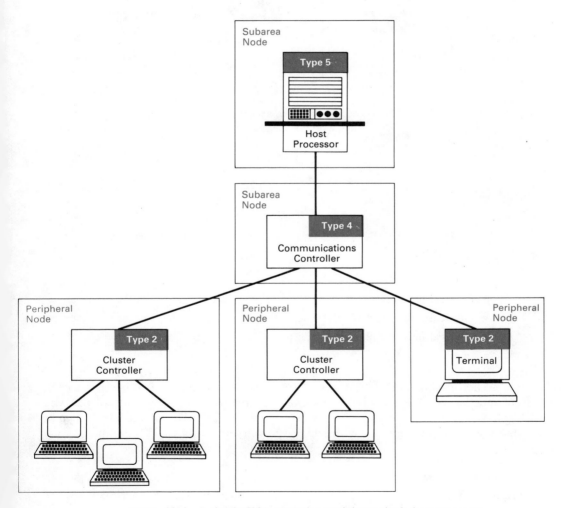

Figure 13.6   A simple SNA network containing a single host processor.

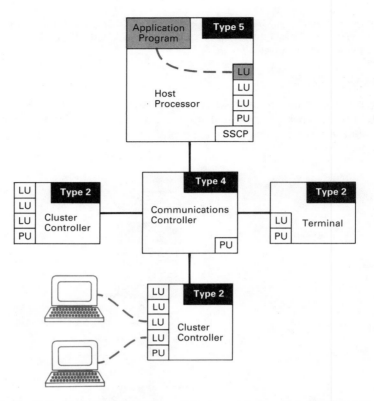

Figure 13.7 Each network node contains one or more network addressable units (NAUs).

- Physical unit type 5 (PU type 5, or PU 5)
- Physical unit type 4 (PU type 4, or PU 4)
- Physical unit type 2 (PU type 2, or PU 2)
- Physical unit type 1 (PU type 1, or PU 1)

The architectural definitions of the various physical unit types have been enhanced as SNA has evolved. For example, the most recent version of the type 2 physical unit is known as PU type 2.1, or PU 2.1. This is the physical unit that is used in conjunction with LU 6.2 in implementing APPC facilities.

A SIMPLE SNA NETWORK

Figure 13.6 shows a simple SNA network. At the top of the figure is a host node (type 5) that manages the network. Connected to the host node is a communi-

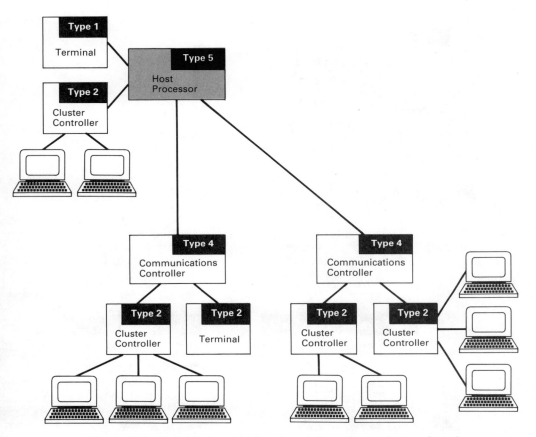

Figure 13.8 A single-domain network contains only one host node and a single system service control point (SSCP).

cations controller node (type 4). There are three peripheral nodes (type 2) attached to the communications controller. Two of the peripheral nodes have terminal devices attached to them; the other peripheral node has a terminal integrated within it.

Figure 13.7 shows the various NAUs that might be contained in the network from Fig. 13.6. The host node contains the SSCP, which provides network management and user interconnection functions. Each of the nodes contains a physical unit (PU), which represents the device and its resources to the network. Some of the nodes also contain logical units (LUs) that provide users with access to the network. Users of this network include the terminal users shown at the bottom of the diagram and the application program running in the host node. As indicated in the diagram, some nodes are capable of supporting concurrent users and thus will contain several logical units.

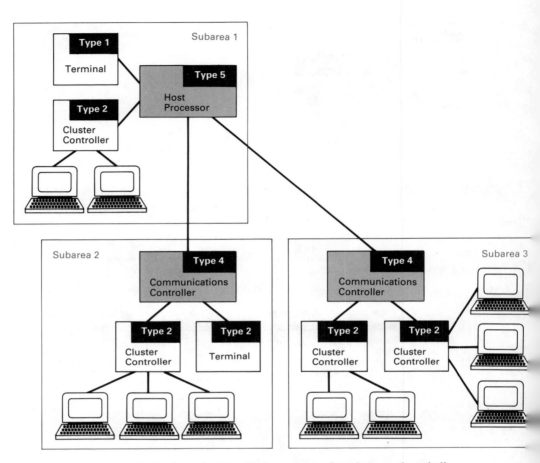

Figure 13.9 Each subarea in a domain is made up of a subarea node and all
the resources it controls.

**DOMAINS AND
SUBAREAS**

Figure 13.8 shows the structure of a somewhat more
complex SNA network. In this network, there is a
single host node, two communications controller
nodes, and six peripheral nodes. All of the devices and nodes (with their resi-
dent NAUs) shown in Fig. 13.8 constitute a single *domain* managed by the host
node. A domain is defined as *the set of SNA resources known to and managed
by an SSCP*. A domain typically consists of numerous *subareas*. A subarea is
defined as one subarea node and all the resources it controls. Figure 13.9 shows
the three subareas that make up the domain from Fig. 13.8.

MULTIPLE-DOMAIN
NETWORKS

The simplest SNA networks have only one domain and consequently only one host node. But this is not the case for all SNA networks; many SNA networks contain several domains. The network shown in Fig. 13.10, for example, has seven domains, each of which is managed by a type 5 host node having its own SSCP. Notice that domains C, D, E, and G do not have communication controllers, and domain C consists of a host node with no subordinate nodes.

When an SNA network consists of multiple domains, a terminal attached to one host processor is able to communicate with an application program running in some other host processor in the network. For example, a terminal in domain A could communicate with an application program running in the host processor in domain C. The host processor in domain A is involved only in establishing a connection between the terminal and the host node. Once the connection is established, the terminal is free to communicate with the program running in the host processor in domain C without any further involvement of the host processor in domain A.

NETWORK
ADDRESSES

The SNA software uses a system of network addresses in establishing connections, or *paths,* between logical units. Each network addressable unit—physical unit, logical unit, or SSCP—has a *network address* that uniquely identifies it within the network. In addition, each network addressable unit has a *network name*. Typically, network users refer to NAUs by network name rather than by network address. The SSCP translates each network name into its corresponding network address. The use of network names helps to shield users from changes that might occur in the physical or logical structure of the network.

SNA
COMMUNICATION
LINKS

As we have seen, messages are passed from one node to the next across a *communication link* that connects the two nodes. There are two types of communication links that can connect nodes. For nodes that are close together (in the same room or the same building), the link can be implemented by a cable that is connected to one of the computing systems' I/O channels. SNA includes protocols that can be used to control data transmission over an I/O channel. If the nodes are far apart, conventional data communication facilities are used to implement the link, such as a voice-grade line or other telecommunications facility.

Data transmission over a telecommunications link is controlled by the Syn-

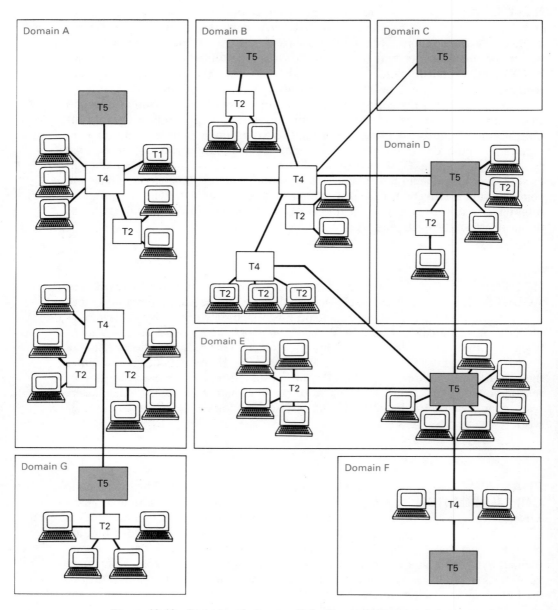

Figure 13.10 Each domain in a multiple-domain SNA network is managed by a host node with its own system service control point (SSCP).

chronous Data Link Control (SDLC) protocol that is defined as part of SNA (see Chapter 9). Although SDLC is the standard SNA data link protocol, other protocols, such as the older binary-synchronous protocol, are supported in certain situations.

SESSIONS

A fundamental concept of SNA is that no communication takes place between network addressable units until a *session* is established between them. Some types of sessions are permanent and are automatically established when the network is brought into operation; they remain established as long as the network is operational. Other types of sessions are dynamic; they are established as required and are broken when they are no longer needed.

At any given moment on an SNA network, it is likely that many concurrent sessions will be established. Many of these separate sessions may share the same physical devices and communication links. For example, a logical unit in a host processor or in a cluster controller might be involved in several sessions at one time. A logical unit located in a terminal device, by contrast, normally participates in only one session at a time with another logical unit.

The most fundamental type of session is one established between two log-

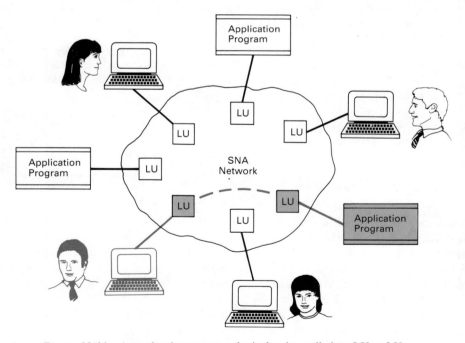

Figure 13.11   A session between two logical units, called an LU-to-LU session, allows two SNA users to communicate via the network.

BOX 13.1   SNA session types

- **LU-to-LU Sessions.** This is the type of session that fulfills the primary purpose of an SNA network. An LU-to-LU session allows users of the network to communicate with each other. LU-to-LU sessions are typically established dynamically as given pairs of users have the need to communicate.

- **SSCP-to-SSCP Sessions.** This type of session applies only to multiple-domain networks. All required SSCP-to-SSCP sessions are normally established automatically when the network is initialized and remain established as long as cross-domain communication between LUs is allowed. SSCP-to-SSCP sessions allow control information to be exchanged between the various host nodes in the network.

- **SSCP-to-PU Sessions.** An SSCP must be permanently in session with each of the PUs in its domain, and these sessions are normally established automatically when the network is initialized. The network administrator can make a particular PU temporarily unavailable by terminating its SSCP-to-PU session. SSCP-to-PU sessions allow control information to be exchanged between the SSCP and the PUs in its domain.

- **SSCP-to-LU Sessions.** An SSCP must also be permanently in session with each of the LUs in its domain. An SSCP-to-LU session must be established before an LU can be accessed by a network user. In most cases, an SSCP-to-LU session is established for each LU when the network is initialized. As with PUs, the network administrator can make an LU temporarily inactive by terminating a particular SSCP-to-LU session.

- **PU-to-PU Sessions.** No specific session types are defined for communication between PUs; however, adjacent PUs may need to exchange network control information. This may need to be done, for example, to transfer a control program from a host processor to a cluster controller or to perform certain activation, deactivation, or testing functions.

ical units; this type of session allows the network users they represent to communicate with each other by means of the network. Figure 13.11 demonstrates this concept, with the dashed line representing the session that has been established between a terminal user and an application program. In addition to sessions between logical units, four other types of sessions can be in operation in the network. Box 13.1 describes all five types of SNA sessions.

An LU-to-LU session is logically similar to a telephone call between two people. To set up a telephone call between myself and you, all I need to know is your telephone number. Assuming that we are both SNA users and have logical units that represent us in the network, all I need to know in order to set

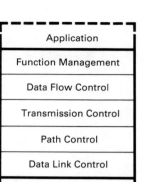

Figure 13.12 A physical control layer runs beneath the data link control layer, and an application layer runs above the function management layer; both are defined outside the SNA architecture.

up an SNA session with you is the network name of your logical unit. In neither case does either of us have to know where the other party is physically. Nor do we have to know how the communication is taking place. The user of an SNA network is no more aware of the complexities of the computer network than a telephone user is aware of the complexities of the telephone system; the network is transparent to the user.

SNA FUNCTIONAL LAYERS

As we saw in Chapter 12, a basic concept underlying network architectures is the division of network functions into well-defined functional layers. As with the OSI model, the functions of SNA are broken into layers, with each layer providing a different group of services. Box 13.2 illustrates the five major SNA functional layers and briefly describes the functions of each.

Operating below SNA's lowest layer, as shown in Fig. 13.12, is a still lower-level layer generally called the *physical control layer*. The physical control layer addresses the transmission of bit streams over a physical circuit. The SNA architecture itself does not define the functions that are performed in the physical control layer and does not specify methods of transmitting bits. Various methods of physical transmission can be employed in an SNA network, including computer channels, telephone lines, satellite links, and microwave transmission.

We can think of a higher-level layer, generally called the *application* layer, operating above function management. The application layer represents the users—the application programs and the people that interface with the SNA network. Although this layer is important, it is defined outside the SNA architecture.

BOX 13.2   SNA functional layers

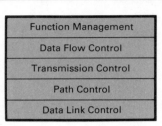

| Function Management |
| Data Flow Control |
| Transmission Control |
| Path Control |
| Data Link Control |

- **Data Link Control.** This layer is responsible for the transmission of data between two nodes over a particular physical link. A primary function of the data link control layer is to detect and recover from the transmission errors that inevitably occur.

- **Path Control.** This layer is concerned with routing data from one node to the next in the path that a message takes through the network. In a complex network, this path often passes over many separate data links through several nodes and may cross several domains.

- **Transmission Control.** This layer keeps track of the status of sessions that are in progress, controls the pacing of data flow within a session, and sees that the units of data that make up a message are sent and received in the proper sequence.

- **Data Flow Control.** This layer is concerned with the overall integrity of the flow of data during a session between two network addressable units. This can involve determining the mode of sending and receiving, managing groups of related messages, and determining what type of response mode to use.

- **Function Management.** This layer performs services for the users of the SNA network and is divided into the following sublayers:

    Function Management Data Services. The services performed by this sublayer include coordinating the interface between the network user and the network, presenting information to the user, and controlling the activities of the network as a whole.

    NAU Services Manager. This sublayer provides services to the function management data services sublayer below it and also to the data flow control and transmission control layers below the function management layer.

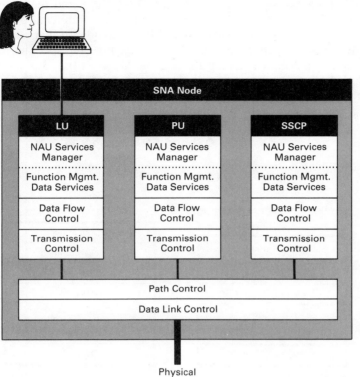

Figure 13.13   Component structure of an SNA node.

SNA LAYERS AND NETWORK COMPONENTS   Figure 13.13 shows how the SNA functional layers relate to the two major SNA components—the network addressable units (NAUs) and the path control network. The NAUs are implemented in the top three layers: function management, data flow control, and transmission control. The services of these layers are primarily concerned with enabling network users to send and receive data through the network and assisting network operators in controlling and managing the network. The path control network component encompasses the bottom two layers: the path control layer and the data link control layer. These layers are concerned with controlling the routing and flow of data through the network and the transmission of data from one node to another.

SNA AND THE OSI MODEL   As we have seen, both SNA and the OSI model use a layered approach to their architectures, and in large part their definitions include similar services. However, there are many differences in the services that are specified and in how the services are distributed among the various layers. Box 13.3 shows how the SNA and OSI layers compare.

BOX 13.3   OSI and SNA compared

SNA	OSI
Application	
Function Management	Application
Data Flow Control	Presentation
Transmission Control	Session
Path Control	Transport
Data Link Control	Network
Physical Control	Data Link
	Physical

- **SNA Function Management.** SNA's function management layer corresponds roughly to the combination of the application layer and the presentation layer in the OSI model. As part of the OSI application layer, a set of application management services are defined; these relate to the management of OSI application processes. In SNA, the management of applications is left to the applications that interface with SNA and is not defined as part of the SNA architecture. However, both SNA and the OSI model include definitions of services related to the overall management of network resources and to the monitoring of their status. In addition to management services, both the OSI model and SNA provide services that relate to the establishment and maintenance of sessions between network users and the formatting and presentation of data.

- **SNA Data Flow Control.** The data flow control layer in SNA is analogous to the session layer in the OSI model. These layers are primarily concerned with the integrity of the overall data flow. These services involve determining and managing the interactions involved in the transmission. These roughly comparable layers also demonstrate how SNA and the OSI model sometimes differ in the way in which services are

BOX 13.3   *(Continued)*

assigned to layers. Two of the services included in the OSI session layer—exception reporting and security—have their counterparts in the transmission control layer in SNA and not in the data flow control layer.

- **SNA Transmission Control.** There is also a rough correspondence between the SNA transmission control layer and the OSI transport layer. Here again there are a number of parallel services, and also a few differences. Monitoring of the quality of service, which is part of the transport layer in the OSI model, finds its counterpart in virtual route control, which is part of SNA's path control layer.

- **SNA Path Control.** The services provided by the network layer of the OSI model are similar to those performed by SNA's path control layer. These services provide transfer of data in a way that makes the physical network structure transparent to the higher layers.

- **Data Link Control.** The OSI data link layer provides the services involved in controlling the transmission of data over a specific physical link. The corresponding SNA services are provided by the data link control layer. SNA uses the Synchronous Data Link Control (SDLC) protocol at this layer, which is effectively a subset of HDLC.

- **The Physical Layer.** The physical layer in the OSI model, which is responsible for the transmission of bits across a physical medium, does not have a counterpart in SNA. Rather than explicitly defining this layer, SNA assumes that this layer is defined outside the SNA architecture using various international standards.

Although we have seen that SNA and the OSI model are quite different, the two architectures need not be viewed as competitive. SNA is an architecture designed to allow IBM to develop a wide range of hardware and software products that can be easily interconnected to form complex networks. The OSI model defines an architecture that is best suited for interconnecting what might otherwise be incompatible systems. The OSI model and its associated standards can be used as a basis for developing individual networks; however, the OSI model can also be used as a basis for interconnecting dissimilar networks.

For example, the OSI model might be used to define architectural guidelines for interconnecting an SNA network with other networks. Moreover, IBM offers support of the CCITT *X.21* and *X.25* recommendations within the SNA product line. It is likely that the SNA and OSI architectures will become more complementary as the two architectures evolve. For example, the protocols used by SNA's Advanced Program-to-Program Communications (APPC) functions have been adopted as one of the standards for the higher-level layers of the OSI model. The APPC protocols are the protocols used with SNA LU 6.2 and PU 2.1 that govern the way intelligent machines communicate in a network.

SNA SOFTWARE   So far we have examined SNA as an architecture that
PRODUCTS   defines formats and protocols independent of any particular product. Next we will look at the key IBM software products used to implement SNA networks. The types of products we will look at fall into the following four categories:

- Telecommunications access methods
- Network control programs
- Application subsystems
- Network management programs

Telecommunications Access Methods

As discussed in Chapter 10, telecommunications access method software resides in a host processor and provides an interface between the host processor and other resources in the network. Figure 13.14 shows the relationship between an SNA telecommunications access method and SNA components. The SSCP in the host node is contained within the access method. Likewise, the host processor physical unit and path control network components are all part of the access method. The logical units are implemented partially within the access method

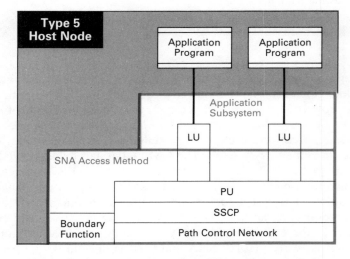

Figure 13.14 Component structure of an SNA telecommunications access method.

and partially within either an application subsystem (described later) or an application program. The three primary SNA telecommunications access methods, discussed in Chapter 10, are ACF/TCAM, ACF/VTAM, and ACF/VTAME.

Network Control Programs

Network control programs (NCPs) are the software subsystems that run in communications controllers. The primary SNA network control program is called Advanced Communication Function for Network Control Program (ACF/NCP). ACF/NCP interfaces with the SNA access method in the host processor to control communication across the network. Figure 13.15 shows how SNA components are incorporated in ACF/NCP. ACF/NCP controls the physical operation of the links in a network and performs routine transmission functions. It also performs bit assembly and disassembly, code translation, polling, routing, error recovery, line tests, device tests, and other physical management functions.

Application Subsystems

SNA application subsystems are generally either transaction processing systems or interactive support systems. Typical SNA transaction processing systems include CICS/VS, IMS/VS, DPPX/DMS, and ACP/TPF. Typical SNA interactive support systems are TSO, VSPC, and VM/VCNA. These systems interface with other SNA products and contain part of the code that implements logical units. Application programs or end users are then able to use the services of the application subsystem; through those services they have access to the SNA network.

A peripheral node typically contains a control program that is implemented in hardware, in software, or in a combination of the two. Figure 13.16 shows the relationships between an application subsystem and the control program in a peripheral node. The control program contains path control network compo-

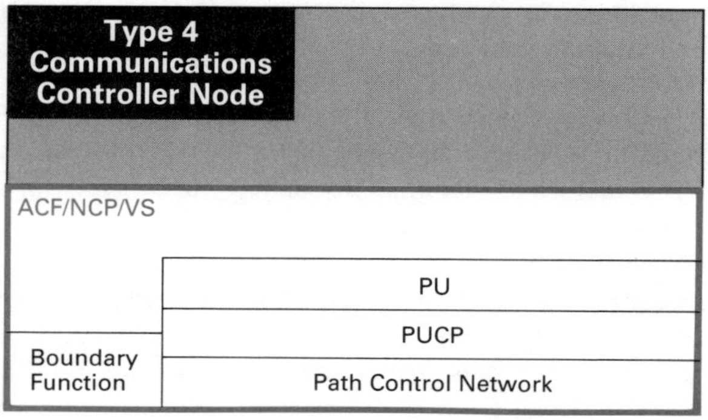

Figure 13.15 Component structure of an SNA network control program (NCP).

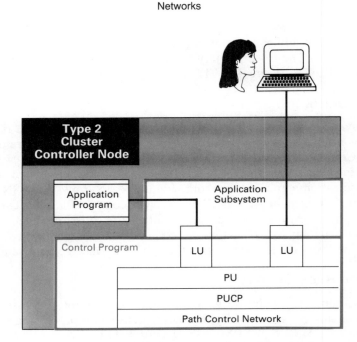

Figure 13.16   Component structure of a peripheral node.

nents, a PUCP, a physical unit, and portions of the code that implements logical units. The application subsystem contains the remainder of the logical unit implementation code. The logical units are then accessed via the application subsystem by either application programs or end users.

Network Management Programs

In addition to telecommunications access methods and network control programs, which support transmission of data throughout the network, there are also a number of application programs that provide network management functions.

- **Network Communication Control Facility (NCCF).** NCCF provides operator control for multiple-domain networks. With NCCF, a network operator can use a single terminal to issue commands to any host processor on the network. NCCF also provides facilities related to collecting, storing, and retrieving data about network errors.

- **Network Problem Determination Application (NPDA).** NPDA is designed to help with online problem determination. It does this by collecting, monitoring, and storing data that relates to network problems and then allowing network operators to display this data.

- **Network Logical Data Manager (NLDM).** NLDM collects information about sessions and routes and allows a central operator to examine that information to help in identifying network problems. NLDM also collects response-time data.

- **Netview.** Netview is a network management product that combines the capabilities of NCCF, NLDM, and NPDA, and provides a number of other functions as well. Netview is designed to make it easier to use these functions in an integrated manner and to provide network operators with greater flexibility in configuring and managing networks.

Other Program Products

The SNA programs we have described are those that play a key role in implementing SNA and are most directly involved with the transmission of data through the network. There are many other IBM program products, however, that are used in SNA networks. There are general-purpose programs, such as operating systems, utilities, and language processors, that are part of the overall computing environment. Many other programs are specifically designed to provide network management or support functions. For further information about SNA, see *SNA: IBM's Networking Solution* by James Martin and Kathleen K. Chapman (Englewood Cliffs, NJ: Prentice Hall, 1987).

Chapter 14 discusses public data networks that provide cost-effective alternatives to private networks. Chapter 14 also introduces the information utilities that can be accessed using public data networks.

14 PUBLIC DATA NETWORKS AND INFORMATION UTILITIES

During the mid-1970s, furious debates ensued among the major common carriers of the world about whether they should build a public data network, what form it should take, and how much they should spend on it. The common carriers and telecommunications administrations desired to provide better service to the computer community. They also perceived that a large revenue, which would grow to tens of billions of dollars worldwide, could go either to themselves or to the computer industry. This is the revenue from the switches, concentrators, multiplexors, polling equipment, line control equipment, and the like used in the interconnection of machines. Common carriers operate the equipment for switching and routing telephone calls; it seemed natural that they should operate the new equipment for switching and routing data.

As discussed in Chapter 7, two main types of switching can be used in creating public computer networks: *fast-connect circuit switching* and *packet switching*.

FAST-CONNECT CIRCUIT SWITCHING

A fast-connect circuit switching network establishes what is, in effect, a physical circuit between communicating machines. The circuit is set up rapidly under computer control; it remains set up while the data passes, which might take a second or less, and is then automatically disconnected so that other users can employ the same facilities. Think of a copper path, carrying electricity, that is set up for a second or so between the communicating machines and is then disconnected.

Circuit switching has been used for decades in telephone exchanges and in the worldwide telex network. The difference with computer networks is that the user circuit is set up and disconnected very quickly. The switched connection is often used only for the time it takes one message to pass, or for one message and an interactive response; sometimes it remains connected for the transmission of a batch of data.

A user of any circuit-switched network can encounter a network busy condition, just as there are busy signals from the telephone network when all circuits are in use. This is different from a packet-switched network in which no busy conditions occur. When a packet-switched network is overloaded, packet delivery time simply gets longer. The designer of a circuit-switched network adds trunks and switching facilities until a sufficiently low proportion of the calls encounter a network busy condition. The probability that an attempted call will be unsuccessful is a basic design parameter of a circuit-switched network. Because the call setup time is fast and most calls are brief, the unit that controls the user connection to the network can retry an unsuccessful call quickly and have a high probability of succeeding on a second attempt.

Fast-connect circuit switching has not been used as much as packet switching in setting up public data networks, although many fast-connect circuit switching networks are in operation.

PACKET SWITCHING

A packet switching network divides the data traffic into blocks, called *packets*. Each packet of user data travels in a data envelope that gives the destination address of the packet and a variety of control information. Each switching node reads the packet into its memory, examines the address, selects the next node to which it shall transmit the packet, and sends it on its way. The packets eventually reach their destination, where their envelopes are stripped off. Then they may have to be reassembled to form the original user messages. A packet switching network operates somewhat like a postal service in which letters in envelopes are passed from one post office to another until they reach their destination. The typical delivery time on today's packet networks is about a tenth of a second. Most of today's public data networks use packet switching techniques.

Most advanced nations now have one or more public packet switching networks. These are becoming interconnected into multinational networks so that packets can travel around the world. The major packet switching public data networks operating in the United States were described in Chapter 4 (see Box 4.3).

We might compare the various types of data networks with a railroad network. With circuit switching, there is an initial operation in which the switches are first set into the desired position. The switches then remain set, and the entire train travels to its destination over the same route. With packet switching, each of the cars of the train is sent separately. When each car arrives at a switch, the decision is made where to send it next. If the network is lightly loaded, the cars will travel to their destination by a route that is close to the optimum. If the network is heavily loaded, the cars may bounce around or take lengthy or zigzag paths, possibly arriving in a different sequence to that in which they departed.

PACKET SWITCHING AND MESSAGE SWITCHING

Packet switching is a form of *store-and-forward* switching. Messages are stored at the switch nodes and then transmitted onward to their destination. Store-and-forward switching has existed for decades in telegraphy message switching systems. Conventional message switching is intended primarily for non-realtime people-to-people traffic; packet switching is intended primarily for realtime machine-to-machine traffic, including terminal-to-computer connections. These differences in purpose are such that there are major differences in operation between message switching and packet switching systems.

NETWORK STRUCTURE

A typical packet switching network is shown in Fig. 14.1. A number of network nodes, each of which implements a specialized network computer called a

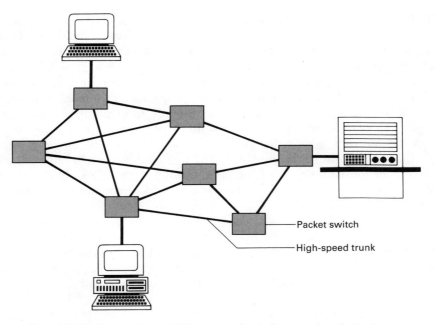

Figure 14.1 In a packet switching network, each network node implements a specialized computer called a packet switch. The packet switches are interconnected by means of high-speed trunks.

packet switch, are connected by means of point-to-point data links. When one user machine sends data to another, it first breaks long messages into pieces, adds control information to each piece to form a packet, and passes the packets to the packet switch at the local network node. Each packet contains the control information needed to transmit the data correctly, and the packets are transmitted from one packet switch to another until they reach their final destination. A packet switch receiving a packet places it in a queue to await attention. When a message reaches the head of the queue, the packet switch examines its destination address, selects the next packet switch on the route, and places the packet in an output queue for that destination. The final packet switch at the destination node passes the received packets to the destination user machine.

PACKETS

The packets might be thought of as envelopes into which data is placed. The envelope contains the destination address and various pieces of control information in the form of a header. The header contains such information as the destination address, the source address, and the packet number. The packet switches in the network do not interfere in any way with the data inside the envelopes.

PAD FUNCTION

Most packet switching networks can vary the routing of packets depending on network conditions. Because of this, it is possible that packets can arrive at their destinations out of sequence. Terminals that are attached directly to a public data network must have enough intelligence and storage to be able to break large messages into packets and to reassemble received packets into the proper sequence. A limited-function terminal that does not have the necessary intelligence to break up and reassemble messages can connect to and use the facilities of a packet switching network through the use of a device that performs a *packet assembly and disassembly* (PAD) function, as shown in Fig. 14.2. The PAD facility can be supplied either by the user or by the operator of the packet switching network. In many cases, the PAD function is performed by the same network computer that handles the packet switching function.

CONTROL FUNCTIONS

The transmission of packets through the network requires three types of control procedures: error control, routing control, and flow control.

- **Error Control Procedures.** Error control procedures are applied to each point-to-point link at the data link level, typically using a bit-oriented data link protocol. When a node receives a packet, it checks its accuracy using error-detecting bits.

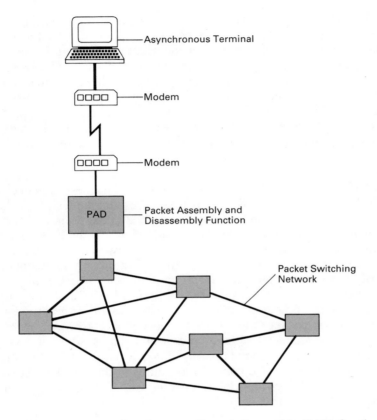

Figure 14.2   An external packet assembly and disassembly (PAD) function can be used to connect an asynchronous terminal to a packet switching network.

- **Routing Control Procedures.** When a packet switching computer receives a packet addressed to another location, it must determine to which of the neighboring nodes of the network it should be sent. The packet switch will have a programmed procedure for routing the packet. A variety of routing strategies are possible.

- **Flow Control Procedures.** Flow control helps avoid traffic jams by preventing too many packets from converging on certain parts of the network. Traffic congestion can be harmful because packets bounce around from node to node, occupying an excessive share of the transmission capacity. The network performance degenerates out of proportion to the increased load, like the roads out of a large city at rush hour.

DATAGRAMS

Because of the extra processing associated with message reassembly, two types of packet switching have evolved. The first handles multipacket messages and has protocols that permit error-free message *assembly* without causing traffic jams. The second handles only single-packet messages, called *datagrams,* and hence avoids complex protocols that increase the network overhead. In a datagram service, users can send messages up to but not exceeding the maximum capacity of one packet. A datagram service is offered as a lower-cost option on some public data networks that also support multipacket messages for users that require them.

NETWORK TRANSPARENCY

It is the intention of the designers of packet switching networks to make the communication techniques as unobtrusive as possible to the users. The network operation should be *independent* of the nature of the computing operations that employ the network. The network should connect two computer processes, perhaps thousands of miles apart, as though they were directly interconnected. This illusion of direct interconnection is referred to as *network transparency.* To make the network appear transparent, the transmission must be fast and the software must hide the complexity of its operations from the process that uses the network. Many packet switching networks define a *network virtual terminal,* which has its own character set and control procedures. The network may then allow a wide variety of incompatible machines to be connected to the network by converting their codes and control procedures to those of the network virtual terminal. This enables customers to interact with a large variety of terminal types without special software having to be written for each.

CCITT RECOMMENDATION X.25

Of particular importance to the technology of packet switching is a recommendation of the CCITT called *Recommendation X.25.* CCITT *Recommendation X.25* defines a standard interface between a packet-switched data network and any user machine connected to that network. Many terminals, computers, and other data communication products have been designed to conform exactly to this interface. All these devices can be successfully attached to a variety of networks in different countries that conform to CCITT *Recommendation X.25.* As shown in Fig. 14.3, *Recommendation X.25* documents standards and protocols that conform to the specifications for the first three layers of the OSI model (physical, data link, and network). *X.25* defines the interface between a user machine that operates in the packet mode and a packet switching network.

An *X.25* network provides a number of useful services for its users, including *permanent virtual circuits* and *virtual calls.*

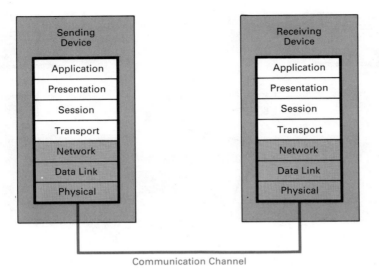

Figure 14.3   CCITT *Recommendation X.25* documents standards for the first three layers of the OSI model.

- **Permanent Virtual Circuits.** A public data network user may wish to be permanently connected to another network user, in much the same way that two users are connected using a leased telephone connection. A permanent virtual circuit, illustrated in Fig. 14.4, provides this facility. The users are permanently connected to their respective network computers. They use the actual communication facilities of the network only when they are actually transmitting data; however, they remain permanently connected as though a physical circuit linked them. Typically, the user of a permanent virtual circuit pays a monthly connect fee plus a charge based on total data transmitted. Users of public data networks are not ordinarily charged on the basis of distance. One of the advantages of using a public data network is that it costs no more to send a message between New York and Los Angeles than it does to send a message across town.

- **Virtual Calls.** When making a virtual call, a user logs onto the network, establishes a virtual circuit with another user, exchanges messages for a time, and then breaks off the connection. Users that make virtual calls are generally charged on the basis of connect time, quantity of data transmitted, or both. In making a virtual call or using a permanent virtual circuit, the user perceives no difference between using a public data network and using ordinary telephone facilities. All the complexities of packet assembly and disassembly and routing through the network are typically transparent to the user.

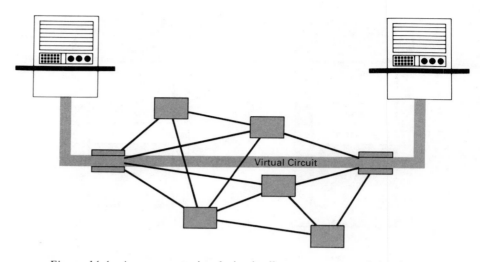

Figure 14.4   A permanent virtual circuit allows two users to have the appearance of a point-to-point permanent connection between them while using transmission capacity only when they are exchanging data.

X.25 PACKET FORMAT

As mentioned earlier, *Recommendation X.25* defines the interface between a user device operating in the packet mode and a packet switching network. This interface consists of a precise definition of the format to which each information packet must conform and the specifications of the various command packets that user machines send and receive to control how the network is used. Box 14.1 describes the format of an *X.25* packet.

The control information in each packet is used by the packet switches at each network node in determining which links to use in routing the packet through the network. As a packet moves through the network, each node places the packet inside a transmission frame in order to transmit it from one network node to the next. Frame transmission at the data link level is handled by one of two bit-oriented data link protocols: *Link Access Protocol* (LAP) or *Link Access Protocol—Balanced* (LAPB). These are functional subsets of the HDLC protocol defined by ISO. As far as the data link protocol is concerned, the information field of the packet and the four control fields are all treated as data as the packet moves across a single point-to-point link. This is shown in Fig. 14.5.

CONNECTIONS BETWEEN NETWORKS

Sometimes it is desirable to employ more than one type of network to achieve a given connection. A dialed telephone call can be made to access the concentrator of a packet-switched network. A multinational call can be set up involving a packet-switched network in one country

BOX 14.1   *X.25 Packet Format*

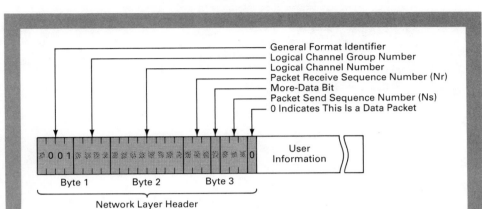

General Format Identifier
Logical Channel Group Number
Logical Channel Number
Packet Receive Sequence Number (Nr)
More-Data Bit
Packet Send Sequence Number (Ns)
0 Indicates This Is a Data Packet

Byte 1   Byte 2   Byte 3

User Information

Network Layer Header

All packets, both information packets and *X.25* commands, follow the same basic format. Each packet begins with 3 bytes that contain the following information:

- **General Format Identifier.** This specifies general information about the format of the packet. For example, this field indicates whether 3-bit or 7-bit sequence numbers are used for flow control.

- **Logical Channel Group.** Each user machine attached to the *X.25* network has one or more channel groups assigned to it. This field identifies which logical channel group is used to transmit this particular packet.

- **Logical Channel Number.** Each logical channel group is made up of up to 255 logical channels. This field identifies which logical channel is used to transmit this particular packet.

- **Packet Type Identifier.** This field identifies the packet's type. A *data packet* is used to contain part of the text of a message that is being transmitted through the network. Several types of *control packets* are used to transmit various types of network commands through the network.

and a circuit-switched network in another. Not all packet networks have identical formats, and messages may need to pass from one network to another.

To deal with network connections, interface machines are needed. The connection between different data networks is called a *gateway*. A gateway is typically implemented in the form of a small computer that appears to each network as though it were a normal node of the network. It takes data in the format of one network and translates it into the format expected by the other. The use of gateways is illustrated in Fig. 14.6.

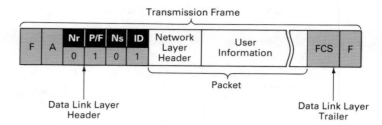

Figure 14.5 Each packet is enclosed in a transmission frame ''envelope'' for transmission from one packet switch to the next in the network.

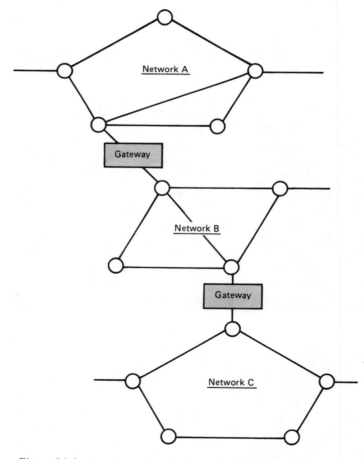

Figure 14.6 A gateway is a device used to interconnect networks.

INFORMATION UTILITIES

We use the term *information utilities* to refer to organizations that provide customers with access to information rather than simply access to data communication services. An information utility generally operates one or more host computers that store information in which their customers are interested. For example, an information utility might provide online access to such information as airline schedules, stock listings, or bibliographic reference data. An information utility might implement its own data network, possibly using packet switching, for connecting customer terminals to its host computers, or it might use one of the public data networks discussed earlier to provide basic communication facilities. Some information utilities offer both forms of access. Box 14.2 lists some of the more popular information utilities and describes the main services they offer.

THE FUTURE OF PUBLIC NETWORKS

Many organizations have announced an intention to build packet switching networks. As public data networks grow, there will continue to be arguments about the relative merits of packet switching and fast-connect circuit switching. It seems likely that the existing packet switching networks will steadily grow, acquiring more traffic and more nodes. When they become very large and ubiquitous, economies of scale may make some form of switched data network replace many of the private leased-line networks that corporations and government departments use today. Packet switching networks will probably evolve in several directions if their traffic grows sufficiently. Some of these future directions are listed in Box 14.3.

We can characterize the years ahead as an *era of great invention* in telecommunications. In an era of great invention, the users need to be protected from the proliferation of new mechanisms. Protection can come from appropriate standards and virtual techniques that make any form of network appear as though it used simple standard interfaces. Users ought to demand such protection, both nationally and internationally. Standards come into existence from government-supported organizations such as the CCITT. Manufacturers or designers, given appropriate standards and protocols, can then be free to invent all manner of ingenious new mechanisms using those standards and protocols.

The virtual call and virtual circuit recommendations of *X.25* relate to packet switching over terrestrial telephone circuits. This may be a dominant technology for a period of time, but, as we have seen, there are many other techniques and uses of telecommunications. If satellites, CATV, fast-connect circuit switching, packet radio, and other new technology play a major role in some countries, virtual operation is desirable, which makes links using these facilities appear to be the same as other types of links. As the transmission of facsimile documents, voice messages, video signals, music, and electronic mail

BOX 14.2 Popular information utilities

- **Bibliographic Research Services (BRS).** BRS offers access to bibliographic data and many full-text databases on more than 70 topics, including finance, business and management, engineering, medicine, physics, computer science, education, books in print, and government documents. BRS can be contacted at 1200 Route 7, Latham, NY 12110.

- **CompuServe Information Service.** CompuServe is a consumer-oriented information utility that provides access to a wide range of services, including airline schedules, financial information, corporate profiles, and news retrieval from newspapers and wire services. CompuServe has many entertainment services, including theater, book, movie, and restaurant reviews, interactive games, and advice columns. Various types of personal computer user groups engage in constant dialogs using computer conferencing services. CompuServe also operates an electronic mail service that is extensively used for sending messages. CompuServe can be contacted at 5000 Arlington Center Blvd., Columbus, OH 43220.

- **Dialog.** Dialog is another bibliographic service that offers access to over 200 databases that summarize data from thousands of publications. Subjects are divided into several major categories, including agriculture and nutrition, bibliography, business/economics, current affairs, education, energy and environment, foundations and grants, law and government, material sciences, medicine and biosciences, patents and trademarks, science and technology, social sciences and humanities. Dialog can be contacted at 3460 Hillview Avenue, Palo Alto, CA 94304.

- **Dow-Jones News Retrieval Service.** The Dow-Jones service is a general-interest information utility that provides a wide range of information services including airline schedules, news stories, the entire text of the *Wall Street Journal,* securities prices, company profiles and 10K extracts, and the complete text of the *Academic American Encyclopedia.* Dow-Jones can be contacted at P.O. Box 300, Princeton, NJ 08540.

- **Merlin Dial Data.** Merlin is an information utility that specializes in providing financial data covering the NYSE, AMEX, NASDAQ, and government issues exchanges, including current and historical information on the prices of stocks, bonds, rights, warrants, commodities, options, and indices. Merlin can be contacted at 1044 Northern Blvd., Roslyn, NY 11576.

- **The Source.** The Source is another consumer-oriented information utility that provides a broad range of information services, including airline schedules, financial information, entertainment services, travel services, news and sports, electronic games, and computer conferencing. The Source, like CompuServe, also offers an electronic mail service for sending and receiving messages.

BOX 14.3 Future directions of packet switching

- The high-speed digital links used by the telephone companies, such as the T1 carrier, will probably become the links used by packet switching networks. Transmission rates of millions of bits per second will permit systems with very fast response times to be built.

- To fill such high-speed links, the networks will have to attract a high traffic volume. Much of this traffic may come from relatively new uses of data communication, such as electronic mail, electronic funds transfer, and other forms of message delivery.

- As networks grow very large, it will be economical for them to become multilevel networks with a hierarchy of switching offices. Just as the telephone network has five classes of offices, so data networks might acquire two, three, and eventually more levels.

- Several classes of priority might be handled, including perhaps immediate delivery (a few milliseconds), 2-second delivery for interactive computing, delivery in minutes, and overnight delivery.

- Some message traffic might be *filed* as on a message switching system. Messages intended to be read on visual display units or spoken over the telephone might be filed until the recipient requests them. Distributed storage rather than centralized storage might be used, especially for bulky data, depending on the relative costs of storage and transmission. A hybrid between message switching and packet switching may thus emerge.

- Fast-connect circuit switching has advantages over packet switching for some types of traffic. The nodes of a large data network may be designed to select whether a circuit-switched or packet-switched path is used. A hybrid between circuit switching and packet switching may evolve.

- The user-interface computer may become separate from the packet switching computers and have an entirely different set of functions. It may be designed to convert the transmission of all terminals to a standard format, code, and protocol so that completely incompatible machines can be interconnected.

- User-interface devices may be designed to receive from and transmit to conventional facsimile machines or other analog devices.

- The interface machines may be designed to compress messages before transmission, to increase the transmission efficiency. This is valuable with data, but especially valuable with facsimile messages.

- Interface machines may be designed to handle packet radio terminals or controllers. Portable data terminals may be linked to the system.

- One of the most cost-effective data transmission facilities will be the satellite, and packet switching networks will probably use satellites. To use future satellites in an optimal fashion will substantially change the topology and protocols of packet switching networks.

(Continued)

BOX 14.3 *(Continued)*

- Economies of scale and flexibility may require that telephone or continuous-channel traffic and burst traffic be intermixed. Networks, especially satellite networks, capable of handling both continuous-channel and packet-switched traffic may emerge.

- An interlinking of separate national networks will occur. Satellites will interlink nodes in many countries, giving users of packet switching the capability to use computers around the world and to send messages worldwide.

- When vast numbers of computers are available on the networks, directory machines will be very important for enabling users to find the facilities they need.

assumes major importance, standards and forms of virtual circuits will be needed for them also.

Now that we have examined the characteristics of public data networks, Chapter 15 discusses the technology of *local area networks,* which allows intelligent machines to be interconnected using extremely high speed links.

15 LOCAL AREA NETWORKS

Most of the technology we have discussed so far in this book has been concerned with conventional data communication systems that most typically connect one or more general-purpose computing systems to large numbers of terminals. In these systems, individual data machines are connected using data links. The data machines and various point-to-point and multipoint data links can be combined to form complex networks. This chapter discusses a relatively new class of protocols that support a fundamentally different type of data communication facility. These protocols are used to implement *local area networks* (LANs). Box 15.1 lists the characteristics of local area networks that distinguish them from conventional data communication networks.

Figure 15.1 contrasts a conventional multipoint data link with a typical local area network. With the multipoint data link, a computer typically communicates with a number of relatively simple terminals. Communication is controlled by the computer, and transmission takes place at relatively slow speed only between the terminals and the computer. With the LAN, each device attached to the communication medium is a relatively intelligent machine, and any device attached to the LAN can communicate with any other device at very high speed.

RESOURCE SHARING

A major purpose of an LAN is to allow flexible resource-sharing networks to be created. Figure 15.2 shows a more detailed look at a typical LAN implementation. One of the stations attached to the LAN supports a high-capacity disk; another drives a high-speed printer. Other stations might be personal computers without disk or printer resources of their own. With appropriate networking software, each of the other stations on the LAN can have access to the high-capacity disk and the high-speed printer just as if it were directly attached to

BOX 15.1   LAN characteristics

- **Station Relationships.** With a typical LAN, all stations that access the common communication facility are peers on the network; there is generally no distinction made between primary stations and secondary stations.

- **Message Exchange.** A LAN is designed to give the appearance of supporting multiple message exchanges at any given time between various pairs of stations, although in actual practice only a single message can be transmitted at any given instant.

- **Transmission Speed.** Transmission speeds are very high, typically in the millions of bits per second.

- **Distance.** A LAN is designed to support communication over a limited geographical area, for example, within a building or a group of related buildings.

- **Transmission Medium.** A LAN typically uses private, user-installed wiring as the communication medium.

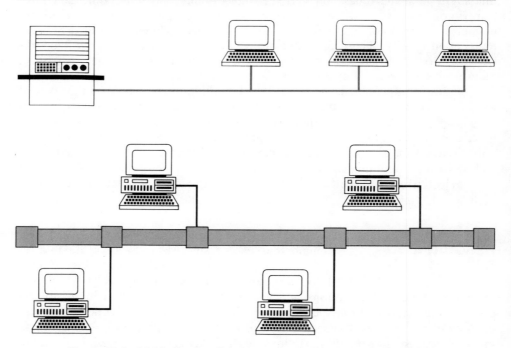

Figure 15.1   Multipoint data link (top) versus local area network (bottom).

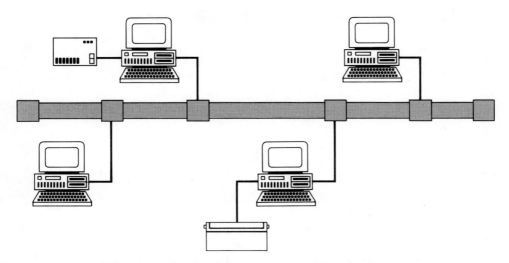

Figure 15.2 A local area network allows intelligent devices to be interconnected for the purposes of resource sharing

that station. The very high speed communication capability of the LAN allows data to be transmitted between stations in such a way that the communication medium itself appears transparent to the user of any station attached to the LAN.

CLASSIFYING LOCAL AREA NETWORKS

A great many hardware and software systems are available for implementing local area networks. All share the general characteristics just discussed, but all are implemented in different ways. In general, local area networks can be classified according to the following criteria:

- Network topology
- Transmission medium
- Transmission technique
- Access protocol

Network Topology

The network topology relates to the logical way in which stations are interconnected. The three major topologies are the *star,* the *ring,* and the *bus.* Box 15.2 describes them.

In many cases, a specific local area network implementation may use combinations of topologies to create hybrid configurations. Figure 15.3 shows an example of a *star-wired logical ring.* Notice that the topology is really that of

BOX 15.2 Network topologies

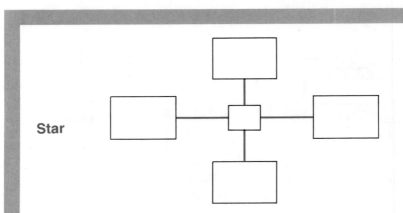

Star

With the star topology, all stations are connected through a central control point. Typical examples of control points are the wiring closets used with some systems or a PABX (private automatic branch exchange) used with systems that employ telephone-type equipment for interconnecting processors. The advantages of the star topology include ease of fault isolation and ease of bypassing and repairing faulty stations. A disadvantage is that the star topology requires more cable than most other topologies to interconnect all stations.

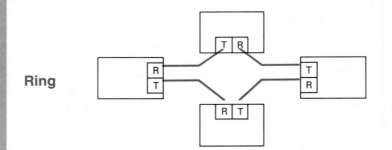

Ring

With a ring, each station is connected to the next one to form a closed loop. Each station has a transmitter and a receiver, and data is transmitted in one direction around the ring. Advantages of the ring include decreased distance sensitivity, since each station regenerates the signal, and ease of implementing distributed control and checking facilities. The disadvantages include sensitivity to station failures (a failed station might break the ring) and difficulty of adding and changing stations.

BOX 15.2 *(Continued)*

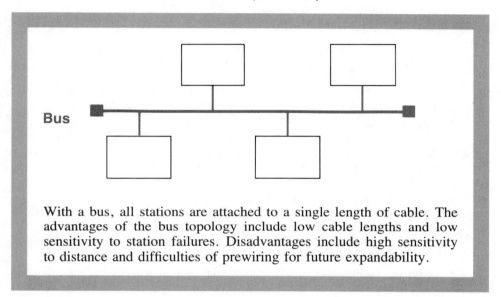

With a bus, all stations are attached to a single length of cable. The advantages of the bus topology include low cable lengths and low sensitivity to station failures. Disadvantages include high sensitivity to distance and difficulties of prewiring for future expandability.

a ring, but the wiring is installed in such a way that the topology physically resembles a star. Such a network might be constructed when cabling is installed using wiring closets, as is done when the IBM Cabling System is used to wire a building.

Transmission Medium

The second criterion by which local area networks can be classified is the type of transmission medium that is used to interconnect processors. Most local area networks use some form of cable to connect the various devices on the network, although LANs that use radio transmission are in use. Box 15.3 describes a few of the various types of media that are used in present-day local area networks.

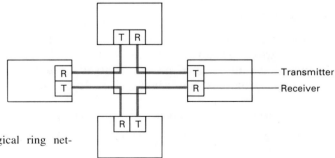

Figure 15.3 Star-wired logical ring network topology.

BOX 15.3   LAN transmission media

- **Unshielded Twisted Pair.** This is the ordinary twisted pair typified by conventional telephone wiring. Its major advantages include low cost and the fact that this type of medium is already installed throughout many existing facilities. Its major disadvantage is that it is typically limited to relatively low transmission speeds (a few megabits per second).

- **Shielded Multiple Twisted Pair.** With this medium, a number of individual twisted pairs are enclosed in a single cable with shielding. The individual twisted pairs are better isolated from noise and other disturbances, but each twisted pair is still limited to relatively low transmission speeds.

- **Coaxial Cable.** With a coaxial cable, a single central conductor is surrounded by an outer tubular conductor. An example of coaxial cable is the cable used to implement cable television systems. For data communication systems, coaxial cable is reasonable in cost and can support very high transmission speeds.

- **Twinaxial Cable.** This is similar to coaxial cable, but instead of a single central conductor, two central conductors are surrounded by an outer tubular conductor.

- **Fiber Optics.** A fiber-optic cable transmits a light beam rather than an electrical signal. Fiber-optic links provide an almost unlimited bandwidth that can support extremely high transmission speeds.

Transmission Technique

The third criterion for classifying local area networks is according to the method that is used for transmitting signals over the cable. There are basically two methods: *baseband* and *broadband*. Box 15.4 describes these two transmission techniques.

Access Protocol

The fourth and final way in which local area networks are classified is according to the protocol that governs the way individual stations access the transmission medium. Any number of access protocols can be devised, but the following three major protocols, described in Box 15.5, dominate the LAN marketplace:

- Carrier sense multiaccess with collision detection (CSMA/CD)
- Carrier sense multiaccess with collision avoidance (CSMA/CA)
- Token passing

BOX 15.4 LAN transmission techniques

- **Baseband.** When a baseband technique is used for transmitting signals, the entire cable is used to propagate a single digital signal. Depending on the transmission medium used, very high transmission speeds can be achieved. An example of a baseband local area network is Ethernet, in which stations communicate using a bus-structured network at approximately 10 million bps. The main advantage of the baseband technique is that interface units are simple and inexpensive; the main disadvantage is that the entire cable is allocated to a single channel.

- **Broadband.** When broadband techniques are used, information is transmitted over the cable in the form of radio-frequency signals. The bandwidth is normally divided into a number of individual channels, each of which is capable of carrying different types of information. An example of a broadband local area network is IBM's PCNET. With PCNET, the various channels can be allocated to computer data and video signals. The disadvantages of the broadband technique are that relatively expensive radio-frequency modems must be incorporated into the interface units and, depending on the distance, the broadband cable may be difficult to install and tune properly.

BOX 15.5 LAN access protocols

- **CSMA/CD.** With the CSMA/CD protocol, all stations attached to the network monitor the transmission medium at all times. When a station needs to transmit data, it waits until the line is quiet and then transmits. If two or more stations transmit at the same instant, a *collision* occurs. Each station detects the collision and then waits for a variable amount of time before testing the medium again and retransmitting. Since each station waits for a different amount of time, the probability is low that the collision will occur the second time.

- **CSMA/CA.** The CSMA/CA protocol is similar to CSMA/CD except that all stations implement an algorithm that helps to avoid collisions rather than simply detect when they occur and then retransmit.

- **Token Passing.** With the token-passing scheme, typically used on ring-structured networks, a special message called the *token* is passed from one station to the next around the ring. When a station receives the token, it either transmits a message, if it has a message to send, or it passes the unused token to the next station on the ring. Each station receives one chance to transmit during the time that it takes for the token to circulate around the ring.

The CSMA/CD protocol is the protocol used by Xerox in its Ethernet LAN, and token passing is used in many of the LAN products offered by IBM. The CSMA/CA protocol is used less often than the other two.

The CSMA/CD protocol is well suited for use with bus-structured networks. It works well because of the typically very high transmission speed of the LAN and because a very small percentage of the total transmission capacity is used. When traffic on the LAN increases, collisions begin to occur for an unacceptably large number of messages, and performance of the LAN degrades. However, many analyses have been done on typical Ethernet LAN implementations. These analyses have found that typical channel utilization even at peak times generally falls in the 10 percent or less category, and more than 99 percent of all transmissions take place without collisions.

With the token-passing protocol, a higher percentage of the total capacity of the medium can be effectively used before the performance of the LAN degrades. However, each station must wait its turn before transmitting, and thus token passing may be less efficient than the CSMA/CD protocol on networks that use a very low percentage of the total transmission capacity.

INTERNATIONAL LAN STANDARDS

An important set of standards for local area networks has been documented by the *Institute of Electrical and Electronics Engineers* (IEEE). The IEEE has published a comprehensive standards document that describes several recommended ways for implementing LANs. The IEEE LAN standards describe implementations of layers 1 and 2 of the OSI Reference Model discussed in Chap-

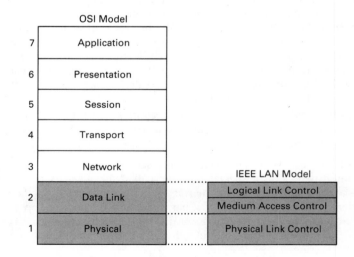

Figure 15.4   The IEEE 802 series of LAN standards pertains to the two lowest levels of the OSI model and divides the data link layer into two sublayers.

ter 12. The IEEE LAN model divides the OSI data link layer into two sublayers, as shown in Fig. 15.4. The *medium access control* sublayer performs the access function for the particular access control method employed by the network. Typical access control methods are the CSMA/CD and token-passing methods discussed earlier. The logical link control sublayer performs functions comparable to conventional data link protocols. These functions include framing, addressing, and error control. The following IEEE standards are important in the local area network marketplace:

- **IEEE Standard 802.2.** This standard describes the functions of the logical link control sublayer of the IEEE LAN architectures.

- **IEEE Standard 802.3.** This standard describes the medium access control sublayer and physical layer functions for a bus-structured network that uses CSMA/CD as an access protocol.

- **IEEE Standard 802.4.** This standard describes the medium access control sublayer and physical layer functions for a bus-structured network that uses the token-passing access protocol.

- **IEEE Standard 802.5.** This standard describes the medium access control sublayer and physical layer functions for a ring-structured LAN that uses token passing as an access protocol.

IEEE Standard 802.3, developed in cooperation with Xerox, describes the techniques used in implementing Ethernet LAN products. Ethernet is a widely used type of local area network, and Ethernet-compatible products are marketed by Xerox and a great many other LAN vendors.

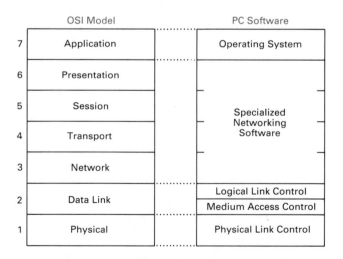

Figure 15.5 Typical implementation of local area network software on a personal computer.

Many of the token-ring LAN products that are marketed by IBM conform to IEEE Standard 802.5.

Figure 15.5 shows how a typical IBM personal computer implementation of a local area network fits into the OSI model. IEEE Standard 802.5 describes the functions that take place at layers 1 and 2, special networking software performs the functions of layers 3 through 6, and the personal computer's operating system runs at layer 7.

Chapter 16 begins Part V of this book, which discusses the design of systems that use data communication. Chapter 16 examines application design issues.

PART **V** DESIGN

16 APPLICATION DESIGN

The main purpose of this chapter is to introduce the steps that are involved in designing application software for data transmission systems and to put into perspective the various tasks that are involved in the design process. Box 16.1 lists the major steps that are involved in the design of a computer system that uses data transmission. In this chapter, we will examine these steps and discuss some of the factors that affect the designer's choices.

THE USER INTERFACE

A first and major factor in the design of a data transmission system is whether the system is designed for human terminal operators. If it is for batch transmission, telemetry, intercomputer communication, or other interlinking of mechanical devices, the design decisions that must be made all depend on technical issues. But where human operators generate the input or carry on a dialog with the system, the psychology and needs of these users will have a major effect on design decisions. The starting point in the design of such a system should be concern for the design of the user interface.

Users come in a variety of types. Some can program; some cannot. Some may be highly trained; some are casual users. Some are highly intelligent; some are less so. Some have a natural ability to communicate with computers; some have only to sit at a terminal for a form of paralysis to set in. (Worse, some seem to cause paralysis in the system itself!)

There is a big difference between a factory worker entering data into a shop-floor terminal and a statistician entering data into a spreadsheet using a personal computer. There is also a difference between an airline ticketing agent sorting out changes in a passenger's itinerary and a high-level manager trying to sort out changes in a customer's order. Airline agents spend the entire day operating terminals; managers, if they operate terminals at all, only do so oc-

BOX 16.1   Steps in data communication system design

1. Determine the needs of the users.
2. Determine the types of messages that will be transmitted.
3. Determine traffic volumes.
4. Establish response-time criteria.
5. Plan the terminal considerations.
    a. Determine terminal locations.
    b. Establish desirable terminal characteristics.
    c. Determine the number of terminals per location.
    d. Determine whether dial-up procedures are required.
    e. Design the user interface.
    f. Determine the number of characters to be transmitted.
6. Resolve network considerations.
    a. Determine locations of intelligent machines.
    b. Determine network structures.
    c. Determine networking software requirements.
    d. Choose network equipment.
7. Build models of a single communication path.
8. Establish a traffic rate table.
9. Establish minimum-cost geographical layout of lines.
10. Make refinements to the network.

casionally in the midst of harassing schedules. These differences will lead to differences in the structure of the user interface. The structures of various types of user interfaces differ *very* widely from system to system. Furthermore, in the future, when more varied communication facilities are available, they will differ still more.

The type of user interface designed has a major influence on the design of the data transmission facilities. If the communication lines are long, and perhaps expensive, this factor may be a constraining one on the permissible user-interface structures. Conversely, some effective but seemingly expensive user interface structures can be employed by restructuring the communication network to make use of intelligent communications controllers, cluster controllers, and concentrators. The considerations of user psychology, then, can affect all aspects of the network design.

OPERATOR ERRORS

All terminal operators make errors occasionally. The errors may be particularly serious if an operator is entering data that is then used for further processing or that resides in the system's files or databases. The percentage of errors made can be affected to a major degree by the structure of the user interface. Once again there is an important relationship between psychological factors and system design.

Where the operators enter data, it is particularly important that facilities for correcting their errors be well thought out. If possible, the system should be designed to catch an error at the time it is made. An error message can then be sent immediately to the operator. In cases where the operator does not have an interactive terminal (as at many factory data collection terminals), errors may be referred later to a special operator or staff with facilities to correct them.

THIRD-PARTY OPERATORS

Where a system is designed to provide information, the persons needing the information need not necessarily operate the terminal. There are a variety of circumstances in which it would be better if they did not. These circumstances are not always recognized by the systems analyst. First, giving everyone terminals may be too expensive. Second, the job of obtaining adequate results from the terminal may be too difficult for the people in question. Systems analysts often tend to overestimate the ability of untrained people to operate terminals. Young people learn to operate them easily, but people set in their ways often do not, particularly when, as is the case with many managers, they cannot afford the time and patience needed to learn. Third, it may be desirable, for security reasons, to allow only certain authorized individuals to operate the terminals.

Where a system is designed to gather information as well as to provide it, the same arguments apply. Sometimes it is even more necessary that the data residing in the files for commercial use be entered by a person trained to be accurate rather than by someone who uses the terminal infrequently.

The people, then, who do not operate a terminal may gain access to a computer either by having assistants who do operate one or by contacting specialist terminal operators. They may obtain information in this way, or they may cause information to be entered into the system. This is exactly what you do when you telephone an airline to make a reservation. You speak to a specialist terminal operator who obtains details of flights and seat availability for you. You need not have access to a terminal yourself to make a reservation (although airline schedules can be consulted and seats can be booked by anyone with access to one of the major information utilities, such as The Source of CompuServe). The same reasoning can apply to management and other persons in an organization who will interact with an information system.

SECURITY

A subject related to the users of the system that will be of increasing concern in data processing is security. Many files and databases contain data that organizations wish to keep confidential. Files and databases also store a wide variety of personal information about private individuals. Keeping such information out of the reach of unauthorized personnel is extremely important. Still more important is the need to prevent unauthorized persons from changing data in the files; otherwise a rich variety of new forms of embezzlement and sabotage would be possible. Many techniques are available for maintaining security. An interlinking set of measures that cover many aspects of the design is required. For the data transmission network, these can include positive identification of the terminal being used; means to prevent wiretapping; a positive identification of the individual using the terminal by means of identification cards, passwords, and other measures; locks on the terminals; authorization tables; security logs; surveillance techniques; and cryptography. In some cases, one of the procedures will be to notify a security officer immediately of any suspected breach in security. Security officers may be used at terminal locations, or, as with the control of errors, a specially trained person or group may be employed in a central location.

TERMINAL CONSIDERATIONS

After analyzing the types of messages that will be transmitted, determining the traffic volumes, and establishing response-time criteria, a very important aspect of the design involves the terminals that will be used. As you can see in Box 16.1, the first terminal-oriented task in the design is to determine where the terminals are to be located.

Location of Terminals

When the terminals are not in the office of the person originating or requiring information, the question arises: Where should they best be positioned? If the user has a telephone link to the person with the terminal, that person could be almost anywhere. It is up to the systems analyst who is designing the system to decide where to put the terminals. We can group them in such a way as to minimize the probability of the user's not receiving immediate service or to minimize queuing delays. We can gather in one room different types of terminals connected to different types of systems, thus combining, perhaps, different types of expertise in the operators. We can build "information rooms" having a variety of functions. Given the constraints imposed by these factors, we will generally locate the terminals so as to minimize the overall system cost.

In a laboratory, for example, each person may not have a separate terminal but may instead go to a communal group of terminals. What is the probability that a user will not find a terminal free when one is needed? Again the systems analyst must determine the grade of service that must be achieved and on this basis do a probability calculation to determine the number of terminals that must be installed.

Number of Characters Transmitted

The last terminal-related factor on the list in Box 16.1 is an important one. Both the quantity of data in a single transmission and the time available to deliver it vary enormously. These two factors together determine the transmission speed that is necessary.

NETWORK CONSIDERATIONS

The choice of communication line types, network structures, and equipment to be used in supporting the application software depends mainly on the following three factors:

- **Space.** The distance between the transmitting and receiving devices or, if there are many of them, their geographical distribution.
- **Time.** The time within which the transmission or message should be sent or within which a response should be received.
- **Quantity.** The number of bits to be sent in a single transmission or message.

In some cases, an examination of these three factors may lead a systems analyst to conclude that data transmission should not be used at all. (Sending diskettes through the mail or by messenger can still be the most cost-effective method for transporting data in many situations.) In addition to these points, there are a number of secondary but still important considerations, such as accuracy of transmission, line failure probability, probability of obtaining a busy signal, whether a device should be connectable to one or many other devices, and how many times the transmission reverses direction (as when many terminals used for terminal dialogs are connected to the same line).

LOCATION OF INTELLIGENT MACHINES

The computers and other intelligent nodes of the network should normally be positioned so as to minimize the overall cost of the total system. If a system covering a large geographical area is to have one central computer center, this computer center should be positioned, if possible, in such a way as to minimize the cost of the other parts of the network. Another factor is whether a single computer should be used with lines linking distant terminals to it or whether several computers with shorter-distance lines should be used. If several computers are decided on, how many should there be, and where should they be located? What is the optimum balance between computer cost and network cost?

To provide a nationwide time-sharing or information service, a computer in each city may be used, or a computer covering a group of cities. By contrast, groups of computers in the same building may serve many locations, the grouping being designed to minimize the probability of a user's not having access to a machine when access is needed. Again, a load-sharing network may be designed; when one computer is fully loaded, jobs may be switched to a different machine. The balance in cost between having many local machines with short-distance transmission or fewer machines with long-distance transmission should be evaluated.

DUPLICATING FILES AND DATABASES

Just as we may have a choice between many localized computers and one centralized one, so there is a choice on some systems between localized databases with duplicate data and one centralized database. Sometimes one single database is desirable because of the need for simultaneous updating from many sources. On other systems, however, the updating may be done at preplanned intervals, which makes it possible to have identical databases in different places, thus reducing transmission cost. The systems analyst should evaluate which is lower in cost, as well as where to position the databases.

DETERMINING THE NETWORK STRUCTURES

Once the basic decisions have been made regarding the location of intelligent devices and files, the structure of the network that is required to tie these together becomes of primary importance. Some data transmission links simply interconnect two points, as in link 1 in Fig. 16.1. More commonly, more than two places have to be linked. They may be linked with a leased line, or ordinary dial-up telephone circuits can be used. A leased line is generally less expensive than a dial-up connection if the line is used for

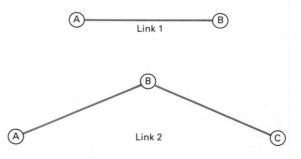

Figure 16.1 Typical network structures.

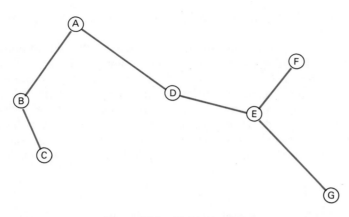

Figure 16.2　Multipoint link.

a high enough proportion of the time. Link 2 in Fig. 16.1 connects three links, and there must be some form of switch at point B to enable A to be connected to B, B to C, or A to C.

When more than a few terminals are used, a multipoint line can be used, as shown in Fig. 16.2. As discussed in Chapter 8, only one terminal is permitted to transmit at once on a multipoint link, so it is normal for one of the locations to have a controlling device, which, like a traffic policeman, instructs the terminals when they may transmit.

Another way of interconnecting the same seven terminals is illustrated in Fig. 16.3. Here all the terminals are connected to a switch, which operates in the same manner as a telephone exchange. Any terminal user can dial any other terminal. The total line distance in Fig. 16.3 is greater than that in Fig. 16.2, which may not matter if the lines are short. If they are long, it will mean that

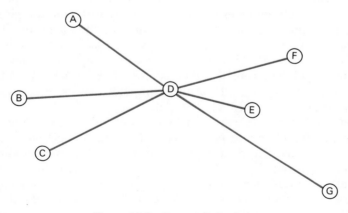

Figure 16.3　Star configuration.

the configuration shown in Fig. 16.3 is substantially more expensive than that of Fig. 16.2.

When large numbers of terminals are connected by leased communication lines, the network configuration can become complex. Figure 16.4 shows terminals in more than 100 cities in the eastern part of the United States connected to a computer center in Chicago. In designing such a network, it is desirable to achieve the minimum line cost within the constraints of other requirements, such as response time. A wide variety of network configurations can be used in designing complex networks. For example, Fig. 16.5 shows the same terminals connected to intermediary locations with individual point-to-point lines.

IN-PLANT AND OUT-PLANT LINES   Communication lines that run exclusively within a user's premises can be laid down by the user rather than leased from a common carrier. These lines are referred to as *in-plant* lines, and those going outside the premises are called *out-plant* lines. The designer thus has three choices: in-plant lines, which have been privately installed; private out-plant lines, which are leased from a common carrier; and public lines, such as those of the public telephone network.

SWITCHING REQUIREMENTS   In many systems, a terminal is installed for one purpose only; it will communicate with only one application running in one computer. This is the case with many terminals for special commercial functions, such as those in banks, airlines, stockbrokerages, and terminals in specialized information systems. Sometimes terminals on general-purpose, time-sharing systems are installed to communicate with many applications, but all running in the same computer. In other cases, however, a terminal can be linked to many different computers. If such is the case, there must be some means of switching the connection between the different machines. The most common way of doing so today is to use the public telephone network. The operator dials the telephone number of the desired computer, and the terminal is then connected to it. A terminal used by one person for programming in APL on one computer may be used by another for accessing a database on a different computer.

Although the public telephone network is useful for switching the connection, because of the ubiquitousness of the telephone connections, other switching means may be used to give access to machines within a building complex or within an organization. The latter are often constructed from leased or privately installed communication facilities. The need for communication with more than one computer center is a parameter that will affect the design.

Figure 16.4 Complex network.

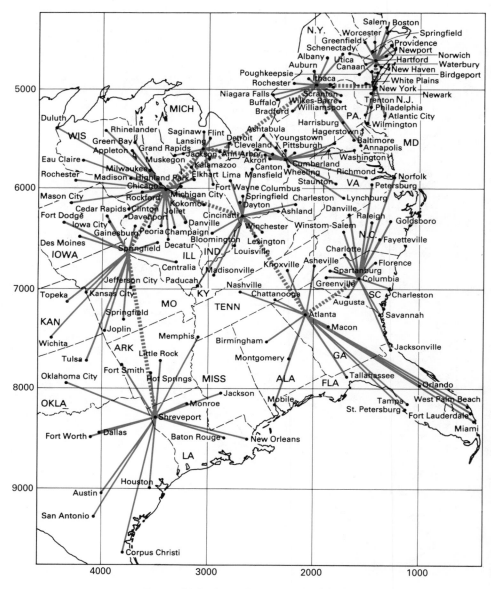

Figure 16.5 Point-to-point configuration.

BUSY SIGNALS

In a switched network, there will be a certain probability of receiving a busy signal. The busy signal may occur because the computer dialed has no more free ports or because there are no free trunks or paths through an exchange. The systems analyst must determine what probability of being denied access to the computer is acceptable and must then design the trunks, exchanges, and computer facilities so as to achieve this condition.

ERROR RATES

A certain number of errors will occur in data transmitted over telecommunications lines. For most types of lines, statistics are available giving the distributions of error rates that can be expected. On some systems, the numbers of errors that can be expected from the terminal operators far exceed those caused by line errors, and the same checking means may be used for dealing with both operator errors and line errors. When the data originates from a machine, however, we generally expect their transmission to be correct.

As discussed in Chapter 8, error-detecting or error-correcting codes are normally employed in data transmission systems. Error-detecting codes give the higher measure of safety. When they are used and an error is detected, the message containing it is ordinarily retransmitted. If a large number of errors occur, a large amount of time will be spent in retransmission. This situation can be controlled by adjusting transmission block size and by selecting transmission means with appropriate speed and error characteristics. Such factors may also be under the control of the system designer.

NETWORK AVAILABILITY

In some systems, it is necessary to have a high degree of certainty of obtaining access to the computer. This is true in military systems and is important on some commercial systems as well. To achieve high system availability, the computers, and occasionally the data in the databases, are sometimes duplicated. It is also necessary to design a communication network that will not fail to establish the necessary connection. In such cases, leased lines that do not pass through switching equipment are normally used. Several terminals are often connected to one leased line. Every such line will enter the computer so that there is no possibility of blocking. In this way, the possibility of receiving busy signals is eliminated.

A further problem remains—that of line failure. If the probability of leased-line failure is deemed unacceptably high, alternative routing must be planned. The public telephone network can often be used to provide backup for a leased-line system.

THE REMAINING STEPS

After the initial design work is done regarding the terminals and the network configuration, the remaining steps consist of technical tasks (see Box 16.1). These often involve the use of the computer in running mathematical models or computer simulations of various parts of the design.

THE MASTER PLAN

An organization making extensive use of data transmission today is likely to have a wide diversity of needs. It will use many different types of both online systems and batch data transmission. Different online systems may have fundamentally different modes of operation. In addition to the data transmission, organizations spend enormous amounts of money on ordinary voice communication.

Ideally and theoretically, it would be best to have one integrated network that handles all the organization's information transmission. This is the goal of ISDN technology (see Chapter 20). However, in today's environment, many large organizations have a proliferation of separate networks. The proliferation has grown up over a period of years with a variety of reasons for installing new facilities.

Typically, a new computer system is installed with its own particular requirements. It is economical for it to use new transmission facilities rather than an extension of the old ones. But the old ones are still in use for a different purpose and are not dismantled. There are also *current* reasons for using separate networks, and these are based on the costs of contemporary technology.

In particular, the choice of the services used in various networks is dependent on the facilities available and their costs. Some computer systems need high-speed lines. Others can operate at the maximum speed of voice lines. Some data transmission devices need the communication line continuously or very frequently, and it is economic for them to have a private leased line. Others need the connection only occasionally, and the lowest-cost answer is thus a dial-up line. Where an organization has many calls, data or voice, that are placed between certain locations, it may use a mechanism for switching separate calls onto leased lines connecting these points.

Many organizations make substantial use of leased voice lines (often called *tie lines*). In this case, the ability to use the leased-line network may become a major factor in designing the data transmission facilities. Often, however, the data transmission network is set up independently using separate facilities.

Probably the most important reason for the growth of separate transmission networks concerns the difficulty of implementing complex computer systems. A data processing team does not implement all the systems required by a large organization in one gigantic integrated step. Doing so would be far too complex. Instead, the organization's data processing facilities evolve step by step, each step being concerned with the installation of a new system or a change to an existing system, which can be implemented by the available staff. If the staff members attempt to bite off more than they can chew at any one step, grave difficulties lie ahead. In a large organization, however, several steps may be proceeding simultaneously. The result is a patchwork of computer systems interlinked in a variety of ways.

Although different systems may evolve separately, it is desirable that, as far as possible, the data processing designers have a *master plan* for the future evolution of data transmission facilities in their organization. Only in this way can there be an adequate measure of compatibility between the systems. This is particularly important in systems for performing commercial or administrative operations. Without such advanced planning, the systems become more difficult to link together, often more difficult for the terminal operators to use, more cumbersome in the database planning, and more expensive in application of resources and in telecommunications costs.

Adherence to a neatly conceived master plan has rarely been achieved in reality. The state of the art is moved by unpredictable tides strong enough to distort the best-laid plans. A certain machine or software package suddenly becomes available. One approach works and another fails. Natural selection takes over, and we have a process of evolution dominated by the survival of whatever is most practical.

The master plan, then, must not be too rigid. It must permit systems to evolve in their own ways. The master plan may call for defined interfaces between separately evolving systems. The separate systems should each be of a level of complexity that is currently practicable. Components of the plan should be designed, as far as possible, with proliferation in mind. A master plan for the communication network may exist separately from a master plan for the evolution of computer systems. Its purpose would be to lower the overall cost of the data transmission and other telecommunications links.

Designers of new systems should be expected to use the planned communication facilities where it is reasonable for them to do so. The saving can be worthwhile, especially in large nationwide corporations, which often spend many millions of dollars per month on telecommunications. Any data network can be constructed in a variety of ways to meet the needs of different types of users.

Now that we have introduced the steps that are involved in the designing of a data communication system, Chapter 17 introduces the aspects of the design that are associated with the way the user interfaces with the system.

17 USER-INTERFACE DESIGN

Where the system is primarily oriented toward communication with human beings, it is often desirable that the design process *begin* with the planning of the user interface. This will determine the types of terminal used, the communication line speeds, the probability of obtaining the desired service at the first attempt, and the response times to be achieved. These factors will in turn lead to different choices in the configuration of the data transmission network. Box 17.1 discusses aspects of a terminal-oriented system that have direct bearing on the design of the user interface.

USER-INTERFACE STRUCTURE

The choice of a user-interface structure is of particular importance in the design of the user interface. The structure of the terminal dialog can differ widely on seemingly similar systems. There are many approaches to the design of the dialog. We will discuss a number of approaches that can guide the development of the user interface. We will begin with guidelines that pertain to alphanumeric dialogs, the most prevalent in today's systems. We will then go on to examine an example of a graphics-oriented user interface and then discuss the use of color in the design of the user interface.

PROGRAMMING-LANGUAGE DIALOGS

Many systems analysts, when they first think of a terminal dialog, think of time-sharing systems and programming. Most computer languages are now available in an appropriate form at terminals, and many programming languages have been devised specifically for terminal use, including many of the fourth-generation languages (4GLs) that are now in common use. It is important for the designer to realize, however, that the majority

BOX 17.1 Aspects of user-interface design

- **Dedicated or Casual Operator?** On some online systems, the operator spends the whole working day sitting in front of the terminal. On other systems, the terminal is used only occasionally by someone who spends most of the day doing entirely different work. The user interface must be designed very differently for these two categories.

- **Media Used.** Common methods of input at a terminal for human interaction are a keyboard and a pointing device, such as a mouse or a light pen. Common means for output are printing, display of characters or graphics images on a screen, and voice answerback. The designer must select the most suitable media for the application, taking into consideration terminal cost, communication network cost, and user psychology.

- **Language and Response Structure.** The designer specifies exactly what the user will say to the system and the form in which the system will respond. There are innumerable possible structures for terminal dialogs. The choice will depend on the nature of the application, the terminal, and the operator.

- **Speed of Terminal.** The speed of the terminal has a major effect on its possible interactive users. A conversation involving many lengthy responses requires a terminal capable of displaying information quickly.

- **Response Time.** Certain applications are very sensitive to the response time of the system. For some terminal uses, a very fast response time is necessary; for others, it is not. Response-time considerations are discussed in detail in Chapter 18.

- **Availability.** Availability of the system refers to the probability that the terminal is usable at the time the operator wishes to use it. Some systems are designed so that the terminals will always receive service when they request it, except in a period of equipment failure. This, however, may be unnecessarily expensive, especially when the terminals have low utilization.

- **Control of Errors.** The likelihood of errors often depends to a large extent on human factors. A well-designed conversation structure minimizes errors. Error-detecting formats can be devised, and the information being entered can be checked against existing files.

- **Security.** When information in a database can be read or changed by operators at terminals, it is necessary to prevent unauthorized persons from reading information that does not concern them and from modifying data or creating new records. Steps should be taken to prevent unauthorized access to a system.

of persons who will be using a data communication system are not programmers. Most of them do not want to program, have little aptitude for it, and would make a mess of it if they tried. We need a different form of terminal dialog for the vast numbers of nontechnical workers who need to use computers in their work.

NATURAL-LANGUAGE DIALOG

To converse with computers in the same manner as we talk with other human beings would in many ways be the ideal form of communication. Many systems have been built that allow the terminal user to converse with the computer using some form of natural-language dialog. While there is no difficulty in making the computer *respond* in English, it is extremely difficult to program it to *comprehend* English input, although this has been done on a limited basis. The INTELLECT query language allows the user to enter database queries using natural language. The following is an example of a query that INTELLECT understands:

```
Show me a vertical display of the name, age, city, and salary
of typists living in Illinois.
```

Although systems have been designed to process natural language, the designer should not underestimate the difficulty of this in deciding to design a human interface that attempts to understand natural language. The INTELLECT system took years to develop and is being constantly refined.

The language we speak is in a very disorderly state. Its words are ambiguous; its syntax, confused. Many sentences are imperfect expressions of thought because the language is only partly rational. Mechanized parsing is difficult because many words can be a verb at one time and a noun at another, and the language is full of irregularities and exceptions. Recognizing the meaning of sentences sometimes requires a wealth of prior knowledge, making it very difficult to program this ordinary human function.

The difficulties with natural language are an extreme case of a more general dilemma with user-interface design. We need to design the dialog structure so that it is as easy as possible for humans to use. The degree to which we achieve this condition will determine the acceptability of the systems we create. However, the more freedom we give the operator in phrase structuring, the more complexity will be necessary in the programming to interpret what the operator enters. The objective of making the dialog as fluid as possible is generally at odds with the objective of making the input from the human operator precise.

LIMITED ENGLISH INPUT

Although natural-language input suffers from an imprecision that often defeats the simple-minded computer, a user interface can be designed that understands a small number of ordinary words, provided that these words are defined with exactness. The advantage in this type of user interface is that the user employs familiar words. The disadvantage is that the operator may be tempted to overestimate the intelligence of the machine and to overstep the tight restrictions on input wording. Worse, in some cases the user might obtain an incorrect answer because a word or phrase is entered that is not in the computer's dictionary. Thus the request

```
List all Chicago branch managers with police convictions.
```

might provide a list of all innocent Chicago branch managers if the words *police* and *convictions* are not in the dictionary. A misspelled word would be similarly ignored.

    The problem of misinterpretation can be overcome in part by displaying on the screen the condensed version of the request (i.e., "List Chicago branch managers"). Another school of thought advocates that *no* word should be permitted that is not in the dictionary. If null words are to be permitted, an acceptable set of them should be in the dictionary along with the key words. Queries that use words not in the dictionary can then be rejected, accompanied by an error message.

DIALOG USING MNEMONICS

Many online systems are built for handling a particular application that will be used by trained operators. In such a case, mnemonics are often used to shorten the input that the operator has to enter. Mnemonics are simple codes that both the operator and the system understand. The disadvantage of using mnemonics is that the user has to remember them. This disadvantage can become prohibitive if there are a large number of codes. It can also be a severe disadvantage if the operators are not adequately trained or do not use the system constantly.

    In a few areas, mnemonic codes have been in use before the installation of computerized systems, and these same mnemonics are then incorporated into the user interface when online systems are installed. The airlines, for example, have for some time had an international code for cabling information relating to seat reservations. This same code was then used to advantage in some parts of the dialog used in today's airline reservation systems.

    The following is an example of a typical command entry that the user of an airline reservation system might enter to display a flight booking:

```
*21/25 mar-goldsmith. w
```

The * indicates a display request, "21" is the flight number, "25 mar" is the date, and the - indicates that the name "goldsmith. w" follows. The system might display the following for W. Goldsmith's booking:

```
1.    21F   25 MAR   LAXJFK   HS1   856A430P
2.   112F   27 MAR   JFKLAX   HS1   900A1230P
```

The airline agent would then interpret the codes in the first line of the display as representing Goldsmith's first flight. The flight number is 21, in first class, on March 25, flying from Los Angeles International to New York JFK; one seat is reserved; the flight leaves at 8:56 A.M., and it is scheduled to arrive at 4:30 P.M.

PROGRAMMING-LIKE STATEMENTS

On some systems, the use of mnemonics builds up into statements that look as if they were part of a programming language. There are diverse examples of this. Some database query languages use mnemonics in a program-like fashion.

The following illustration of a dialog designed for financial analysts looks like an interactive program. It is, however, designed for a specific application and does not have the flexibility of a programming language. Such a dialog is often produced in the form of subroutines in a conventional programming language that can be used at the same terminal.

The dialog begins when the analyst calls a routine named IIR (Interactive Information Retriever). The input entered by the analyst is shown in lower case, the output displayed by the computer in upper case.

```
call iir;
IIR. PROCEED:
r1 = 100 * nfc / equity;
PROCEED:
```

Here the analyst is defining a ratio that will be used in the future. The code *nfc* ("net for common") and *equity* are already defined, and the analyst must know this. The computer stores the definition for "r1" in its dictionary. The analyst proceeds:

```
get r1 (abc) for 1968 to 1972;
1968    1969    1970    1971    1972
18.24   16.91   15.13   17.31   20.12
```

A language of this type is fairly simple for a financial analyst to learn and use. It enables the user quickly to display comparisons, averages, ratios, statistics functions, and a variety of facts in the accessible database using a simple set of easily learned programming-like statements.

MENUS

Systems for casual users should ordinarily be designed to avoid the use of mnemonics or programming-like statements. One way to do this is to design the user interface so that it is always the computer rather than the operator that leads.

A dialog consists of pairs of messages—a question or statement (sometimes a set of statements) followed by a response. In any terminal dialog, the first message of each pair can come either from the user or from the computer. The former is an *operator-initiated* dialog and the latter a *computer-initiated* dialog.

If the dialog is operator-initiated, as in our financial example, users have to know exactly what to do. They must be familiar with the necessary mnemonics, procedures, and formats. If a dialog is computer-initiated, the computer can tell the user precisely what to do. A computer-initiated dialog is often less flexible, since the user has to follow a predetermined path. The path can, however, have many branches in it—at each step, if necessary.

One form of computer-initiated dialog uses *menus* to request information from the user. The menus are normally structured in a hierarchical fashion, each level of menu taking the user farther down in the menu structure.

The following is an example of a simple menu:

```
ENTER LINE NUMBER OF CUSTOMER TYPE:

1.        MANUFACTURING
2.        SERVICE INDUSTRY
3.        RETAILER/WHOLESALER
4.        TRANSPORTATION
5.        BANKING
6.        EDUCATIONAL
7.        GOVERNMENT
8.        MILITARY
9.        OTHER

==>  _
```

Complete and complex applications have been implemented using this technique. The operator needs little training and cannot go far wrong. Such a method is very useful for the "casual" operator. However, multiple levels of menus are frustrating for trained operators. In some systems that implement menus, some mechanism exists for bypassing the menus, possibly using keywords or mnemonic codes, when the user becomes more familiar with the system.

Workstations that support a graphics screen and a mouse or other type of pointing device are particularly well suited to implementing dialogs that use menus. We will look more closely at such a user interface later in this chapter when we discuss user interfaces that use graphics.

FORM FILLING

There are many types of computer-initiated dialogs, just as there are many types of operator-initiated dialogs. Another common type of computer-initiated dialog is one that asks the user to fill in a form on the screen. A display is presented that has variable fields, initially filled with blanks, that the user fills in, as in the following example:

```
CUSTOMER DATA

ENTER THE FOLLOWING INFORMATION ABOUT THE CUSTOMER

LAST NAME _____    FIRST NAME _____

STREET      _____    CITY      _____
STATE       __  ZIP _____ ____     PHONE (___) ___ ____
```

Some systems use a combination of menus and form filling to guide the user through the dialog structure.

HYBRID DIALOGS

Although the majority of dialogs are either entirely computer-initiated or entirely operator-initiated, some are a mixture of the two. This is the case in the following illustration, which again is designed for a financial analyst.

We begin in a user-initiated fashion, by asking for a set of statistical analysis programs *(sam)*, of which we are going to use a specific one called *scatter*. Notice that the computer assists us but that we are also required to know what to enter at certain points in the dialog:

```
call sam;
PROCEED:
call scatter;
DEFINE DATA:
STOCK LIST A23;
DEFINE Y AXIS:
pe = price for mar 22 1972/ eps for 1972;
DEFINE X AXIS:
epsg = growth (eps);
FOR WHAT DATES?
1968-1972;
SPECIFY CONSTRAINTS;
epsg greater than 0;
PROCEED:
call linear fit;
DO THE PREVIOUS DEFINITIONS HOLD?
yes;
PE = 10.7 + 0.67*EPSG
PROCEED:
call correlation coef;
DO THE PREVIOUS DEFINITIONS HOLD?
y;
R = 0.61
PROCEED:
end;
```

SPECIAL TERMINAL HARDWARE

One approach to designing a user interface for a specific purpose is to use specially built hardware with keys and lights labeled with elements of the dialog. The computerized cash registers that are used in many fast-food restaurants are examples of these. Often other devices are also used, such as badge readers and bar-code readers; this has been done on many systems. The temptation to have unique terminals for a particular application is often strong. In some cases, the special-purpose terminal has been complex and expensive. It seems likely that we will see many more attempts to use special terminals in the future. For example, most banks are now using specially designed terminals that allow simple transactions to be entered by the general public at all hours of day and night.

A major disadvantage of using special equipment in many cases is cost. Machines that are specially constructed and that have small sales will be expensive, particularly when reliability and maintenance are taken into consideration. The second disadvantage is inflexibility. Commercial computer applications are subject to a high rate of change. It is often difficult for the designer to anticipate what change will occur or how rapidly it will come. If the user interface is designed around a custom-built terminal, the designer is building resistance to change into the system. Indeed, most user interfaces other than the simplest have changed drastically after the system is initially installed—this tends to be the rule rather than the exception. The difficulty of changing terminal hardware three months after a system is installed is much greater than that of changing programs.

SYSTEMS FOR A TOTALLY UNTRAINED OPERATOR

We have much in our favor if we can *train* the user of an online system, even if only for a fairly brief time. However, there are *many* potential applications for which we would like a totally untrained person to use the terminal. This condition has been achieved with great success on certain systems (such as the banking systems mentioned earlier). The key to success again lies in the user-interface design.

Dialogs for totally untrained operators are almost always computer-initiated rather than operator-initiated. The first essential for dialog with a totally untrained operator is to stop the user from saying anything that the computer cannot interpret. There are several ways to do this. The most effective is to restrict the means of input by providing a limited number of keys. If we do not give the user an alphabetic keyboard, the user cannot compose verbal messages.

Another way of restricting the user's input is to confine the dialog to simple menu selection techniques. A terminal with keys at the side of the screen designed for menu selection would have a wide range of applications. Most banking terminals designed to be used by the general public employ this technique.

An additional essential for dialog with an untrained operator is designing the computer responses so that they have the utmost clarity. They should leave the user with no doubt about what is to be done next.

FIXED-FRAME RESPONSES
In some systems that use computer-initiated dialogs, it is possible to carry out the entire operation with a set of unvarying computer responses. The computer does not *compose* a response; it merely *selects* one from a predetermined set. The set, in some cases, is large.

This approach simplifies the programming and raises the possibility of avoiding transmission of the actual computer responses over expensive communication links. The responses could be stored in small local machines near the terminal locations. The computer would indicate which response was to be sent to a terminal by transmitting only a coded identification. The local machine would generate the requisite response. Although the frames may be stored ready for use at peripheral locations, they can also be maintained centrally. The system can be designed so that a new or changed frame can be transmitted from the central computer to the peripheral devices.

A feature of computer-initiated dialogs that makes this scheme attractive is that the dialog is usually very one-sided. The computer gives lengthy responses and the operator very short ones, sometimes only one character.

USER INTERFACES WITH GRAPHICS DISPLAYS
With today's advanced computing systems, high-resolution graphics displays are replacing the alphanumeric displays of days past. When a graphics display is available, information can be displayed in the form of pictures instead of words. This is making possible new applications that would not be feasible using alphanumeric terminals. The availability of graphics displays, often providing color capabilities, makes the job of the user-interface designer much more difficult than when an alphanumeric dialog was the only option.

GENERAL-PURPOSE GRAPHICS USER INTERFACES
Many of today's computing systems implement a general-purpose graphics-oriented user interface. The best known of these, at the time of writing, is the user interface employed by Apple's Macintosh line of small computers. The Macintosh user interface had its beginnings in research begun by Alan Kay at the Xerox Palo Alto Research Center (PARC). Kay's vision was a computer he called the *Dynabook*, a computing system with the power and speed of a mainframe in the size and shape of a notebook. The system would have a flat screen and be capable of storing

vast amounts of data internally, as well as being able to communicate with networks. It would be so easy to use that anyone would be able to tap its power.

ALTO AND STAR   Though it has not yet produced Dynabook, research at Xerox has resulted in a number of revolutionary computers. One, the *Alto,* was released in the mid-1970s with a price tag of over $30,000. Another, released somewhat later, was the *Star,* with a price tag of roughly $16,000. A variation of the Star still has many enthusiastic users. Both the Alto and the Star used a *mouse* as a pointing device, displayed information on the screen in the form of *windows,* and supported *pop-up menus* that were instantly available on the screen.

Legend has it that in the late 1970s, about the time that Apple Computer's *Lisa* project was beginning, Steve Jobs, one of the founders of Apple Computer, was touring the PARC development laboratories with a number of other people from Apple. The PARC people demonstrated some prototype equipment that implemented windows, pop-up menus, and a mouse as a pointing device. Jobs is said to have pointed to the machine and said to the people accompanying him: "I want a machine like that." According to the story, that was when the concept for the Lisa, and later the Macintosh, was born.

LISA AND   The Lisa was released in January 1983. It supported
MACINTOSH   all the user-interface features now familiar to Macintosh users. It was a revolutionary machine, but it was not a success in the marketplace. Most people agree that the price was simply too high. The Macintosh was then introduced in January 1984.

We will next describe the general characteristics of the user interface implemented on Apple's Macintosh line of computers. Many features of the Macintosh user interface, which were pioneered by those at Xerox's PARC, have been implemented by others as well. Today, graphics user interfaces featuring mouse, windows, and instantly available menus are available for most types of small computers.

The primary method a Macintosh computer uses for communicating with the user is displaying information on a screen that supports relatively high resolution graphics. The user communicates with the Macintosh via a keyboard and a pointing device called a *mouse*.

THE MOUSE   A typical mouse is a hand-held device that contains a small rubber ball that rolls as the device is moved across a flat surface. As the ball rolls, the mouse generates control signals that are sent to the computer. A pointer displayed on the graphics screen closely follows the movement of the mouse. The mouse used with the Macintosh contains a single button. Some other computers use a two-button or a three-button mouse. There are four actions the user can perform with the Macintosh's single-button mouse: clicking, double clicking, pressing, and dragging. These actions are described in Box 17.2.

POINTER SHAPES   Macintosh application programs use various pointer shapes to give the user a visual cue concerning the types of actions that are appropriate in a given situation. For example, a pointer shaped like an arrowhead indicates that objects can be pointed to and selected, and a pointer shaped like a wristwatch indicates that the user should wait for some event to be completed before initiating any new actions.

THE KEYBOARD   The Macintosh keyboard is used primarily for entering text and numeric data. It can also be used for issuing commands as an alternative to using pull-down menus. Various types of keyboards are available for the Macintosh, both from Apple and from other vendors. Some have keys for controlling the cursor and a variety of function keys. Others are quite simple and contain little more than the keys required for text entry.

BOX 17.2   Mouse actions

- **Clicking.** In performing the *clicking* action, the user points at a screen object and briefly presses and immediately releases the mouse button. Clicking a screen object generally signifies that the user intends to perform some action on that object.

- **Double Clicking.** The user *double-clicks* by clicking on an object twice in rapid succession. Double clicking is normally an enhancement, superset, or extension of the particular feature selected by clicking a screen object.

- **Pressing.** Pressing involves holding down the mouse button while keeping the screen pointer positioned over a screen object. Pressing often means the same thing as clicking an object repeatedly.

- **Dragging.** Dragging involves moving the mouse while pressing the mouse button. When an object is dragged, the object, or an outline of it, generally attaches itself to the screen pointer and moves with it as the mouse is moved. When the user releases the mouse button, the object remains at the new location.

THE GRAPHICS SCREEN

Macintosh computers support graphics displays of various sizes. All information is displayed on the screen in graphics mode using a system software subsystem called *Quickdraw*. The Macintosh does not support a text mode; text is drawn on the screen using Quickdraw in the same manner as any other type of information.

CONCEPTUAL MODELS

The purpose of a computing system is to manipulate information. The central concepts surrounding the Macintosh user interface all relate to the functions of creating, accessing, displaying, moving, duplicating, modifying, and deleting information. The Macintosh user interface implements six conceptual models, described in Box 17.3, that make it easy for users to perform the above functions:

- **Desktop**—the working environment
- **Document**—the information itself
- **File**—an entity that *contains* information
- **Application**—a program that *manipulates* information
- **Resource**—an entity that *modifies* the behavior of an application
- **Window**—an area of the screen that *presents* information

OVERLAPPING WINDOWS

The desktop can contain any number of open windows. Windows can overlap one another in any desired way. When windows overlap, there is a simulated front-to-back ordering of the windows. Only one window, called the *active window,* is on top. When the user selects a window by clicking it with the mouse, it becomes the active window and is moved to the front of the pile of overlapping windows. The other windows retain their original front-to-back order.

THE ACTIVE WINDOW

Generally, the last window to be opened or selected is the active window. The active window is always highlighted in some way. For example, in the screen shown in Fig. 17.1, the active window is distinguished from the inactive windows by rows of horizontal highlighting lines in the window's title bar. All commands and data that are entered apply to the application that is in control of the active window.

BOX 17.3   Macintosh conceptual models

- **Desktop.** The desktop is the Macintosh's working environment. We can have any number of objects on the desktop, such as file folders and documents. We can open these objects, close them, and manipulate the information in them, just as we can with real file folders and documents on an ordinary desk.

- **Document.** A *document* is an organized collection of information, such as a letter created with a text editor, an illustration created with a graphics editor, or a ledger sheet created with a spreadsheet program. A document as viewed through a window on the display screen generally closely resembles the document as it will appear when printed.

- **File.** A *file* is a container of information. For example, documents are stored in files. Files can also be used to store *applications* and *resources*.

- **Application.** *Applications* are the Macintosh counterparts to application programs. A file that contains an application can be used to access and manipulate the information contained in other files. Each document file is associated with a principal application. When we open a text file that was created using a text editor, the text editor that was used to create it is automatically called up and is used to display the document in its window.

- **Resource.** *Resources* are sets of information that application programs use to modify their behavior. For example, a font file is a resource that an application uses to display information using a particular type font. Resource files are created by applications also, but these applications are not normally employed by the typical user. Resource files are normally created and manipulated by specialized applications called resource editors. For example, there exists a font editor that can be used to create and modify font resource files.

- **Window.** *Windows* are objects on the desktop that are used to display information. Several windows are shown in Figs. 17.1, 17.2, and 17.3.

DOCUMENT WINDOWS

Although many specialized windows are displayed by the Macintosh, the most common form of window is that displayed by an application that works with a document. Document display windows, and the windows the system software uses to display the contents of disks and folders, are generally similar. Figure 17.2 shows an example of the document window displayed by a spreadsheet application.

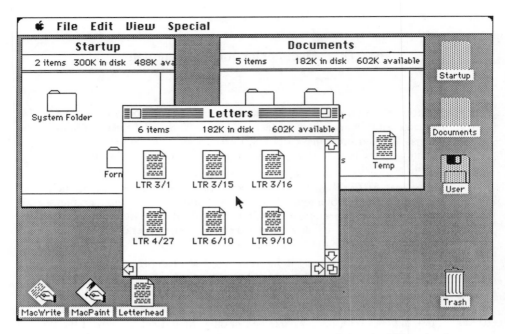

Figure 17.1 On the Macintosh desktop, the active window is differentiated from inactive windows by rows of horizontal highlighting lines.

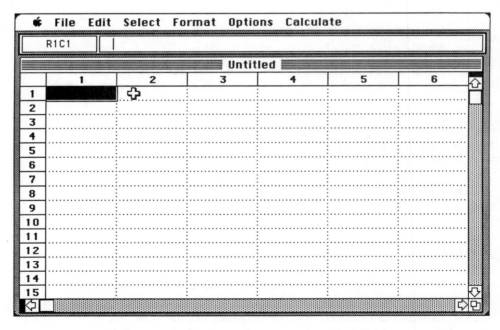

Figure 17.2 A typical Macintosh document window, displayed by a spreadsheet application.

COMMANDS AND MENUS
The primary method of command entry on the Macintosh is through the use of *pull-down menus*. A menu bar is displayed at all times across the top of the screen. The user pulls a window down by pointing at the menu's name and pressing the mouse button. The user issues a command by selecting a menu item. This is done by dragging the pointer to the name of the command to be executed and releasing the mouse button. Figure 17.3 shows an example of a menu bar with one of the menus pulled down.

ICONS
When possible, most Macintosh applications display information in the form of small pictures, called *icons*. An icon is a fundamental object implemented by the Macintosh user interface. Some sample icons are shown in Fig. 17.4.

DIALOG AND ALERT BOXES
Dialog boxes and alert boxes are used when the application program needs to inform the user about something, when the program requires information from the user, or when an error or other special event has occurred. A dialog box can be used to prompt the user for information, as shown in Fig. 17.5.

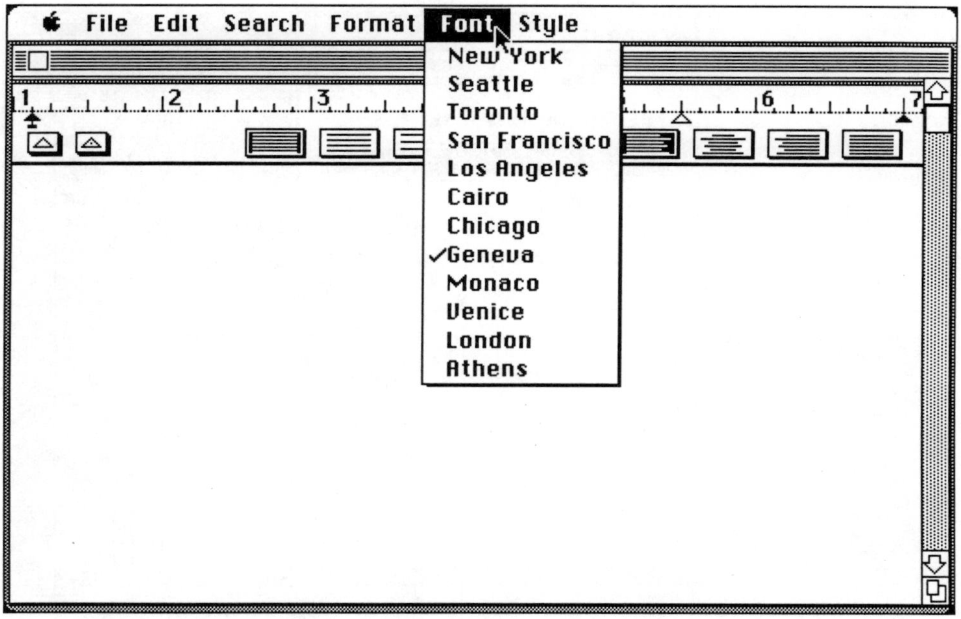

Figure 17.3 A typical Macintosh pull-down menu.

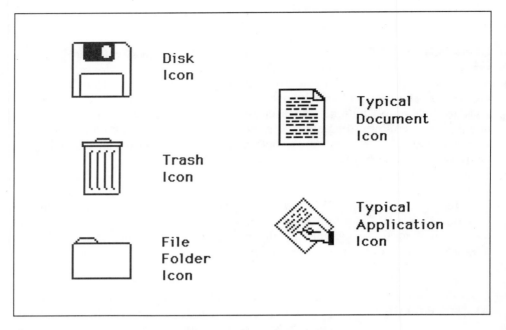

Figure 17.4 Typical Macintosh icons.

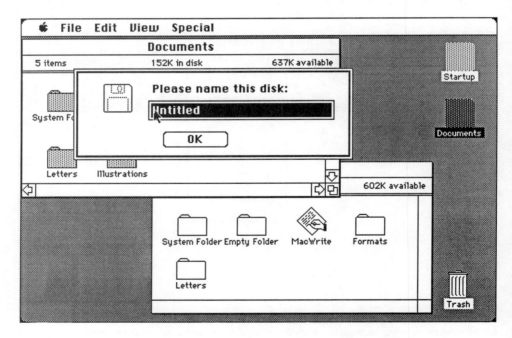

Figure 17.5 A dialog box asking the user to identify a diskette that has just been formatted.

MODELESS OPERATION

One of the underlying principles in the Macintosh user interface is that an application program should operate as much as possible in a *modeless fashion*. A *mode* of an interactive system can be defined as the state of the user interface that lasts for some period of time, is not associated with any particular object, and has no role other than to place an interpretation on user input.

When a computer system operates in multiple modes, the user often gets confused, especially when the system changes modes without the user's being aware of it. Confusion results because the user continually finds the computer in the wrong mode.

It is necessary for a general-purpose computing system to operate in a variety of modes, but mode switching must be completely comprehensible to the user at all times. In general, there are three cases when mode switching is acceptable:

- **Long-Term Modes.** When we call up a word processing program, we expect that the computer will then begin operating in text-editing mode. When we exit the word processor and call up the graphics editor, we expect the computer to switch to graphics-editing mode. This is entirely acceptable and understandable to the user.

- **Short-Term Modes.** This type of mode change occurs when the user initiates a short-term event, as by pressing the mouse button and holding it down. This is also desirable. A short-term mode can be referred to as a "spring-loaded" mode. When we let go of the button, the mode instantaneously changes back.

- **Alert Modes.** Alert modes are often used in error situations. When an application program enters an alert mode, it may temporarily stop accepting normal input and accept only a narrow range of inputs relating directly to the error condition. Alert modes are acceptable, but they must be implemented in such a way that the user immediately recognizes that something unusual has happened.

Application programs must sometimes change modes for periods of time to implement functions that are not covered by these three situations. When a change in mode occurs, a Macintosh application normally makes the mode change clearly visible and obvious to the user. Acceptable and desirable mode changes within an application program normally meet one or more of the following requirements:

- The mode change is indicative of the normal operation of a simulated real-life object. For example, in drawing lines with a graphics editor, we might like the user to be able to change the shape of a simulated paintbrush. Each change of shape causes the editor to change its line-drawing mode.

- The mode change should affect only the attributes of something, not its operation. For example, when we change the shape of the paintbrush, the user still draws lines in the same manner; only the shape of the pattern being drawn changes.

- When in the new mode, the software should prevent the user from taking actions not related to the new mode. For example, if the user gets dangerously close to using up all available space on a disk, the program should alert the user and stop accepting normal input until the user has saved the work in progress and has made sufficient space available.

USER-INTERFACE HINTS

Apple Computer provides the following advice to application developers grappling with the user-interface issues that surround the development of new applications. These tips provide sound advice that might be followed by the developer of an application for any type of computer.

- A given action should always produce the same sort of result each time the user performs it. Avoid surprising the user.
- Avoid giving the user too many alternatives for performing the same action. For example, a command in a pull-down menu and an alternative command key shortcut are sufficient in most cases. A third or fourth alternative tends to confuse the user.
- Avoid overloading an application with esoteric features. According to Apple, featurism is the single major contributor to system complexity and user intimidation.
- Avoid changing the state of the application without making the user aware of it. The environment should be consistent and predictable.
- Avoid a cluttered screen display.
- Avoid the use of multiple modes wherever possible.

THE USE OF COLOR

The widespread availability of color displays has caused an explosion in the use of color in interactive computer systems. Color can be a powerful tool in making information easier to understand. It can also be overused and make computer displays harder to understand and even hard on the eyes. Much research is necessary in the area of the use of color in the design of the user interface.

The different colors that are available on the terminal should be analyzed, and only the color combinations that result in the most readable displays should be used. In general, using black characters on a colored background tends to result in clearer displays than using bright text on a black background. On many terminals, certain color combinations result in particularly fuzzy displays due to the color fringing that occurs around the edges of characters and other screen objects. For example, on many of the displays used with IBM terminals and small computers, green or cyan (light blue) text or graphics on a brown background is a particularly bad combination, while black text and graphics on a brown background is particularly clear. Black text on a cyan background is another particularly clear combination.

In general, colors should be used sparingly, and the number of different colors on the screen at any one time should be minimized. Displays that overuse colors tend to be garish and confusing to the user. Some colors have connotations to most users that can be exploited in the design of the user interface. For example, all help screens might display black text on a green background, since green seems to be associated in most people's minds with assistance. By the same token, black text on a red background might be used for all error messages, since red tends to be a warning color.

In the final analysis, color tends to be partly subjective, and people have their own color preferences. In many cases, the capability should be provided for allowing people to choose their own colors and to tailor their displays to their own tastes, unless, of course, particular colors have precise meanings in the user interface being designed.

Now that we have examined the general principles that should guide the design of the user interface, Chapter 18 discusses response time, an important aspect of all user interfaces.

18 RESPONSE-TIME REQUIREMENTS

As mentioned in Chapter 17, one of the main parameters in the design of a data transmission system is the required response time. This factor is especially important in online systems. When a response to a user at a terminal is needed, the permissible time for the response will affect in a major way the network organization and the equipment selected.

Response time is the time a system takes to respond to a given input. We define it for an operator using a terminal keyboard as the interval between the operator's pressing the *last* key of the input message and the terminal's displaying the *first* part of the reply. In a typical system that uses data communication, the response time achieved will be the sum of three major time elements:

- The time associated with the data transmission network
- The time associated with accessing the database system
- The time associated with computer processing of the retrieved data

In some computer systems, the terminal response time is almost entirely dependent on the computer and its files. The communication lines may each support a single terminal and thus have little effect on response time. In other systems, especially those with large numbers of terminals or geographically extensive networks, the communication system may make a much greater contribution to the overall response time than the computer system.

The cost of providing a very short response time can be high. This may be true because of computer and file considerations. It will often be true because of the communication network.

DIFFERING RESPONSE TIMES

The response time for all transactions need not be identical. Sometimes certain terminals will be given a higher response time than others. Sometimes—and this case is often important—different types of transactions require a shorter response time than other types of transactions. For example, an inquiry about certain data may be given a much faster response time than a transaction that updates that data.

Similarly, if we instruct the system to execute a command, we should receive confirmation very quickly that the command has been accepted and understood and can be complied with. However, the processing itself might take much longer.

The systems analyst needs to go through all the functions the system will perform and determine the desired response time for each of them, recognizing that they can be different.

ECONOMIC FACTORS

One of the factors that should be considered when planning response-time requirements is economic. If the processing of an online transaction needs several conversation elements—that is, messages to the computer followed by responses to them—a lengthy response time will delay the overall transaction processing. The longer a transaction takes, the more terminals will be needed to handle a given volume of work. A lengthy response time may tie up other equipment, such as buffers or components in the communication network. A lengthy response time may result in people's being kept waiting, and it may be possible to place an economic value on this. A shop supervisor making entries many times per day may lose a significant amount of time. Lengthy transaction processing may result in queues developing. Customers may be kept waiting and, in some cases, may be lost.

PSYCHOLOGICAL FACTORS

Factors relating to human psychology must also be considered if the system is to be accepted by its potential users.

Behavioral psychologists have identified two requirements concerned with terminal response time. First, there is the user's natural expectancy of a response. In human conversation, one expects a response within about 2 seconds. The response may be no more than a grunt or a facial expression, but lack of response for, say, 4 seconds would be an unnatural break in the conversation. One would want to know the reason for the delay. In conditioning experiments, a response within 2 seconds has been shown to constitute an important boundary in the effectiveness of feedback.

Second, human beings spontaneously organize their activity into *clumps* that can easily be completed. There is a sense of completion when such a clump of activity is terminated. Writing one sentence, or occasionally two, of this book is one such clump. Dialing a telephone number would also be followed by a temporary sense of completion, or *closure,* as psychologists call it. In the same way, segments of a terminal conversation are followed by a closure. The main reason is that a certain amount of information—the telephone number being dialed, for example—must be held in *short-term memory,* a sort of human buffer storage. When I dial a telephone number, for instance, I retain it in my buffer until I finish dialing the number and then, on closure, it becomes erased. Similarly, when I am entering information into a computer terminal, throughout the action I am holding the data in my short-term memory. During this period, I do not want to be interrupted; otherwise I will lose what I am remembering in my buffer. An interruption or a delay in achieving closure is frustrating. However, a much longer delay can be tolerated after closure has occurred following a string of related interactions.

There are different degrees of psychological closure. Completing the dialing of a telephone number is a simple closure, completing the entry of a detailed transaction into a system is more elaborate, and completing a problem-solving operation is a much more final closure.

Different elements in a terminal conversation may, then, require different response times, and it is sometimes possible to take advantage of this fact in the design of the system. When many interactions are linked to perform a single task, a response time much longer than 2 seconds to each individual interaction would be frustrating. But after a sequence of interactions has been completed and closure occurs, a much longer response time can be tolerated.

As we have seen, in some cases, a response time longer than 2 seconds is acceptable. However, there are many situations when a 2-second response time would be extremely frustrating. Many types of interaction with graphics terminals using a mouse or other pointing device require response times in the sub-second and even decisecond (less than a tenth of a second) ranges, especially for thought-intensive work, such as computer-aided design.

There are certain ranges of response time that are important in determining the response time requirements of a terminal dialog. These ranges are summarized in Box 18.1.

INTERIM RESPONSES

If it is not possible to give a response to an interaction within 2 seconds when user psychology dictates that the user will expect one within that amount of time, the situation can be ameliorated somewhat by providing an interim response—saying, in effect, "I heard what you said; wait a minute while I formulate the reply." This would appear as a word or a phrase on the terminal. For lengthy delays, more than one interim response might be desirable. A simple response such as "working" displayed every few seconds is reassuring that the user hasn't been forgotten.

An interim response produced in this way does not, of course, solve the problem when the reason for requiring a fast response is continuity of the user's thinking.

BOX 18.1 Response-time ranges

- **Greater than 15 seconds.** In general, delays greater than 15 seconds rule out conversational interaction. Certain types of employees may be content to sit at a terminal for more than 15 seconds waiting for the answer to a single simple inquiry. However, for a busy person, captivity for more than 15 seconds seems intolerable. If delays of more than 15 seconds will occur, the system should be designed so that the user can turn to other activities and request the response at some later time.

- **Greater than 4 seconds.** Delays greater than 4 seconds are generally too long for a conversation requiring the operator to retain information in short-term memory. They would be very inhibiting in problem-solving activity and frustrating in data entry activity. However, after a major closure, delays of from 4 to 15 seconds can be tolerated.

- **2 to 4 seconds.** A delay longer than 2 seconds can be inhibiting to terminal operations demanding a high level of concentration. A wait of 2 to 4 seconds at a terminal can seem surprisingly long when the user is absorbed and emotionally committed to complete what he or she is doing. Again, a delay in this range may be acceptable after a minor closure has occurred.

- **Less than 2 seconds.** When the terminal user has to remember information throughout several responses, the response time must be short. The more detailed the information remembered, the greater the need for responses of less than 2 seconds. For elaborate terminal activities, 2 seconds represents an important response-time limit.

- **Subsecond response times.** Certain types of thought-intensive work, especially with graphics terminals, require very short response times to maintain the user's interest and attention for long periods of time.

- **Decisecond response times.** A response to the pressing of a key and seeing the character displayed on the screen or clicking a screen object with a mouse needs to be almost instantaneous—less than 0.1 second after the action. Interaction with a mouse requires extremely fast interaction if the designer is to avoid the use of alien syntax (one with commands, mnemonic, punctuation, etc.). Subsecond and decisecond response times cannot typically be achieved if data must be transmitted from the terminal to a central computer and back again to support the interaction. Such short response times are normally provided by functions performed in the terminal itself.

TOO SHORT A RESPONSE TIME
In some cases, too *short* a response time can be psychologically bad. It can have a harassing effect on the user if every machine response comes back instantaneously. Subconsciously the user may feel coerced into an attempt to keep up with the machine. On some systems, a built-in delay has been used to ensure that responses to complex queries are not displayed in less than about 1.5 seconds. On telecommunications-based systems, however, the designer is more likely to be worried about long response times than short ones.

SPECIFIC RESPONSE SITUATIONS
In determining the response-time requirements of individual transactions, the situation in which the transaction takes place is a major factor. As we have seen, in certain situations, a response time of 2 seconds or less is an absolute requirement. Given other situations, such a short response time is not required at all. The following are some of the situations that are likely to occur in online systems.

1. Response to "System, Are You Listening?"

When we pick up the telephone and listen for the dial tone, we are in effect asking this question. We expect to hear the dial tone within a second or so because that is what we are accustomed to. When a session with a computer is being *initialized,* a wait of 3 seconds or longer would generally be acceptable. This will affect the design of automatic dialing and switching on data networks. If the system is *not* listening, some form of busy signal is desirable, as on the telephone networks.

2. Response to Initialization

When users are taking initialization action, they are able to tolerate longer delays than they will when they become locked into conversation or problem solving. Sometimes the initialization or sign-on procedure may involve a wait of many seconds while facilities are being set up or programs are being read into storage. Here a fairly quick interim response, followed by a wait of up to half a minute, would usually be acceptable.

3. Error Messages

When the user makes a mistake that is detected by the system, an error message is generally sent back. The user should always be allowed to complete the current segment of thought before being informed of the error. It is offensive to be interrupted in mid-thought and abruptly told of an error. It is, in fact, desirable to have a brief pause after this temporary closure rather than bang back the error message instantly. The response time of an error message should be about 2 seconds. An error message tends to be more acceptable after the sense of completion that comes with the 2-second pause. Very short response times in error situations tend to make the user feel inferior to the machine.

4. Response to a Single-Step Inquiry

When there is a solitary response to a simple question like "Part No. 574138: How many in stock?" or "What is the last traded price of CDC stock?" a response time of lengthy duration may be acceptable. It may be made more acceptable if there is an interim quick response. If, however, a person uses the terminal frequently (several times per hour), it will be frustrating if the response time is, say, 15 seconds.

In situations with single-step inquiries, much depends on the situation surrounding the inquiry and, in particular, on whether other work has to stop until the response is received. If the terminal user is talking to a customer when making the inquiry, a quick response is required. A stockbroker would become very annoyed with a terminal giving a 6-second response because of the urgency of the inquiry. A storekeeper, by contrast, might be unconcerned about a 10-second response.

5. Response to Chained Questions

When the user is attempting to answer a question that needs a linked series of inquiries, a response time of 2 seconds or less becomes necessary for maintaining continuity of attention. The more complex the thought process, the more important this point is. It is particularly important where there is ambiguity in the results. Suppose, for example, that an airline agent is using a terminal for booking a journey from New York to Rome and that the passenger wants to stop at some Caribbean island on the way. What are the best flights? There are many possible answers to this question, and most of them involve flying with more than one carrier. The airline agent will use the terminal to explore the alternatives. Since there will be many linked queries, response times longer than 2 seconds will be frustrating.

6. Browsing

Suppose that the user is leafing through information looking for a particular factory item, much as a person looks through a telephone directory or list of technical reports. This browsing operation may proceed very rapidly at a screen, with the screen being filled in a second or less. The user will probably not read every word on the screen before requesting the next screen; rather, the user's eye quickly scans the information. In this circumstance, the next screen must be displayed very quickly, preferably with a response time of no longer than 1 second. If the user's requests for the next frame are typically sequential, the data transmission system can anticipate them, sending them to a buffer in the terminal or its control unit.

7. Keyboard Entry Versus Pointer Device Entry

An operator using a mouse or a light pen typically expects a quicker response than an operator using a keyboard. Part of the reason for this is that when performing a selection using a pointing device, the user's attention is fixed on the screen all during the interaction. With a keyboard, there is an adaptation time of as long as a second or more when the user shifts attention from the keyboard to the screen. A 2-second delay in response to a mouse selection of a screen item can seem much longer than the same type of interaction using the keyboard. A 1-second or less response to a selection with a pointer device is desirable if it can be achieved.

8. Graphic Response to a Pointing Device

A graphic response to a pointing-device action can take a variety of forms:

- Lines are drawn on the screen with the mouse or light pen. Here the line should appear on the screen almost instantaneously. There should be no perceptible variability in delay.

- An image is built up from a menu of image parts displayed on the screen. The user may select one of the symbols and move it to the required position. Here a delay of up to a second may be acceptable.

- An entire new image may be called for. In this case, the considerations are much the same as the preceding ones requiring a nongraphic response. To avoid a break in continuity of thinking, the image should appear in 2 seconds or less. If continuity of thinking is not involved, the user can wait longer.

9. Graphic Manipulation of Models and Structures

Advanced graphics applications can become complicated, with users carrying out manipulations that require them to retain much information in short-term memory. A fast response time is needed in order to permit this type of interactive thinking. It is possible to maintain a high level of mental activity at a computer terminal for short periods. Responses of 1 second or so are needed for such activity when the attention is fixed constantly on the screen.

10. Response to a "Go" Command

The user may key a lengthy series of entries into a system with some interactive dialog and then, at the end of this operation, instruct the machine to execute a complex operation with these entries. The user may be entering the details of a problem, the parameters of a file search that is required, or the instructions of a program to be executed. When the user finally says "Go" at the end of such a sequence, this is usually a point at which the user is prepared to sit back and relax. The user's short-term memory clears. A fast response to the problem is not required, although an acknowledgment of the "Go" command should be sent within 2 seconds.

VARIATION IN   Many systems will not give the same response time
RESPONSE TIME   to each request of the same type. Some, in fact, be-
                         cause of the nature of the system design, will give a
wide range of response times. The mean response time might be 2 seconds, but
10 percent of the response times are more than 4 seconds, 5 percent more than
6 seconds, and 1 percent more than 8 seconds.

Ideally, for most applications, we would like the dispersion of response times to be low. Too high a standard deviation means that the operator will occasionally become frustrated. If an operator is accustomed to a 2-second response and the system sometimes takes 6 seconds, he or she may wonder whether the computer is going to respond at all this time. The 6 seconds will seem unnaturally long. The user may even initiate the action again or pummel some key on the terminal, which could cause problems.

In many cases, the configuration of the communication network has an effect on response time and other aspects of the user interface. Chapter 19 brings to a conclusion the design part of this book by discussing the design of the data communication network.

19 NETWORK DESIGN

As increasing numbers of terminals are used with data communication systems, the need to devise means of lowering the overall cost of the network grows. In this chapter, we will attempt to summarize the various approaches that can be used in organizing a network by discussing many of the factors that must be considered in determining the overall structure of the network and in refining that structure to achieve a minimum-cost geographical layout of lines.

LINE LENGTH FACTORS
The techniques used depend on the lengths, and hence the cost, of the communication lines and on the number of terminals. If the lines are very long, they are expensive, so techniques for minimizing the cost of the lines may dominate the network design. If the lines are short, their cost is of less concern, and the cost of the terminals and devices attached to the lines is of greater importance. Where the lines are very short—as with a typical local area network— their cost is of little significance in the design, and we often find their bandwidth being used quite wantonly. If a system has a large number of terminals, the terminal cost becomes of major importance, and the network organization should use schemes that enable inexpensive terminals to be used.

SYSTEMS WITH VERY SHORT PRIVATE LINES
We will begin our discussion with the situation in which the lines are so short that we can almost ignore their cost. With typical local area networks, as discussed in Chapter 15, a very high transmission speed is used, typically millions of bits per second. In many cases, the high-speed connections are idle much of the time; much of the transmission capacity is

wasted. However, the lines are short, and once they are installed, there is little additional cost for maintaining them.

SYSTEMS WITH SHORT PUBLIC LINES

We cannot be as wanton in our use of public lines or lines leased from the common carrier. Nevertheless, on short lines, the terminal cost still dominates the design. Short public lines are normally used at efficiencies far below those of which they are capable.

It is indeed intriguing to reflect on how inefficiently local telephone lines are used. The two wires from the telephone in your home probably travel to the local central office in a cable, which carries hundreds of other such pairs. One pair of wires is for your exclusive use as long as you pay your telephone bill. Nobody else shares it. This practice seems inefficient, for such a pair of wires has a bandwidth capable of carrying 24 or more telephone conversations at the same time. Furthermore, your telephone is likely to be in use no more than an hour in total in an average week—0.6 percent utilization. One could say that the line carries $1/24 \times 0.6/100 = 0.00025$ of the voice transmission it is capable of carrying. Rarely in engineering can one find such an expensive facility as a nation's local telephone lines used so inefficiently.

SYSTEMS WITH LONG LINES

When longer lines are used, the techniques change. Now the lines are more costly, and it is desirable to use them more efficiently. If the lines are more than about 100 miles long, the cost of the lines themselves usually dominates the network design.

The first step to efficient line utilization is good modem design. Modems alone, however, do not completely solve the problem. On many commercial systems, we wish to connect to the long lines terminals or other devices that cannot utilize the full line capacity. Suppose that terminals are to be situated at nine locations, as shown in Fig. 19.1, and connected to a computer many miles away. If the terminals have a high usage, it may be cheaper to have a leased line to them rather than a dial-up line. One approach would be to have a leased line to each of them, as shown in Fig. 19.2. Such lines, however, are likely to be inefficiently utilized for the following reasons:

- Most of the terminals will not be transmitting or receiving constantly. The line may then be unused much of the time.

- The line, equipped with suitable modems, has a certain maximum transmission speed. The terminals may not be able to make use of the available line speed.

- The messages we send to the terminals may contain repetitive information or information that could be coded less redundantly. By building some form of

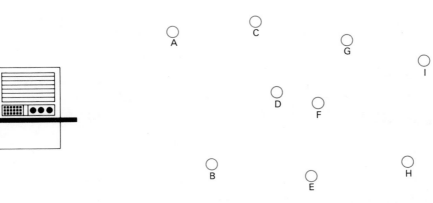

Figure 19.1   A number of terminal locations that must be connected to a computer.

intelligence into the network away from the computer, we could lessen this repetitive or redundant transmission.

As discussed in Part II, a variety of devices and techniques are available for achieving these ends. Their objective is to minimize network cost. Without such methods, a large network would have prohibitively expensive line costs. We will next summarize some of the methods available. Techniques are often combined in practice.

USING A PRIVATE EXCHANGE

The total line mileage can be cut greatly by using line switching. In Fig. 19.3, a switching mechanism is placed at location D. Messages from the computer to

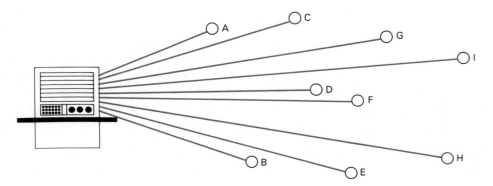

Figure 19.2   Connecting the terminal locations using point-to-point links.

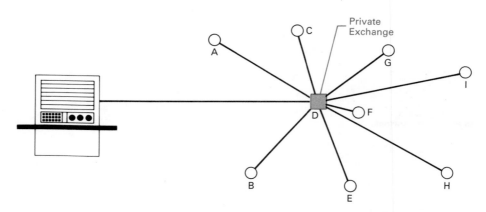

Figure 19.3   Connecting the terminal locations with a private exchange.

a terminal go through this switch. The messages might be preceded by addressing characters that cause the line from the computer to be physically connected to the line to the appropriate terminal. Similarly, when the terminal sends a message to the computer, the appropriate connection must be established. There may be more than one line from the exchange to the computer, and the switching mechanism must be able to hunt for a free one.

The switching mechanism may be a privately owned switching device, such as a private branch exchange at location D, or it might be a mechanism installed in the local telephone exchange at D.

The disadvantage of using an exchange in this way is that a terminal operator may be unable to obtain a line to the computer when one is needed because all are busy. Figure 19.3 shows one line from the exchange to the computer. In practice, there may be more terminals and more lines. The designer must calculate the probability of the terminal operator's not being able to make a connection and being kept waiting for a long time.

USING MULTIPOINT LINES

The total line mileage can be cut further by using a multipoint line. The terminals can be in different locations, with the line taking the shortest path between them, as in Fig. 19.4. The total line mileage in Fig. 19.4 is lower than in the previous diagram.

As we saw in Chapter 8, only one terminal at a time can transmit or receive on a multipoint line. A discipline must be established on the line whereby the devices wait their turns to transmit. If a terminal wishes to transmit, it must wait until the line is free. The terminal cost will be somewhat higher because it needs circuits for recognizing its address and carrying out the data link control procedures.

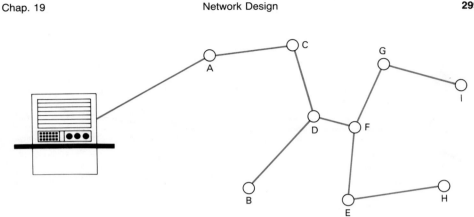

Figure 19.4   Connecting the terminal locations with a single multipoint link.

The terminal user may therefore be kept waiting on a multipoint line just as on a system using an exchange. However, the wait may not be as long. A multipoint line is occupied only for the duration of one message. However, if a switching device is used, the connection from one terminal to the computer may remain unbroken for the duration of a conversation.

A single multipoint line might also be overloaded, so two multipoint lines might be used to connect the nine terminal locations shown. This situation is illustrated in Fig. 19.5. The line configuration here is arranged to give a balanced loading and again to take the shortest path.

USING MULTIPLEXORS

Use of a multiplexor with our nine terminal locations is shown in Fig. 19.6. A single wideband line is being split up into eight separate channels, each ca-

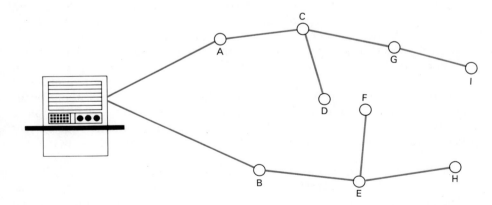

Figure 19.5   Connecting the terminal locations with two multipoint links.

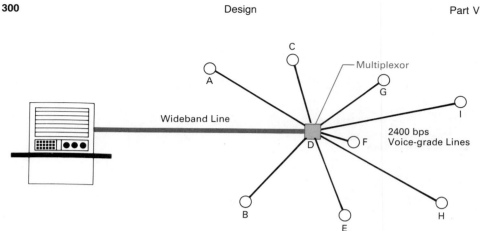

Figure 19.6   Connecting the terminal locations with a multiplexor.

pable of transmitting 2400 bps in this example. We can think of this configuration as being equivalent to using separate lines to each terminal. The fact that the channels are grouped together by multiplexing does not affect the system performance or the programming. This is one of the attractive features of using a multiplexor. The response time or line availability is in no way degraded, as it would be with a multipoint line or a configuration using an exchange. No addressing or polling messages are needed, nor are headers for operating an exchange or making a terminal recognize that a message is addressed to it. The programmer need not even know that multiplexing is being used.

USING BUFFERED DEVICES

Most transmitting and receiving devices operate at their own speeds—speeds that are usually different from the optimum speed of the line. An extreme example is a keyboard operator. If you are operating an asynchronous terminal, you press the keys at your own rate, and the characters are transmitted at this rate, regardless of the capacity of the line. You are tying up the communication line while you wait and think. By contrast, with a synchronous terminal that has a buffer, your hesitant typing could be filling up the buffer without occupying the telecommunications link; the line could be used for transmitting other data. When you finally press the ENTER key, requesting that a message be sent to the computer, the contents of the buffer would then be sent at the maximum speed of the line.

The use of buffers is clearly of value when the line has many different devices contending for transmission. The buffer increases the cost of the terminal. The cost must be balanced against the savings, and the longer the lines, the more likely it is that terminal buffers save money. With today's technology, buffered terminals cost very little more than simple asynchronous terminals, and the extra cost is justified in many applications.

In addition to saving money, terminal buffers can have a major effect on the time an operator is kept waiting at a terminal. Suppose that a typical operator keys data into a terminal at 1.5 characters per second on a multipoint line that transmits at 15 cps. Suppose that an average length for a message keyed in is 75 characters and that you are waiting for another terminal to transmit. If there is no buffering, you will wait 50 seconds. With buffering, you will wait 5 seconds. If a voice line is used at a speed of 150 cps and buffering is used, you will wait only half a second.

USING CONCENTRATORS

As we saw in Chapter 9, synchronous transmission is more efficient than asynchronous transmission. Therefore, we often find network configurations in which asynchronous terminals are attached to a concentration point, as in Fig. 19.7, and from there on the data is carried by synchronous transmission. Similarly, a concentrator may link slow lines to a wideband line. It may link lines that are inefficiently or intermittently used to a line on which the transmission is organized as efficiently as possible.

Two types of concentrators can be used. The first is a device that does not change the speed of lines but simply links many lines from terminals (or telephones) to a smaller number of outgoing lines. When a terminal attempts to contact a computer, for example, the signal may reach a concentrator of this type, which then searches for a free line to the computer. The second type is more commonly used today in data communications. It is a device, often called a *protocol converter*, that stores messages arriving on low-speed lines and then transmits them to a computer in a modified form on a more tightly organized high-speed line.

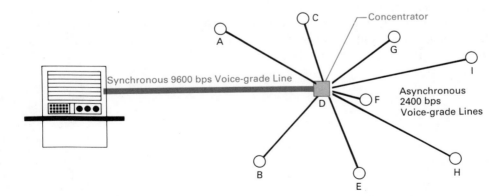

Figure 19.7　Connecting the terminal locations with a concentrator.

Concentrators can also be used in conjunction with multipoint lines to increase line utilization. For example, the concentrators can themselves share a multipoint line. They must then have the logic necessary for responding to polling messages, recognizing messages addressed to them, and performing other line control functions. Also, the low-speed lines downstream of the concentrators can each be multipoint lines attached to several terminals. There can be more than one level of concentration in some large networks. Common control units may feed voice lines that link into concentrators on wideband lines.

USING MESSAGE SWITCHING TECHNIQUES

As we discussed in Chapter 7, there is a fundamental difference between line switching and message switching. With line switching, a physical connection is made between the circuit paths, as in a telephone exchange. With message switching, no physical connection is made; instead the message is stored and then passed on to its destination. In a message switching system, the terminals are not interconnected and enabled to respond to each other directly, in real time. Message switching can give a much better line utilization than line switching.

Today, if the traffic volume is high enough to warrant it, computers are used for message switching. A message switching system sometimes becomes an important part of a computer network.

USING PACKET SWITCHING TECHNIQUES

Message switching systems have traditionally been used to relay messages that do not need a fast delivery time. Packet switching systems, by contrast, operate in a similar manner to message switching systems but relay their messages in a few milliseconds. Packet switching systems can provide a very high degree of line sharing because they allow many users to have access to the same network.

We conclude this book in Chapter 20 by discussing the future. In the future both voice and high-speed data communication will be handled with a worldwide integrated services digital network (ISDN).

EPILOGUE

20 THE FUTURE: ISDN TECHNOLOGY

As we saw in Chapters 2 and 3, the world's analog telecommunications plant is rapidly being replaced by more efficient and cost-effective digital facilities. It is important to realize that the installation of digital telecommunications facilities involves two complementary technologies: digital *transmission* and digital *switching*. Both technologies are well established. The first T-carrier transmission system was introduced by AT&T in 1962, and the first large-scale digital switch to use time-division multiplexing was the Western Electric 4ESS switch, first implemented in 1976. Digital transmission and digital switching complement each other and can provide a powerful, high-bit-rate network.

CONVENTIONAL ANALOG NETWORK

Figure 20.1 shows the conceptual structure of a conventional analog telecommunications network. Typically, this type of network is designed and managed by two separate organizations. The transmission facilities have traditionally been referred to by the common carrier as *outside plant*, while the switching facilities are typically called *inside plant*. The wideband signal that is transmitted from one switching office to another must be demultiplexed before it is switched and then must be remultiplexed before a new wideband signal can be sent on to the next switching office.

INTEGRATED DIGITAL NETWORK (IDN)

Contrast the conventional analog network configuration with the network shown in Fig. 20.2, which uses both digital transmission and digital switching. In such a network, voice signals that enter the network at one end are digitized by equipment in the switching office. The signal can then be sent in this digital form through any number of intermediate switching

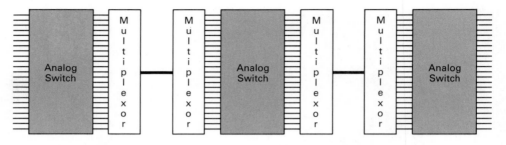

Figure 20.1   With analog transmission and switching, signals must be de-multiplexed and remultiplexed each time they are switched.

offices without having to be decoded. Only when the signal arrives at its destination is it converted into its original analog form. Although digital transmission and switching are advantageous even for voice communication, digital technologies provide even greater benefit for data communication. This is because the digital data signals do not have to be converted from their original digital form into analog signals for transmission or for switching and because very high bit rates can be economically sent over digital transmission facilities.

The conversion of the world's telecommunications facilities into an *integrated digital network* (IDN) is well under way, and most observers agree that a worldwide integrated digital network will eventually become a reality. The economies inherent in digital technologies make this inevitable. It is important to realize, however, that the creation of an integrated digital network is of the most benefit to the common carrier. The end user is most often given an ordinary analog channel that happens to be converted into digital form once it reaches a common carrier's switching office. The end user benefits indirectly, of course, by sharing in the cost savings that digital facilities provide.

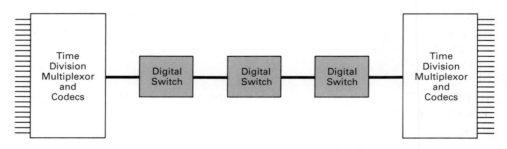

Figure 20.2   With digital transmission and switching, a high degree of integration can be achieved.

INTEGRATED SERVICES DIGITAL NETWORK (ISDN)

A major step in the evolution of common carrier facilities from an analog environment to a completely digital environment lies in the creation of an *integrated services digital network* (ISDN) on top of the IDN. With the ISDN, a digital channel is provided directly to the end user. In such a network, equipment on the user's premises performs any necessary signal conversion that might be necessary to create a digital signal. The digital signal is then transmitted directly to the common carrier's switching office over local loops that are engineered to carry signals in digital form. The interface to the network is documented in the form of international standards.

Because all signals handled by the ISDN will be digital, the user can connect any desired equipment to the network, as long as that equipment is capable of generating a digital bit stream that conforms to ISDN standards. It is the stated goal of ISDN technology to allow any type of equipment to be connected to the network, permitting it to communicate with a complementary device at the other end. The ISDN will be able to detect the nature of the terminals that are connected to it and will be able automatically to supply the type of service that is required by the user. For example, one user of the ISDN might plug a digital telephone into the wall socket and dial up another digital telephone connected to the network. Another user might plug in a terminal, yet another a facsimile machine, and so on. The ISDN would automatically supply the type of channel required to support the connection and would allow any two users to conduct a conversation in the same manner as two users of today's public telephone network.

The only difference between the use of the ISDN and the use of today's public network for ordinary voice telephony would be in the equipment that would be required by the two users. Each user's telephone would require the circuitry needed to convert the analog voice signal to and from the digital form necessary for transmission and switching within the network. This signal conversion is performed by a device called a *codec*. Since codecs have already been implemented on a single silicon chip, the cost of the codec should not significantly increase the cost of the telephone instrument.

The individual telephone user might not perceive a great deal of difference between the ISDN and a conventional analog network, although the ISDN will allow additional services to be offered that are not offered today. But the *data* user will derive enormous benefits. The user of a data terminal could dial up another data terminal user, and the two could exchange messages at high bit rates over the same channel that is used for voice. As we will see, the basic channel provided by the ISDN will support a bit rate of 64 kbps. The ISDN will also provide much higher bit rates than 64 kbps for users that need them.

ISDN STANDARDS

The creation of a worldwide ISDN is not a problem of technology—the technology already exists; the challenge lies in creating the necessary *standards* and getting all countries to agree to them. The main coordinating body for ISDN standards development is the CCITT. Box 20.1 shows how the CCITT describes the ISDN in terms of six attributes that are governing the development of ISDN standards and of the worldwide ISDN itself.

ISDN CHANNELS   The main building block of the ISDN is a 64 kbps channel that is known as the *B channel*. Many channels in the United States are already capable of carrying a 64 kbps bit rate. However, U.S. common carriers typically use a portion of the 64 kbps bit stream for control and signaling purposes and provide only 56 kbps to the user. An ISDN B channel is a *clear channel* that provides a full 64 kbps to the user.

With the ISDN, signaling is handled in a separate *D channel*. D channels are typically packet-switched and provide a bit rate of either 16 kbps or 64 kbps, depending on the level of service that is desired. Other types of channels are also being considered. The incompatibility between the 64-kbps B channel and the 56-kbps channel provided in the United States is a major stumbling block to the rapid deployment of a worldwide ISDN, and this issue is currently under study by the CCITT.

BOX 20.1   Six ISDN attributes

- The ISDN must evolve from the telephone networks that are already in operation throughout the world. The existing networks are themselves in the process of evolving from analog networks into IDNs.

- New services that are to be offered in the ISDN environment must be compatible with the basic 64-kbps switched digital channel.

- A worldwide ISDN will probably not be fully operational until the end of the 1990s and possibly later, although some ISDN services are already available in some areas.

- During the transition period, the ISDN will rely heavily on interconnections between national ISDNs and existing non-ISDN public data networks.

- The ISDN will implement intelligence in order to perform such functions as maintenance, system control, and network management.

- The ISDN will use a set of layered protocols that conform to the OSI Reference Model (see Chapter 12).

ISDN LEVELS OF SERVICE

Although many levels of service are under study by the CCITT, one of two alternative levels of service is likely to be used by the majority of ISDN customers. These two levels of service are the *basic access interface* and the *primary access interface*.

- **Basic Access Interface.** The basic access interface level of service defines a bit rate of 144 kbps, which is divided into two 64-kbps B channels and one 16-kbps D channel. This is the level of service that an individual residential or small business subscriber would most likely use for voice and data applications. The basic access interface would allow a typical user to conduct a voice telephone call and a data call simultaneously over the same telephone line.

- **Primary Access Interface.** The primary access interface level of service defines a bit rate of 1.536 Mbps, which is divided into twenty-three 64-kbps B channels and one 64-kbps D channel. This is the level of service that might be used by a larger company to connect a digital PBX to the central switching office. The primary access interface might also be used to connect a high-speed data machine directly to the ISDN.

ISDN USER INTERFACE

To make it easy to connect various devices to the ISDN, it is important that a limited number of types of connection points be defined for the network and that these connection points be well standardized. Figure 20.3 shows the interface points that have been defined for the ISDN. The boxes in the diagram represent the groupings of functions that have been identified for the equipment

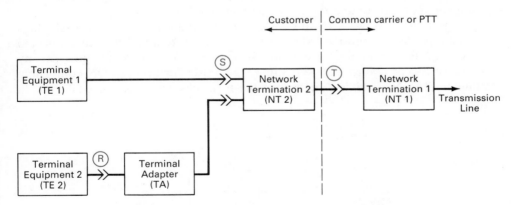

Figure 20.3 The ISDN reference model defines functional groupings and interface points to the network.

that will be used to connect to the network. These functional groupings are as follows:

- **Network Termination 1 (NT1).** The NT1 functional grouping will be implemented in a device that will probably be owned by the common carrier. It will be installed at the end of the local loop that provides ISDN service to an individual customer.

- **Network Termination 2 (NT2).** The NT2 functional grouping will be implemented in a device that will most likely be owned by the ISDN customer, not by the common carrier. It will allow a number of ISDN terminals to be connected to a single ISDN connection.

- **Network Termination 12 (NT12).** This functional grouping will typically be used in regulatory environments such as exist in many European countries. The NT12 grouping combines the functions of NT1 and NT2.

- **Terminal Adapter (TA).** This functional grouping will be implemented in a device that allows a non-ISDN terminal to be attached to the ISDN.

- **Terminal Equipment 1 (TE1).** A TE1 is a terminal that conforms to ISDN standards. Examples are digital telephones, ISDN-compatible data terminals, and ISDN-compatible facsimile machines.

- **Terminal Equipment 2 (TE2).** A TE2 is a terminal that is not compatible with the ISDN, such as one that implements the X.21 or RS-232-C physical-level interface.

The simplest way for a customer to connect a device to the ISDN is to plug an ISDN terminal (TE1) into the ISDN at point T. This is shown in Fig. 20.4. In this case, the NT2 grouping is implemented by a set of wires directly connecting a terminal to the ISDN at interface point T. In the United States, point T will most likely define the dividing line between the equipment supplied by the common carrier and the equipment supplied by the user.

Figure 20.5 shows a more complex arrangement in which the user plugs an NT2-type device into the ISDN at point T. Each terminal is then connected to the NT2 device at interface point S. The NT2 device might provide any number of S-type connection points into which users can plug ISDN-compatible terminals. The NT2 device might take the form physically of a digital PBX, a

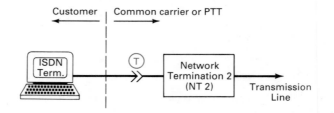

Figure 20.4   Connecting a terminal to the ISDN at interface point T.

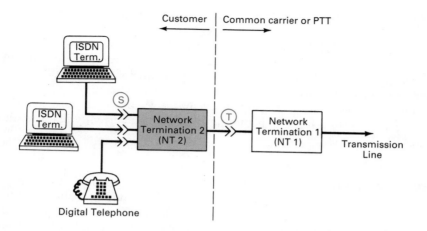

Figure 20.5   Connecting terminals to the ISDN at interface point S.

terminal controller, or even a local area network. As shown in Fig. 20.6, a non-ISDN terminal might also be connected to the NT2 via a terminal adapter that connects to the NT2 device at point S. The non-ISDN terminal is connected to the TA device at interface point R.

The same physical connector will be used for both interface point S and interface point T. For the ISDN basic access interface, the S and T interface will probably take the form physically of a small plastic plug similar to the modular plug that is used today to connect a device to the telephone network. It will probably contain eight wires rather than the four typically used for analog

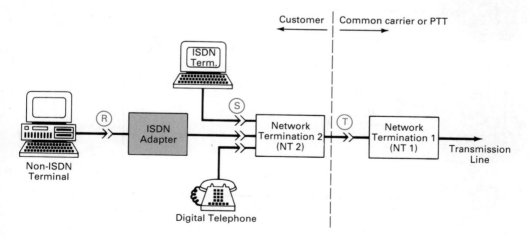

Figure 20.6   Connecting a non-ISDN terminal to the ISDN at interface point R.

telephony. The connector may be different for the higher-speed primary access interface.

The initial ISDN recommendations also allow for an analog terminal, such as an ordinary telephone, to be connected to the NT1 device, as shown in Fig. 20.7. Compatibility with conventional analog channels will be important for the interim period as the world evolves to the ISDN. The way in which analog channels of all types are to be supported by the ISDN, such as voice channels and the channels used for television transmission, are currently being studied by the CCITT.

ISDN SERVICES

In addition to providing telephone services in a more economical fashion and providing better facilities for data communication, it is envisioned that the ISDN will make possible a number of additional services that are either not available today or are available only on a limited basis. Box 20.2 lists a number of services that could be offered in conjunction with the ISDN.

Most ISDN services could be provided using the 64-kbps B channel, although some services would require the use of higher-speed facilities. Some services that common carriers offer today might require even higher bit rates than would be provided by the ISDN primary access interface. In some cases,

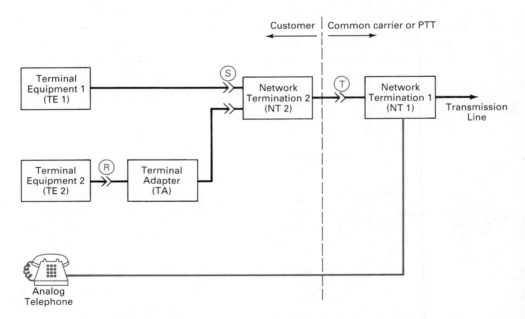

Figure 20.7   Conventional analog telephones will also be supported by the ISDN.

BOX 20.2 Potential ISDN services

- Local voice telephone service
- National long-distance services
- International long-distance services
- Malicious call blocking
- Automatic call transferring
- Abbreviated dialing
- Prerecorded messages
- Conference calls
- Camp on busy
- Restricting outgoing toll calls
- Hot lines
- Detailed billing information
- Automatic wake-up or reminder calls
- Leased voice circuits
- Information retrieval using speech recognition
- Music transmission
- Packet-switched data services
- Circuit-switching data services
- Leased channels
- One-way telemetry services
- Electronic funds transfer
- Information retrieval
- Electronic mail
- Alarm services
- High-speed computer communication
- Automatic call dialing
- Automatic call answering
- Closed user groups
- Calling line identification
- Called line identification
- Automatic call transferring
- Teletext services
- Videotext services
- Facsimile services

BOX 20.3   ISDN evolution

1. New transition services will be introduced first, offering facilities similar to those that will be provided by a true ISDN. These new services will allow the common carriers to test the marketplace in a cost-effective manner.
2. As ISDN-like services become more widely used, equipment will begin to be replaced with equipment that conforms to the emerging ISDN standards.
3. True ISDN services will then be provided in selected market areas that have the highest concentration of users who are likely to need ISDN facilities. ISDN facilities will be made available to customers outside the initial areas through various types of remote access arrangements.
4. Finally, ISDN services will be provided universally to all the customers of a common carrier.

these services might be provided by higher-speed channels that operate outside the ISDN, such as long-distance transmission of television signals. However, it is possible that these services would be controlled by the ISDN and might even share some of the same transmission links that are used to implement the ISDN.

EVOLUTION
TOWARD ISDN

Conversion to the ISDN will be an expensive, time-consuming process. It will necessarily be done a piece at a time, with ISDN facilities being made available first to those that have a specific need for ISDN services and are willing to pay for them. Box 20.3 shows how the evolution toward an ISDN environment is likely to take place in the United States.

At the time of this writing, there is no common agreement about how long it will take to implement a worldwide ISDN; in fact, some observers are doubtful that it will ever happen. However, most experts agree that worldwide deployment of the ISDN is only a matter of time. The end of the 1990s is the time frame most often mentioned for its completion.

It is impossible to determine for sure, at this point in time, exactly what form the ISDN will take and what types of services will be offered. The ISDN will be driven by the market, not by technology, and common carriers will offer the services that they feel users are willing to pay for. Many new services will be offered, and some of these will possibly fail when common carriers discover that customers do not use them.

GLOSSARY

ACCUNET. Trademark of AT&T that refers to a collection of digital data transmission services offered in the U.S.

ACOUSTICAL COUPLER. A particular type of modem that contains a microphone and speaker and interfaces with a communication channel using audio tones and a standard telephone handset.

ADCCP. (*See* **Advanced Data Communication Control Procedure.**)

ADDRESS. A coded representation of the destination of data or of its originating location. Multiple devices on one communication line, for example, must have unique addresses. There is a distinction between a station's data link address, which must be unique on a single data link, and a station's network address, which must be unique within an entire network.

ADVANCED DATA COMMUNICATION CONTROL PROCEDURE (ADCCP). A bit-oriented data link protocol standardized by the American National Standards Association (ANSI) and documented in ANSI Standard X3.66 and in Federal Standard 1003. ADCCP is similar to HDLC. (*See also* **High-Level Data Link Control.**)

ALPHABET. A table of correspondence between an agreed set of characters and the signals that represent them. Often called a *data code* or *character set*.

ALTERNATE ROUTING. (*See* **Routing, alternate.**)

AMERICAN STANDARD CODE FOR INFORMATION INTERCHANGE (ASCII). Usually pronounced "ask'-ee." A 7-bit code for data transfer adopted by the American Standards Association to achieve compatibility between data devices. ASCII is a variation of the CCITT International Alphabet No. 5.

AMPLIFIER. An electronic circuit used on an analog transmission facility that detects a weak signal and makes it stronger. An amplifier often amplifies the noise on the channel as well as the original signal.

AMPLITUDE MODULATION. One method of modifying a sine-wave signal in order to make it "carry" information. The sine wave, or carrier, has its amplitude modified in accordance with the information to be transmitted.

ANALOG DATA. Data in the form of continuously variable physical quantities. Compare with **Digital data.**

ANALOG TRANSMISSION. Transmission of a continuously variable signal as opposed to a discretely variable signal. Physical quantities, such as temperature, are continuously variable and so are described as "analog." Data characters, by contrast, are coded in discrete pulses or signal levels and are referred to as "digital."

ARCHITECTURE. An overall scheme or plan that may not necessarily be fully implemented. An architecture represents the goal toward which its implementors strive. The term *architecture* is often used to describe database management systems, operating systems, data communication systems, and other highly complex software/hardware mechanisms. A good architecture relates primarily to the needs of the end users rather than to enthusiasms for particular techniques.

ASCII. (*See* **American Standard Code for Information Interchange.**)

ASYNCHRONOUS TRANSMISSION. Data transmission in which each group of code elements corresponding to an alphabetic signal is preceded by a start signal that serves to prepare the receiving mechanism for the reception and registration of a character and is followed by a stop signal that serves to bring the receiving mechanism to rest in preparation for the reception of the next character. Contrast with **Synchronous transmission**. Asynchronous transmission is also called *start-stop transmission.*

ATTENUATION. Decrease in the magnitude of current, voltage, or power of a signal in transmission between two points. Can be expressed in decibels.

ATTENUATION EQUALIZER. (*See* **Equalizer.**)

AUDIO FREQUENCIES. Frequencies that can be heard by the human ear (typically 30 to 20,000 hertz).

BANDWIDTH. The range of frequencies available for signaling. The difference expressed in hertz (cycles per second) between the highest and lowest frequencies of a frequency band.

BASEBAND SIGNALING. Transmission of a signal at its original frequencies; that is, a signal not changed by modulation.

BAUD. Unit of signaling speed. The speed in baud is the number of discrete conditions, or signal events, per second. If a signal event represents only one bit condition, the line speed in baud is the same as the bit rate in bits per second. When each signal event represents other than one bit, baud does not equal bits per second.

BAUDOT CODE. A code for the transmission of data in which 5 equal-length bits represent one character. This code is used with some teletype machines.

BCC. (*See* **Block check character.**)

BEL. 10 decibels. (*See* **Decibel.**)

BINARY-SYNCHRONOUS PROTOCOL. A data link protocol, defined by IBM, that uses synchronous transmission to transmit frames of arbitrary length. The binary-synchronous protocol is a character-oriented protocol that uses either the ASCII or EBCDIC character set to define control functions. A character-stuffing procedure may be used to make it possible to carry any desired character in the data portion of the transmission frame.

BIT. Contraction of *binary digit*, the smallest unit of information in a binary system.

BIT-ORIENTED PROTOCOL. A class of data link protocols that are independent of any given code set. Protocol control functions are specified in particular positions of the transmission frame, thus allowing any desired bit stream to be carried in the data portion of the frame. A flag bit configuration (0111 1110) identifies the beginning and ending of each frame, and a zero-bit insertion procedure ensures that 6 consecutive one bits never appear in the frame itself.

BIT RATE. The speed at which bits are transmitted, usually expressed in bits per second. Compare with **Baud.**

BIT REPEATER. (*See* **Repeater, regenerative.**)

BIT STUFFING. (*See* **Zero-bit insertion.**)

BITS PER SECOND. Measure of the bit rate (data carrying speed) of a data transmission channel. Compare with **Baud.**

BLOCK CHECK CHARACTER (BCC). A set of bits (usually 16) carried at the end of a binary-synchronous transmission frame that is used in error detection. The sending station puts each character of the data portion of the frame through an arithmetic algorithm to develop the BCC character value. The receiver puts each character of the received frame through the same algorithm and compares the calculated BCC value with the received BCC value. If the values are different, the receiving station transmits a negative acknowledgment, thus requesting that the frame be retransmitted.

BROADBAND. (*See* **Wideband.**)

BROADCAST ADDRESS. A data link or network address that indicates that all stations on the data link or network are to receive a transmission.

BUFFER. A storage device used to compensate for a difference in rate of data flow or time of occurrence of events when transmitting data from one device to another.

CABLE. An assembly of one or more conductors within an enveloping protective sheath, constructed to permit the conductors to be used separately or in groups.

CARRIER. A continuous frequency capable of being modulated, or impressed with a second (information-carrying) signal.

CARRIER, COMMUNICATION COMMON. A company that furnishes communication services to the general public and is regulated by appropriate local, state, or federal agencies.

CARRIER SYSTEM. A means of obtaining a number of channels over a single path by modulating each channel on a different carrier frequency and demodulating at the receiving point to restore the signals to their original form.

CCITT. (*See* **International Telegraph and Telephone Consultative Committee.**)

CENTRAL OFFICE. The place where communication common carriers terminate customer lines and locate the switching equipment that interconnects those lines. Also referred to as an *exchange, end office,* or *local central office.*

CENTRONICS INTERFACE. A data link protocol originally developed by the Centronics Corporation for parallel transmission of data over a direct cable connection. The Centronics interface generally employs a 36-pin connector and is often used for connecting a printer to a computer.

CHANNEL. A path for electrical transmission between two or more points. Also called a *circuit, line, link, path,* or *facility.*

CHANNEL, ANALOG. A channel on which the information transmitted can take any value between the minimum and maximum limits defined by the channel.

CHANNEL, VOICE-GRADE. A channel suitable for transmission of speech, digital or analog data, or facsimile, generally with a frequency range of about 300 to 3100 cycles per second.

CHANNEL GROUP. The assembly of 12 telephone channels in a carrier system, occupying adjacent bands in the spectrum for the purposes of simultaneous modulation or demodulation.

CHARACTER. Letter, figure, number, punctuation mark, or other sign contained in a message. Besides such characters, there may be characters for special symbols and control functions.

CHARACTER STUFFING. A technique used by the binary-synchronous data link protocol for allowing any desired character (including control characters) to be carried in the data portion of a transmission frame.

CIRCUIT. A means of communication between two points. (*See also* **Channel.**)

CIRCUIT, FOUR-WIRE. A metallic circuit in which four wires (two for each direction of transmission) are presented to the station equipment. (*See also* **Duplex transmission.**)

CIRCUIT, TWO-WIRE. A metallic circuit formed by two conductors insulated from each other. It is possible to use the two conductors as a simplex transmission path, a half-duplex path, or a full-duplex path.

CIRCUIT SWITCHING. Switching in which a physical path is set up between the incoming and outgoing lines. Contrast with **Message switching,** in which no physical path is established. With circuit switching, an actual physical circuit is established between the sender and the receiver for the duration of a transmission.

CLUSTER CONTROLLER. A device, often a stored-program computer, that is used to control the functions of a group of terminals generally located in close physical proximity.

CODEC. Contraction of *coder/decoder.* A codec is a device that is used to convert a telephone voice signal into a digital bit stream. A codec generally uses pulse code modulation (PCM) to perform the conversion. (*See also* **Pulse code modulation.**)

CODER/DECODER. (*See* **Codec.**)

COMITÉ CONSULTATIF INTERNATIONAL TÉLÉGRAPHIQUE ET TÉLÉPHONIQUE (CCITT). (*See* **International Telegraph and Telephone Consultative Committee.**)

COMMON CARRIER. (*See* **Carrier, communication common.**)

COMMUNICATIONS CONTROLLER. A device, generally a stored-program computer, that attaches to a host computer and has as its function to control data communication functions.

COMMUNICATION NETWORK ARCHITECTURE. (*See* **Network architecture.**)

COMMUNICATIONS SATELLITE. A device, generally in geosynchronous orbit, that is essentially a microwave relay in the sky. Devices called transponders in the satellite receive microwave signals from a sending earth station and retransmit the signals to receiving earth stations. (*See also* **Earth station, Transponder.**)

CONDITIONING. The addition of equipment to a leased voice-grade channel to provide minimum values of line characteristics required for data transmission.

CONTENTION. A method of line control in which the terminals request to transmit. If the channel in question is free, transmission proceeds; if it is not free, the terminal waits until the channel becomes free.

CONTROL CHARACTER. A character whose occurrence in a particular context initiates, modifies, or stops a control operation—for example, a character to control carriage return.

CONTROL MODE. The state that all terminals on a line must be in to allow line control actions or terminal selection to occur. When all terminals on a line are in the control mode, characters on the line are viewed as control characters performing line discipline, that is, polling or addressing.

CONTROL STATION. (*See* **Primary station.**)

CROSSTALK. The unwanted transfer of energy from one circuit, called the disturbing circuit, to another circuit, called the disturbed circuit.

CYCLICAL REDUNDANCY CHECK. Use of a particular type of arithmetic algorithm for generating error detection bits in a data link protocol.

DATA CIRCUIT-TERMINATING EQUIPMENT (DCE). Class of device that interfaces between a device of the class *data terminal equipment* (DTE) and a data transmission facility. A DCE normally performs some type of signal conversion between the terminal device and the transmission facility.

DATA COMMUNICATION. The electronic transmission of data, including information generated by computers and other forms of data, including telegraph and telemetry signals.

DATA LINK. A communication facility, and related line termination equipment, that allows data to be transmitted over the facility.

DATA LINK PROTOCOL. A standard that governs the way in which communicating machines interact at the data link level. A set of rules that all devices on the data link follow in controlling transmission over the link.

DATA SET. A device that performs the modulation, demodulation, and control functions necessary to provide compatibility between business machines and communication facilities. (*See also* **Modem.**)

DATA TERMINAL EQUIPMENT (DTE). The portion of a data processing machine that is capable of transmitting digital data over a communication circuit. A DTE is generally attached to a DCE (data circuit-terminating equipment) in order to send and receive data over a communication facility. (*See also* **Data circuit-terminating equipment.**)

DATA TRANSMISSION. (*See* **Data communication.**)

DATAGRAM. A message sent over a packet-switched network that consists of a single packet only. (*See also* **Packet, Packet switching.**)

DATAPHONE. Both a service mark and a trademark of AT&T. As a service mark it indicates the transmission of data over the telephone network. As a trademark it identifies the communication equipment furnished by AT&T for data communication services.

DATAPHONE DIGITAL SERVICE (DDS). A data communication service offered by AT&T that provides digital channels of various bit rates to its users.

DCE. (*See* **Data circuit-terminating equipment.**)

DDS. (*See* **Dataphone Digital Service.**)

DECIBEL (db). One-tenth of a bel. A unit for measuring relative strength of a signal parameter, such as power or voltage. The number of decibels is 10 times the logarithm (base 10) of the ratio of the measured quantity to the reference level. The reference level must always be indicated, such as 1 milliwatt for power ratio.

DEMODULATION. The process of retrieving intelligence (data) from a modulated carrier wave; the reverse of *modulation*.

DIAL-UP. The use of a dial or push-button telephone to initiate a station-to-station telephone call.

DIBIT. A group of 2 bits. In four-phase modulation, each possible dibit is encoded as one of four unique carrier phase shifts. The four possible states of a dibit are 00, 01, 10, and 11.

DIGITAL DATA. Information represented by a code consisting of a sequence of discrete elements. Compare with **Analog transmission.**

DIGITAL SIGNAL. A discrete or discontinuous signal; one whose various states are discrete intervals apart. Compare with **Analog transmission.**

DIGITAL SPEECH INTERPOLATION (DSI). A form of dynamic channel assignment for increasing the utilization of a digital voice channel in which channel capacity is assigned to a user only when that user is actually speaking. (*See also* **Dynamic channel assignment, Time assignment speech interpolation.**)

DISCONNECT SIGNAL. A signal transmitted from one end of a subscriber line or trunk to indicate at the other end that the established connection should be disconnected.

DISTORTION. The unwanted change in waveform that occurs between two points in a transmission system.

DSI. (*See* **Digital speech interpolation.**)

DTE. (*See* **Data terminal equipment.**)

DUPLEX TRANSMISSION. Simultaneous two-way independent transmission; also called *full-duplex transmission*. Compare with **Half-duplex transmission.**

DUPLEXING. The use of duplicate computers, files, or circuitry so that if one component should fail, an alternative one can enable the system to carry on its work.

DYNAMIC CHANNEL ALLOCATION. A technique in which channel capacity is assigned to a user only when the user actually requires it.

EARTH STATION. The part of a communications satellite transmission system that resides on the ground. A sending earth station transmits a signal up to a communications satellite in earth orbit; a receiving earth station receives a signal that is retransmitted by the satellite.

EBCDIC. (*See* **Extended Binary-coded Decimal Interchange Code.**)

EIA. (*See* **Electronics Industry Association.**)

END OFFICE. (*See* **Central office.**)

EQUALIZATION. Compensation for the attenuation (signal loss) increase with frequency. Its purpose is to produce a flat frequency response while the temperature remains constant.

EQUALIZER. Any combination (usually adjustable) of coils, capacitors, and/or resistors inserted in a transmission line or amplifier circuit to improve its frequency response.

ERROR-CORRECTING CODE. A code incorporating sufficient additional signaling elements to enable the nature of some or all of the errors to be indicated and corrected entirely at the receiving end.

ERROR-DETECTING CODE. A code in which each signal conforms to specific rules of construction so that any departure from this construction in the received signals can be automatically detected. Such codes necessarily require more signaling elements than are required to convey the basic information.

ESCAPE MECHANISM. A mechanism in a data code that permits a control character (the escape character) to signify that one or more following characters are to be given an alternative interpretation.

EVEN PARITY CHECK. (*See* **Parity check.**)

EXCHANGE. A unit established by a communication common carrier for the administration of communication service in a specified area, usually embracing a city, town, or village and its environs. It consists of one or more central offices together with the associated equipment used in furnishing communication service. (This term is often used as a synonym for *central office.*)

EXCHANGE, PRIVATE AUTOMATIC (PAX). A dial telephone exchange that provides private telephone service to an organization and does not allow calls to be transmitted to or from the public telephone network.

EXCHANGE, PRIVATE AUTOMATIC BRANCH (PABX). An automatic exchange connected to the public telephone network on the user's premises.

EXCHANGE, PRIVATE BRANCH (PBX). A manual or automatic exchange connected to the public telephone network on the user's premises.

EXTENDED BINARY-CODED DECIMAL INTERCHANGE CODE (EBCDIC). An 8-bit data code that is used on much IBM equipment both internally and sometimes for data communication purposes.

FACSIMILE (FAX). A system for the transmission of images. The image is scanned at the transmitter, reconstructed at the receiving station, and duplicated on paper.

FAST-CONNECT CIRCUIT SWITCHING. A form of circuit switching, well suited to use on computer networks, in which connections are established in milliseconds.

FCC. (*See* **Federal Communications Commission.**)

FD *or* FDX. Full-duplex. (*See* **Duplex.**)

FDM. (*See* **Frequency-division multiplexing.**)

FEDERAL COMMUNICATIONS COMMISSION (FCC). A board of seven commissioners appointed by the president under the Communications Act of 1934, having the power to regulate all interstate and foreign electrical communication systems originating in the United States.

FIBER OPTICS. A generic term for the technology that allows data to be transmitted over a thin strand of glass using a modulated light beam.

FILTER. A network designed to transmit currents of frequencies within one or more frequency bands and to attenuate currents of other frequencies.

FLOW CONTROL. A mechanism in a data communication system for regulating the flow of data over the network. (*See also* **Pacing.**)

FOREIGN EXCHANGE SERVICE. A service that connects a customer's telephone to a telephone company central office normally not serving the customer's location.

FORWARD ERROR CORRECTION. A form of error handling in which sufficient redundancy is built into each message that the receiving station can both detect and automatically correct errors that occur during transmission.

FRAME. The unit of data that is handled by the data link–level layer of software in a data communication system.

FREQUENCY-DIVISION MULTIPLEXING. A multiplexing system in which the available transmission frequency range is divided into narrower bands, each used for a separate channel.

FREQUENCY MODULATION. One method of modifying a sine-wave signal to make it "carry" information. The sine wave or "carrier" has its frequency modified in accordance with the information to be transmitted. The frequency function of the modulated wave may be continuous or discontinuous. In the latter case, two or more particular frequencies may correspond each to one significant condition.

FULL-DUPLEX TRANSMISSION. (*See* **Duplex transmission.**)

GATEWAY. A device that serves as a bridge between two networks.

GEOSYNCHRONOUS ORBIT. An earth orbit 22,282 miles high at which point a satellite above the equator travels around the earth in exactly the time it takes for the earth to rotate on its axis. A satellite in geosynchronous orbit appears to hang stationary over a particular point on the earth.

GRADE OF SERVICE. The probability of receiving a network busy signal on a communication network.

GROUP. (*See* **Channel group.**)

GROUP ADDRESS. A data link or network address that specifies a collection of stations on the data link or network.

GUARD BAND. Range of frequencies that separate one subchannel from another when frequency-division multiplexing is used.

HALF-DUPLEX CIRCUIT. A circuit designed for transmission in either direction but not both directions simultaneously.

HALF-DUPLEX TRANSMISSION. (*See* **Half-duplex circuit.**)

HANDSHAKING. Exchange of predetermined signals for purposes of control when a connection is established over a data link.

HD *or* **HDX.** Half-duplex. (*See* **Half-duplex circuit.**)

HDLC. (*See* **High-Level Data Link Control.**)

HERTZ (Hz). A measure of frequency or bandwidth. The same as cycles per second.

HIGH-LEVEL DATA LINK CONTROL (HDLC). A bit-oriented data link protocol standardized by the International Standards Organization (ISO) and documented in ISO Standards 3309 and 4435.

HUB POLLING. A form of polling in which the polling signal is sent from one terminal to the next on the data link.

IDN. (*See* **Integrated digital network.**)

IEEE. (*See* **Institute of Electrical and Electronics Engineers.**)

INFORMATION UTILITY. A company that is in the business of providing information to its customers typically via computer terminals connected to a public data network.

IN-PLANT SYSTEM. A system whose parts, including remote terminals, are all situated in one building or a localized area. The term is also used for communication systems spanning several buildings and sometimes covering a large distance but in which no common carrier facilities are used.

INSTITUTE OF ELECTRICAL AND ELECTRONICS ENGINEERS (IEEE). An organization that, among other activities, produces data communication standards. Particularly important are the IEEE 802 group of standards for various types of local area networks.

INTERNATIONAL ALPHABET NO. 2. A 5-bit character code, standardized by the CCITT, widely used in telegraphy.

INTERNATIONAL ALPHABET NO. 5. A 7-bit character code widely used in data transmission. ASCII is a dialect of International Alphabet No. 5.

INTERNATIONAL STANDARDS ORGANIZATION (ISO). An international organization for standardization. ISO publishes many standards that are important for data communication. The OSI Reference Model is being developed by the ISO. (*See also* **Reference Model for Open Systems Interconnection**.)

INTERNATIONAL TELECOMMUNICATION UNION (ITU). The telecommunications agency of the United Nations, established to provide standardized communication procedures and practices including frequency allocation and radio regulations on a worldwide basis. The CCITT is part of the ITU. (*See also* **International Telegraph and Telephone Consultative Committee.**)

INTERNATIONAL TELEGRAPH AND TELEPHONE CONSULTATIVE COMMITTEE (CCITT). An organization in the International Telecommunication Union that publishes recommendations of importance to data communication. *Recommendation X.25* is published by the CCITT.

INTEGRATED DIGITAL NETWORK (IDN). A communication network that combines the technologies of digital switching and digital transmission of information. (*See also* **Integrated services digital network.**)

INTEGRATED SERVICES DIGITAL NETWORK (ISDN). A communication network that uses an integrated digital network (IDN) to carry all forms of traffic, such as voice, computer data, and facsimile. (*See also* **Integrated digital network.**)

INTEROFFICE TRUNK. A trunk between toll offices in different telephone exchanges.

IRMA BOARD. Circuit board for personal computers that permits 3270 terminal emulation.

ISDN. (*See* **Integrated services digital network.**)

ISO. (*See* **International Standards Organization.**)

ITU. (*See* **International Telecommunication Union.**)

JUMBOGROUP. The assembly of six mastergroups (3600 telephone channels) in a carrier system, occupying adjacent bands in the spectrum, for the purposes of simultaneous modulation or demodulation. (*See also* **Mastergroup.**)

JUMBOGROUP MULTIPLEX. The assembly of three jumbogroups (10,800 telephone channels) in a carrier system, occupying adjacent bands in the spectrum, for the purposes of simultaneous modulation or demodulation. (*See also* **Jumbogroup.**)

LEASED FACILITY. A facility reserved for sole use of a single leasing customer. (*See also* **Private line.**)

LAP *and* LAPB. (*See* **Link Access Protocol.**)

LINE CONDITIONING. (*See* **Conditioning.**)

LINE SWITCHING. (*See* **Circuit switching.**)

LINE TERMINATION DEVICE. A device, such as a modem or service unit, used to attach a data machine to a transmission facility. (*See also* **Data circuit-terminating equipment.**)

LINK ACCESS PROTOCOL (LAP) *and* LINK ACCESS PROTOCOL—BALANCED (LAPB). Bit-oriented data link protocols standardized by the CCITT that specify the functions of the data link level of CCITT *Recommendation X.25.* LAP and LAPB are compatible subsets of HDLC. (*See also* **High-Level Data Link Control.**)

LOADING. Adding inductance (load coils) to a transmission line to minimize amplitude distortion.

LOCAL AREA NETWORK (LAN). A data communication network, usually operating at high speeds (typically hundreds of thousands or millions of bits per second), over a limited geographical area (typically within a building or group of buildings), using privately installed communication media.

LOCAL EXCHANGE *or* LOCAL CENTRAL OFFICE. An exchange in which subscribers' lines terminate. Also referred to as an *end office.*

LOCAL LOOP. A channel connecting the subscriber's equipment to the line-terminating equipment in the central office exchange. Usually a two-wire or four-wire twisted-pair circuit.

LONGITUDINAL REDUNDANCY CHECK (LRC). A system of error control based on the formation of a block check following preset rules. The check formation rule is applied in the same manner to each character.

LOOP CONFIGURATION. Data link configuration in which the stations are arranged in a ring.

LRC. (*See* **Longitudinal redundancy check.**)

MARK. Presence of signal. In telegraph communication, a mark represents the closed condition or current flowing. A mark impulse is equivalent to binary 1.

MASTERGROUP. The assembly of 10 supergroups (600 telephone channels) in a carrier system, occupying adjacent bands in the spectrum, for the purposes of simultaneous modulation or demodulation. (*See also* **Supergroup.**)

MASTERGROUP MULTIPLEX. The assembly of three mastergroups (1800 telephone channels) in a carrier system, occupying adjacent bands in the spectrum, for the purposes of simultaneous modulation or demodulation. (*See also* **Mastergroup.**)

MASTER STATION. (*See* **Primary station.**)

MEASURED-USE SERVICE. A data communication service for which a common carrier or PTT charges only for time the service is used by the customer. Placing a call on the public telephone system is an example of employing a measured-use communication service.

MESSAGE SWITCHING. The technique of receiving a message, storing it until the proper outgoing line is available, and then retransmitting it. No direct connection between the incoming and outgoing lines is set up as in line switching.

MICROWAVE. Any electromagnetic wave in the radio-frequency spectrum above 890 megahertz.

MODEM. Contraction of *modulator/demodulator*. The term may be used when the modulator and the demodulator are associated in the same signal-conversion equipment. (*See also* **Modulation.**)

MODULATION. The process by which some characteristic of one wave is varied in accordance with another wave or signal. This technique is used in modems to make data machine signals compatible with communication facilities.

MODULATOR/DEMODULATOR. (*See* **Modem.**)

MULTIDROP LINE. (*See* **Multipoint line.**)

MULTIPLEXING. Use of a common channel in order to make two or more channels, either by splitting the frequency band transmitted by the common channel into narrower bands, each of which is used to constitute a distinct channel (frequency-division multiplexing), or by allotting this common channel to several information channels, one at a time (time-division multiplexing).

MULTIPLEXOR. A device that uses several communication channels at the same time and transmits and receives messages and controls the communication lines.

MULTIPOINT LINE. A line or circuit interconnecting several stations. Also called a *multidrop line*.

NETWORK ARCHITECTURE. An overall plan that governs the design of hardware and software components that make up a data communication system.

NOISE. Random electrical signals, introduced by circuit components or natural disturbances, that tend to degrade the performance of a communication channel.

NULL MODEM. RS-232-C cable with the appropriate circuits crossed allowing a DTE to be attached to a DTE or a DCE to be attached to a DCE.

ODD PARITY CHECK. (*See* **Parity check.**)

OFF HOOK. Activated (in regard to a telephone set). By extension, a modem automatically answering on a public switched system is said to go "off hook." Compare with **On hook.**

ON HOOK. Deactivated (in regard to a telephone set). A telephone (or modem) not in use is "on hook." Compare with **Off hook.**

ONLINE. An online system can be defined as one in which the input data enters the computer directly from its point of origin and/or output data is transmitted directly to where it is used. The intermediate stages, such as writing magnetic tapes or diskettes or offline printing, are largely avoided.

OPEN SYSTEMS INTERCONNECT REFERENCE MODEL. (*See* **Reference Model for Open Systems Interconnection.**)

OPEN WIRE. A conductor separately supported (on insulators) above the surface of the ground.

OPEN-WIRE LINE. A pole line whose conductors are principally in the form of open wire.

OPTICAL FIBER. A thin strand of glass over which data can be transmitted using a modulated light beam.

OSI REFERENCE MODEL. (*See* **Reference Model for Open Systems Interconnection.**)

PABX. Private automatic branch exchange. (*See* **Exchange, private automatic branch.**)

PACING. A mechanism on a data communication system for regulating the timing of message flow through the network. (*See also* **Flow control.**)

PACKET. The unit of data, of some fixed maximum size, that is transmitted over a packet switching data network. A packet carries a header containing control information such as a packet sequence number, the network address of the station that originated the packet, and the network address of the packet's destination. (*See also* **Packet switching.**)

PACKET ASSEMBLY AND DISASSEMBLY (PAD). The process of dividing a message into packets for transmission over a packet switching network and then reassembling the packets into the original message. PAD also refers to a device that performs the packet assembly and disassembly function. (*See also* **Packet, Packet switching.**)

PACKET SWITCH. A device that accepts an incoming packet and determines from information contained in the packet's header the next node in a packet switching network to which the packet should be transmitted.

PACKET SWITCHING. The technique of transmitting units of data (called packets) of some fixed maximum size through a mesh-structured network from an originating station to a destination station. In packet switching, a physical path is not set up between the originating and destination station. Instead, the packet is relayed from one node of the network to the next until it finally reaches its destination. Contrast with **Circuit switching.** (*See also* **Packet, Packet switch.**)

PAD. (*See* **Packet assembly and disassembly.**)

PAM. (*See* **Pulse amplitude modulation.**)

PARALLEL TRANSMISSION. Simultaneous transmission of the bits making up a character or byte, either over separate channels or on different carrier frequencies on the channel. The simultaneous transmission of a certain number of signal elements constituting the same telegraph or data signal. For example, use of a code according to which each signal is characterized by a combination of 3 out of 12 frequencies simultaneously transmitted over the channel.

PARITY CHECK. Addition of noninformation bits to data, making the number of one bits in a grouping of bits either always even or always odd. This permits detection of bit groupings that contain single errors. It may be applied to characters, blocks, or any convenient bit grouping.

PARITY CHECK, HORIZONTAL. A parity check applied to the group of certain bits from every character in a block. (*See also* **Longitudinal redundancy check.**)

PARITY CHECK, VERTICAL. A parity check applied to the group that is all bits in one character. Also called *vertical redundancy check*.

PAX. Private automatic exchange. (*See* **Exchange, private automatic.**)

PBX. Private branch exchange. (*See* **Exchange, private branch.**)

PCM. (*See* **Pulse code modulation.**)

PHASE MODULATION. One method of modifying a sine-wave signal to make it "carry" information. The sine wave, or "carrier," has its phase changed in accordance with the information to be transmitted.

POINT-TO-POINT CONFIGURATION. A network configuration in which two communicating stations are connected by a single communication channel that is not shared by any other stations.

POLLING. A means of controlling communication lines. The communication control device sends signals to a terminal saying, "Terminal A, have you anything to send?" If not, "Terminal B, have you anything to send?" and so on. Polling is an alternative to contention. It makes sure that no terminal is kept waiting for a long time.

POLLING LIST. The polling signal will usually be sent under program control. The program maintains a list for each channel that tells the sequence in which the terminals are to be polled.

PRIMARY STATION. The station on a data link that is responsible for controlling transmission on the data link. Also called a *master station* or *control station*. Contrast with **Secondary station.**

PRIVATE AUTOMATIC BRANCH EXCHANGE. (*See* **Exchange, private automatic branch.**)

PRIVATE AUTOMATIC EXCHANGE. (*See* **Exchange, private automatic.**)

PRIVATE BRANCH EXCHANGE (PBX). (*See* **Exchange, private branch.**)

PRIVATE LINE. The channel and channel equipment furnished to a customer as a unit for that customer's exclusive use, without interexchange switching arrangements.

PROPAGATION DELAY. The time necessary for a signal to travel from one point on a circuit to another.

PROTOCOL. Rules that govern communication at a given layer in a network architecture.

PROTOCOL CONVERTER. A network device that attaches devices that use one data link protocol to a communication facility that uses some other data link protocol. A protocol converter typically combines the individual transmissions from multiple, simple asynchronous terminals for transmission over a communication facility using a more efficient synchronous data link protocol.

PUBLIC. Provided by a common carrier for use by many customers.

PUBLIC DATA NETWORK. A communication network, designed specifically for the transmission of computer data, that is used by many individual subscribers. Most public data networks use the technique of packet switching rather than circuit switching. (*See also* **Packet switching.**)

PUBLIC SWITCHED NETWORK. Any switching system that provides circuit switching to many customers.

PULSE-AMPLITUDE MODULATION (PAM). A modulation technique in which an analog signal, such as speech, is converted into pulses whose amplitudes are proportional to the amplitude of the signal at the sampling instant.

PULSE-CODE MODULATION (PCM). A modulation technique in which a pulse train is created in accordance with a code. With PCM, the input signal is first quantized, and the signal amplitude at a particular instant in time is represented by a binary number that can be transmitted over a digital communication channel as a series of pulses of some fixed amplitude. PCM is used to convert an analog signal, such as telephone voice, into a digital bit stream. (*See also* **Codec.**)

PULSE MODULATION. Transmission of information by modulation of a pulsed or intermittent carrier. Pulse width, count, position, phase, and/or amplitude can be the varied characteristic.

PUSH-BUTTON DIALING. The use of keys or push buttons instead of a rotary dial to generate a sequence of digits to establish a circuit connection. The signal form is usually multiple tones. Also called *tone dialing, Touch-call, Touch-tone*.

REALTIME. A realtime computer system can be defined as one that controls an environment by receiving data, processing it, and returning the results quickly enough to affect the functioning of the environment at that time.

REASONABLENESS CHECKS. Tests made on information reaching a realtime system or being transmitted from it to ensure that the data in question lies within a given range. It is one of the means of protecting a system from data transmission errors.

RECOMMENDATION X.25. (*See* **X.25.**)

REDUNDANCY CHECK. An automatic or programmed check based on the systematic insertion of components or characters used especially for checking purposes.

REDUNDANT CODE. A code using more signal elements than necessary to represent the intrinsic information.

REFERENCE MODEL FOR OPEN SYSTEMS INTERCONNECTION (OSI MODEL). A network architecture being developed by the International Standards Organization (ISO) that provides a common basis for the coordination of standards development for the purpose of the interconnection of information processing systems. The term *open systems interconnection* (OSI) qualifies standards for the exchange of information among systems that are "open" to one another for this purpose by virtue of their mutual use of applicable standards.

REGENERATIVE REPEATER. (*See* **Repeater, regenerative.**)

REPEATER, REGENERATIVE. A device whose function is to retime and retransmit the received signal impulses restored to their original strength. Also called a *bit repeater*.

RESPONSE TIME. The time a system takes to react to a given input. If a message is keyed into a terminal by an operator, and the reply from a computer, when it comes, is displayed at the same terminal, response time can be defined as the time interval between the operator's pressing the last key of the input and the terminal's displaying the first character of the reply.

ROLL CALL POLLING. A polling technique in which the primary station on a multipoint communication facility consults a polling list to determine the order in which to send polling signals to each of the secondary stations attached to the communication facility.

ROUTING. The assignment of the communication path by which a message will reach its destination.

ROUTING, ALTERNATE. Assignment of a secondary communication path to a destination when the primary path is unavailable.

RS-232-C. A physical-level standard, developed by the Electronics Industry Association (EIA), that defines 25 circuits that can be used to connect two communicating stations and describes the electrical characteristics of the signals carried over those circuits. The RS-232-C interface allows for serial transmission at speeds up to about 20,000 bits per second at a distance of typically 50 feet or less.

SDLC. (*See* **Synchronous Data Link Control.**)

SECONDARY STATION. A station on a data link that cannot initiate a transmission. A secondary station transmits data only when given permission by the station in control of the data link. Also called a *tributary* or *slave* station. Contrast with **Primary station.**

SELECTION. Addressing a terminal and/or a component on a selective calling circuit.

SELECTIVE CALLING. The ability of the transmitting station to specify which of several stations on the same line is to receive a message.

SELF-CHECKING NUMBERS. Numbers that contain redundant information so that an error in them, caused, for example, by noise on a transmission line, can be detected.

SERIAL PORT. A circuit installed in a computer that allows the computer to be attached to a line termination device such as a modem or line driver for the purpose of data communication.

SERIAL TRANSMISSION. Used to identify a system wherein the bits of a character occur serially in time. Implies only a single transmission channel. Also called *serial by bit*.

SHANNON'S LAW. Mathematical formula for determining the theoretical maximum signaling rate of a given communication channel.

SIDEBAND. The frequency band on either the upper or lower side of the carrier frequency within which fall the frequencies produced by the process of modulation.

SIGNAL-TO-NOISE RATIO (S/N). Relative power of the signal to the noise in a channel.

SIMPLEX CIRCUIT. A circuit permitting transmission in one specific direction only.

SIMPLEX MODE. Operation of a communication channel in one direction only, with no capacity for reversing.

SLAVE STATION. (*See* **Secondary station.**)

SLOW-SCAN TRANSMISSION. Type of transmission that allows a signal to be transmitted over a communication channel of lower bandwidth than the original signal.

SNA. (*See* **Systems Network Architecture.**)

SPACE. (1) An impulse that, in a neutral circuit, causes the loop to open or causes absence of signal, while in a polar circuit causes the loop current to flow in a direction opposite to that for a mark impulse. A space impulse is equivalent to a binary 0. (2) In some codes, a character that causes a printer or display screen to leave a character width with no printed symbol.

SPECTRUM. (1) A continuous, usually wide range of frequencies within which waves have some specific common characteristics. (2) A graphical representation of the distribution of the amplitude (and sometimes the phase) of the components of a wave as a function of frequency. A spectrum can be continuous or may contain only points corresponding to certain discrete values.

START BIT. The first bit of a character in asynchronous (start-stop) transmission, used to permit synchronization.

START ELEMENT. (*See* **Start bit.**)

START-STOP TRANSMISSION. (*See* **Asynchronous transmission.**)

STATE PUBLIC UTILITIES COMMISSIONS. State agencies that are responsible for regulating telecommunications within a given state in the United States.

STATION. One of the input or output points of a communication system—for example, the telephone set in a telephone system or a terminal or computer in a data communication system.

STATISTICAL MULTIPLEXOR. A multiplexor that uses intelligence and buffer storage to combine several signals or bit streams into a combined signal or bit stream of lower bandwidth or bit rate than the total of the combined bandwidth or bit rate of the individual signals or bit streams.

STOP BIT. The last bit of a character in asynchronous (start-stop) transmission, used to ensure recognition of the next start bit.

STOP ELEMENT. (*See* **Stop bit.**)

STORE AND FORWARD. The interruption of data flow from the origination terminal to the designated receiver by storing the information en route and forwarding it at a later time. (*See* **Message switching.**)

SUBSCRIBER'S LINE. (*See* **Local loop.**)

SUB-VOICE-GRADE CHANNEL. A channel of bandwidth narrower than that of voice-grade channels. Such channels are usually subchannels of a voice-grade line.

SUPERGROUP. The assembly of five 12-channel groups, occupying adjacent bands in the spectrum.

SWITCHING CENTER. A location that terminates multiple circuits and is capable of interconnecting circuits.

SYNCHRONOUS. Having a constant time interval between successive bits, characters, or events. The term implies that all equipment is in step.

SYNCHRONOUS DATA LINK CONTROL (SDLC). A bit-oriented data link protocol standardized by IBM as part of IBM's Systems Network Architecture (SNA). SDLC is a compatible subset of HDLC. (*See also* **High-Level Data Link Control.**)

SYNCHRONOUS TRANSMISSION. Data transmission in which the sending and receiving instruments are operating continuously at substantially the same frequency and are maintained, by means of correction if necessary, in a desired phase relationship. Compare with **Start-stop transmission.**

SYSTEMS NETWORK ARCHITECTURE (SNA). Network architecture that defines the formats and protocols used by IBM computing system equipment and software in performing data communication functions.

T1 CARRIER. Digital data transmission carrier that supports a bit rate of 1,544,000 bits per second. T1 carriers are used by common carriers for long-distance telephone service and by individual subscribers for voice and data communication.

TARIFF. The published rate for a specific unit of equipment, facility, or type of service provided by a communication common carrier. Also, the vehicle by which the regulating agencies approve or disapprove such facilities or services.

TASI. (*See* **Time assignment speech interpolation.**)

TELECOMMUNICATIONS. The electronic transmission of any kind of electronic information, including telephone calls, television signals, data communication of all forms, electronic mail, facsimile transmission, and telemetry from spacecraft.

TELECOMMUNICATIONS ACCESS METHOD. Software subsystem that supplements conventional operating system services by providing low-level programming support for data communication functions.

TELEPHONE FREQUENCY. (*See* **Voice frequency.**)

TELEPROCESSING. A form of information handling in which a data processing system uses communication facilities. (Originally, but no longer, an IBM trademark.)

TELEPROCESSING MONITOR. Software subsystem that uses the services of a telecommunications access method to provide high-level programming support for data communication functions.

TELETYPE. Trademark of Teletype Corporation, usually referring to a series of different types of teleprinter equipment, such as tape punches, reperforators, and page printers, used for communication systems.

TELETYPEWRITER EXCHANGE SERVICE (TWX). An AT&T public, switched teletypewriter service in which suitably arranged teletypewriter stations are provided with lines to a central office to other stations throughout North America.

TELEX SERVICE. A dial-up telegraph service enabling its subscribers to communicate directly and temporarily among themselves by means of start-stop apparatus and circuits of the public telegraph network. The service operates worldwide. Computers can be connected to the telex network.

TERMINAL. Any device capable of sending and/or receiving information over a communication channel. The means by which data is entered into a computer system and by which the decisions of the system are communicated to the environment it affects.

TIE LINE. A private-line communication channel of the type provided by communication common carriers for linking two or more points.

TIME ASSIGNMENT SPEECH INTERPOLATION (TASI). A particular form of dynamic channel assignment for increasing the utilization of an analog voice channel in which channel capacity is assigned to a user only when that user is actually speaking. (*See also* **Dynamic channel assignment, Digital speech interpolation.**)

TIME-DIVISION MULTIPLEXING. A system in which a channel is established by connecting intermittently, generally at regular intervals and by means of an automatic distribution, its terminal equipment to a common channel. At times when these connections are not established, the section of the common channel between distributors can be used to establish other channels in turn.

TIMEOUT. A predefined period of time that elapses before the initiation of an expected event.

TOLL CENTER. Basic toll switching entity; a central office where channels and toll message circuits terminate. While this is usually one particular central office in a city, larger cities may have several central offices where toll messages circuits terminate.

TOLL CIRCUIT (**AMERICAN**). (*See* **Trunk circuit** (British).)

TOLL SWITCHING TRUNK (**AMERICAN**). (*See* **Trunk junction** (British).)

TONE DIALING. (*See* **Push-button dialing.**)

TOUCH-TONE. AT&T term for push-button dialing.

TRANSCEIVER. A terminal that can transmit and receive traffic. On some local area networks, the device that attaches to the transmission medium for transmitting and receiving data.

TRANSLATOR. A device that converts information from one system of representation into equivalent information in another system of representation. In telephone equipment, it is the device that converts dialed digits into call-routing information.

TRANSPARENT. A facility, device, or function is transparent if it appears not to exist but in fact does.

TRANSPARENT TEXT MODE. Mode of a data link protocol that allows the message text to contain all possible bit configurations. Bit-oriented data link protocols always operate in transparent text mode. Some character-oriented data link protocols support transparent text mode as an option.

TRANSPONDER. Device in a communications satellite that receives a signal from a sending earth station and retransmits the signal to one or more receiving earth stations.

TRIBIT. A group of 3 bits. The eight possible states of a tribit are 000, 001, 010, 011, 100, 101, 110, and 111.

TRIBUTARY STATION. (*See* **Secondary station.**)

TRUNK CIRCUIT (BRITISH), TOLL CIRCUIT (AMERICAN). A circuit connecting two exchanges in different localities. *Note:* in Great Britain, a truck circuit is approximately 15 miles long. A circuit connecting two exchanges less than 15 miles apart is called a *junction circuit*.

TRUNK EXCHANGE (BRITISH), TOLL OFFICE (AMERICAN). An exchange with the function of controlling the switching of trunk (British), or toll (American) traffic.

TRUNK GROUP. Those trunks between two points both of which are switching centers and/or individual message distribution points, and which employ the same multiplex terminal equipment.

TRUNK JUNCTION (BRITISH), TOLL SWITCHING TRUNK (AMERICAN). A line connecting a truck exchange to a local exchange and permitting a trunk operator to call a subscriber to establish a trunk call.

TWX. (*See* **Teletypewriter exchange service.**)

VERTICAL PARITY *or* REDUNDANCY CHECK. (*See* **Parity check, vertical.**)

VIRTUAL. A virtual device, facility, or function is one that appears to exist but in fact does not.

VIRTUAL CHANNEL. A channel that appears to be a simple, direct connection but in fact is implemented in a more complex manner.

VOICE FREQUENCY *or* TELEPHONE FREQUENCY. Any frequency within the part of the audio frequency range (300–3100 hertz) essential for the transmission of speech of commercial quality.

VOICE-GRADE CHANNEL. (*See* **Channel, voice-grade.**)

VRC. Vertical redundancy check. (*See* **Parity check, vertical.**)

WIDE AREA TELEPHONE SERVICE (WATS). A service provided by telephone companies in the United States that permits a customer, by use of an access line, to make calls to telephones in a specific zone on a dial basis for a flat monthly charge. Monthly charges are based on the size of the area in which calls are placed, not on the number or length of calls.

WIDEBAND. Communication channel having a bandwidth greater than a voice-grade channel and therefore capable of higher-speed data transmission. Sometimes called *broadband*.

X.25. A recommendation of the CCITT specifying the protocols and message formats that define the interface between a terminal operating in the packet mode and a packet switching network. (*See also* **Packet, Packet switching.**)

XMODEM PROTOCOL. A data link protocol employed with asynchronous transmission for the purposes of transferring data files from one computer to another.

ZERO-BIT INSERTION. The technique employed with bit-oriented protocols to ensure that 6 consecutive one bits never appear between the two flags that define the beginning and the ending of a transmission frame. When 5 consecutive one bits occur in any part of the frame other than the beginning or ending flag, the sending station inserts an extra zero bit. When the receiving station detects 5 one bits followed by a zero bit, it removes the extra zero bit, thus restoring the bit stream to its original value.

INDEX

TEAR OUT THIS PAGE TO ORDER OTHER TITLES BY JAMES MARTIN
THE JAMES MARTIN BOOKS

Quantity	Title	Title Code	Price	Total $
_____	Action Diagrams: Clearly Structured Program Design	00330–1	$38.50	_____
_____	Application Development Without Programmers	03894–3	$54.95	_____
	A Breakthrough In Making Computers Friendly:			
_____	The Macintosh Computer (paper)	08157–0	$25.00	_____
_____	(case)	08158–8	$31.95	_____
_____	Communications Satellite Systems	15316–3	$59.95	_____
_____	Computer Data-Base Organization, 2nd Edition	16542–3	$54.95	_____
_____	The Computerized Society	16597–7	$26.95	_____
_____	Computer Networks and Distributed Processing:	16525–8	$54.95	_____
	Software, Techniques and Architecture			
_____	Data Communication Technology	19664–2	$36.75	_____
_____	Design and Strategy of Distributed Data Processing	20165–7	$57.95	_____
_____	Design of Man-Computer Dialogues	20125–1	$54.95	_____
_____	Design of Real-Time Computer Systems	20140–0	$54.95	_____
_____	Diagramming Techniques for Analysts and Programmers	20879–3	$49.95	_____
_____	An End User's Guide to Data Base	27712–9	$42.95	_____
_____	Fourth-Generation Languages, Vol. I: Principles	32967–2	$42.95	_____
_____	Fourth-Generation Languages, Vol. II: Representative 4GLs	32974–8	$42.95	_____
	Fourth-Generation Languages, Vol. III: 4GLs from IBM	32976–3	$42.95	
	Future Developments in Telecommunications, 2nd Edition	34585–0	$56.95	_____
_____	An Information Systems Manifesto	46476–8	$49.95	
_____	Introduction to Teleprocessing	49981–4	$44.95	
_____	Managing the Data-Base Environment	55058–2	$57.95	
_____	Principles of Data-Base Management	70891–7	$44.95	
_____	Principles of Data Communication	70989–9	$44.00	
_____	Programming Real-Time Computer Systems	73050–7	$46.95	
	Recommended Diagramming Standards for Analysts and Programmers	76737–6	$45.00	_____
_____	Security, Accuracy, and Privacy in Computer Systems	79899–1	$57.95	
_____	SNA: IBM's Networking Solution	81514–2	$44.95	
_____	Software Maintenance: The Problem and Its Solutions	82236–1	$49.95	
_____	Strategic Data Planning Methodologies	85111–3	$43.95	_____
_____	Structured Techniques: The Basis for CASE, Revised Edition	85493–5	$52.00	_____
_____	Systems Analysis for Data Transmission	88130–0	$60.00	_____
_____	System Design from Provably Correct Constructs	88148–2	$49.95	_____
_____	Technology's Crucible (paper)	90202–3	$15.95	_____
_____	Telecommunications and the Computer, 2nd Edition	90249–4	$54.95	_____

(over)

————	Telematic Society: A Challenge for Tomorrow	90246–0	$31.95 ————
————	Teleprocessing Network Organization	90245–2	$34.95 ————
————	Viewdata and the Information Society	94190–6	$41.95 ————
————	VSAM: Access Method Services and Programming Techniques	94417–3	$44.95 ————

Total: ————

-discount (if appropriate) ————

New Total: ————

AND TAKE ADVANTAGE OF THESE SPECIAL OFFERS!

When ordering 3 or 4 copies (of the same or different titles) take 10% off the total list price.

When ordering 5 to 20 (of the same or different titles) take 15% off the total list price.

To receive a greater discount when ordering more than 20 copies, call or write:

Special Sales Department
College Marketing
Prentice Hall
Englewood Cliffs, NJ 07632
(201)592–2046

SAVE!

If payment accompanies order, plus your state's sales tax where applicable, Prentice Hall pays postage and handling charges. Same return privilege refund guarantee. Please do not mail cash.

☐ **PAYMENT ENCLOSED**—shipping and handling to be paid by publisher (please include your state's tax where applicable).

☐ **SEND BOOKS ON 15-DAY TRIAL BASIS** and bill me (with small charge for shipping and handling).

Name ————————————————————————————

Address ——————————————————————————

City ———————————————— State ———————— Zip ————

I prefer to charge my ☐ Visa ☐ MasterCard

Card Number ———————————————— Expiration Date ————————

Signature ——————————————————————

All prices listed are subject to change without notice.
This offer not valid outside U.S.

Mail your order to: Prentice Hall Book Distribution Center
Route 59 at Brook Hill Drive
West Nyack, NY 10994

Announcing . . .

TECHNOLOGY'S
CRUCIBLE

by James Martin

Order Your Copy Using This Form and Receive a *SPECIAL 50% DISCOUNT!*

- How will today's high technology and human nature impact tomorrow's quality of life?
- Through a television series set in the year 2019, a narrator asks the question, "Would the course of history have been different if the public in the 1980s had understood the journey on which they had embarked?"
- In *Technology's Crucible,* James Martin, a renowned computer-industry consultant, world-wide lecturer, and best-selling author of over 30 computer text and reference books, describes the forces that are shaping the environment of tomorrow. This book does not forecast the future; it provides a vehicle for helping people think constructively about the future.

QUANTITY	TITLE/AUTHOR	TITLE CODE	PRICE	TOTAL
_____	*Technology's Crucible* (Martin)	90202-3	$15.95	$_____
			−50%	$_____
			New Total	$_____

SAVE! If payment accompanies order, plus your state's sales tax where applicable, Prentice Hall pays postage and handling charges. Same return privilege refund guaranteed. Please do not mail cash.

☐ PAYMENT ENCLOSED—shipping and handling to be paid by publisher (please include your state's tax where applicable).

☐ SEND BOOKS ON 15-DAY TRIAL BASIS and bill me (with a small charge for shipping and handling).

Name _____

Address _____

City _____ State _____ Zip _____

I prefer to charge my ☐ Visa ☐ MasterCard

Card Number _____ Expiration Date _____

Signature _____

All prices listed are subject to change without notice.
Prices and offer not valid outside the U.S.
For quantity orders and special discounts call either (201)592-2046 or (201) 592-2498

Mail your order to: Prentice Hall Book Distribution Center
Route 59 at Brook Hill Drive
West Nyack, NY 10994

Dept. 1: D-CAJB-YM(4)